The Words of Others

The Words
of Others

From Quotations to Culture

GARY SAUL MORSON

Yale UNIVERSITY PRESS   New Haven and London

Yale University Press books may be purchased in quantity for educational, business, or promotional use. For information, please e-mail sales.press@yale.edu (U.S. office) or sales@yaleup.co.uk (U.K. office).

Set in Minion type by Integrated Publishing Solutions.
Printed in the United States of America.

Library of Congress Cataloging-in-Publication Data

Morson, Gary Saul, 1948–
    The words of others : from quotations to culture / Gary Saul Morson.
        p. cm.
    Includes bibliographical references and index.
    ISBN 978-0-300-16747-4 (alk. paper)
    1. Quotations—History and criticism.   2. Quotation in literature.
3. Epitaphs—History and criticism.   I. Title.
    PN171.Q6M67 2011
    080.9—dc22

                                        2010034293

A catalogue record for this book is available from the British Library.

This paper meets the requirements of ANSI/NISO Z39.48–1992 (Permanence of Paper).

10 9 8 7 6 5 4 3 2 1

For Michael

Have you ever noticed . . . that man is
surrounded by tiny inscriptions, a sprawling anthill
of tiny inscriptions: on forks, spoons, saucers, his pince-nez
frames, his buttons, and his pencils! No one notices
them. They're waging a struggle for survival.

—Yuri Olesha, *Envy*

Contents

Acknowledgments

Though the people are gone, the thoughts and words of Wayne Booth, Victor Erlich, Aron Katsenelinboigen, and Stephen Toulmin continue to shape my thought and expression. I hear their voices as I write. The late Lawrence B. Dumas helped make Northwestern University the sort of place that inspired the best research and teaching.

The idea of writing a book on quotations occurred to me some fifteen years ago, when I imagined that I had at last found a topic I could handle quickly. Fortunately, I was delayed by many whose wisdom, written and spoken, helped me to see complexities I had missed: Elizabeth Cheresh Allen, James Sloane Allen, Robert Alter, Carol Avins, Dan Ben-Amos, Bracht Branham, Bud Bynack, Caryl Emerson, Dilip Gaonkar, Boris Gasparov, Marcia Gealy, Gerald Graff, Thomas Greene, Robert Gundlach, Robert Hariman, the late Dell Hymes, Norman Ingham, Robert Louis Jackson, Barbara Kirshenblatt-Gimblett, Julie Lasky, Robert Lerner, Lawrence Lipking, Daniel Lowenstein, Kathe Marshall, Susan McReynolds-Oddo, Clara Claiborne Park, Janice Pavel, Thomas Pavel, Sarah Pratt, Martin

Price, Alfred Rieber, Kenneth Seeskin, Helen Tartar, Herbert Tucker, Meredith Williams, and Michael Williams.

I cannot possibly list all the former students to whom I owe much, but they include Elena Aleksandrova, Lindsay Sargeant Berg, Wendy Cheng, Michael Denner, Andrew Gruen, the late Robert Gurley, John Mafi, Lori Singer Meyer, Matthew Morrison, Joanne Mulcahy, Karthik Sivashanker, Trish Suchy, Ryan Vogt, Cindy Wang, Justin Weir, and Jennifer Yeung. Nava Cohen and John Knapp continue to offer help, as well as friendship, beyond the call.

As the years go by, I only grow more indebted to, as well as appreciative of, Robert Belknap, Frederick Crews, Robin Feuer Miller, and William Mills Todd. Their generosity and decency, as well as intelligence and insight, serve as a model.

I repeatedly discussed quotations with the always quotable Joseph Epstein, whose powerful writing and wise spirit keep my prose and prosaics much better than they otherwise would be.

At one time or another, I benefited from close reading and important suggestions by Frances Padorr Brent, Emily Morson, Jane Morson, Andrew Wachtel, and the two anonymous readers for Yale University Press.

Jonathan Brent decisively shaped this book from its inception to its completion. Discussion by discussion, he led me to realize that what I had taken to be a mere prologue to my main argument should be a separate book. With his encouragement, I postponed what I had originally planned, and then, with his feedback, arrived at the present title. He and Frances Padorr Brent remind me, in many ways, of what the words of some others can do.

However far he may be, Kenneth Mischel is always close. I can only cite, never imitate, the courage and energy of Dalya

Sachs-Bernstein, and can only repeat, but never adequately, my endless admiration and caring for Michael André Bernstein. Every day brings wonder for the ninety-three gifts of Alexander Morson and Emily Morson. Katharine Porter knows that to express what I owe to her would challenge language.

Prologue
Cleopatra's Nose

Picture commencement at a major Midwestern university. The guest speaker, a well-known legislator, summons the students to live not for themselves but for society. In the tradition of such addresses, he asks the graduates "not to heap up wealth, nor take pride only in your personal achievements, nor remain content to care for a family. Reach out to the world around you and resolve to leave it a better place than you found it. A wise man once said that 'no man is ever an island,' and truer words were never spoken. You are most yourself when attending to someone else. . . ."

A parent who majored in English remembers that "no man is ever an island" is a quotation from John Donne, but can't identify exactly where. Her husband is reminded of the contrary sentiment in the Simon and Garfunkel song, "I am a rock, I am an i-i-island!" while the woman on their right wonders if "Truer words were never spoken" is a quotation, an allusion to a quotation, a saying, or just a cliché; and what exactly is the difference between these categories anyway?

Recalling the maxim that if you don't know the source

of a moral exhortation, assume it comes from Shakespeare, Franklin, or the Bible, a grandfather muses that since the Bible is not "a wise man," and since the language doesn't sound like Shakespeare, the source is probably Franklin. Well, to err is human.

A graduate student studying the social use of language wonders whether something can be a quotation if it has no author. What about proverbs? But of course, she thinks, some proverbs do have authors, like Shakespeare or Pope. Does Solomon count as an author, or just a convention? How about Aesop or Confucius? Discreetly, she taps her iPhone, Googles the phrase "truer words were never spoken," and finds a continuation: "—Ah, but the words leave hearts broken. Truth is only for the wise—lovers ought to stick to lies."

But why is there no source? Is the quotation, with or without the continuation, "anonymous"? And is "anonymous" equivalent to "author unknown"? For that matter, can a line be both anonymous and "attributed"? More searching leads to another site, which defines the phrase and includes a link to "Variety is the spice of life," which leads to "Curiosity killed the cat" and then to "You stole my thunder," whose author turns out to be someone named John Dennis, famous for disliking puns ("A man who would make so vile a pun would not scruple to pick a pocket").

The speaker advises:

> Remember: your youthful idealistic dreams will fade. Plenty makes you poor; and, sooner or later, as water wears down a stone, your dreams turn to dust and you go after the main chance. It's hard to love thy neighbor: others will take what you have earned with the sweat of your brow, and you will be

tempted to repay injuries tit for tat. When you do, you will tell yourself you are merely pursuing justice. *Everyone* who harms others probably tells himself that, and believes it. "One's own anger is always righteous."

It was Martin Luther King who said, "An eye for an eye and the whole world is blind." The Bible bids us "turn the other cheek." And let us add that if you don't end the day with a sore cheek, you have not lived it right.

Heaving a theatrical sigh, one robed professor on the podium whispers to his neighbor: "I wish he would stop doing *this*" (imitating the speaker's gesture of making inverted commas in the air). But his colleague rather enjoys recognizing quotations, supplying authors not given, and, perhaps especially, noticing cited words *not* marked as such but offered with a wink to those "in the know."

A graduate who idolizes Thoreau finds the speaker's smarmy exhortations unbearable. In response, he quotes to himself the essay on civil disobedience: "I have come into this world, not chiefly to make this a good place to live in, but to live in it, good or bad." Scowling at what he imagines to be heads nodding in complacent agreement with the speaker, he thinks: "Any man more right than his neighbors constitutes a majority of one." As if to demonstrate his own disobedience, he "coughs."

He is not alone in his sense of injured superiority. A senior who majored in philosophy rolls his eyes, in just the way his thesis advisor would, at the sentimental claptrap. Maybe we are not islands, he reflects, but each of us is at least a peninsula. After all, "we all die alone"—was that Pascal or Tolstoy?

And are those the actual words, or just how they are usually quoted?—sort of like "Pride goeth before a fall" when the line really is: "Pride goeth before destruction, / And an haughty spirit before the fall." I wonder if "an" ever occurs before "haughty" except in a quotation, or whether you can make anything sound like a quotation by adding a word like "goeth"?

In any case, he reflects, what the speaker asks of us is impossible or—still worse for a philosopher—"incoherent." "It's not even false," as philosophers love to say. The whole history of philosophy shows that everyone always acts out of self-interest, and why not? The student recalls writing his paper on David Hume's scandalous observation that "it is not contrary to reason to prefer the destruction of the whole world to the scratching of my finger," and coming across what seemed like an allusion to Hume in Dostoevsky's *Notes from Underground:* "When they prove to you that one drop of your own fat must be dearer to you than a hundred thousand of your fellow creatures, then you might as well as accept it like a law of mathematics." At least, that was the gist of it. And Adam Smith cautioned that it was "not from the benevolence of the butcher, the brewer, or the baker" that we expect our dinner, but from their self-interest.

The philosophy student grows especially annoyed at the chaplain on stage, who smiles approvingly—it seems, on purpose—and visibly completes quotations with his lips. The chaplain takes mental notes for his next sermon, and plans to invoke Rabbi Hillel: "If I am not for myself, who will be for me? But if I am only for myself, what am I?" Yes, he tells himself, it would be good for a chaplain to quote a rabbi. But he regrets that Dr. King has been credited for words usually attributed to Gandhi, only to wonder whether Gandhi may have received credit for these words in the same way—not because he actually said them, but because, to some audience, he was the one most worthy of having said them.

A cell phone rings just long enough to play the tsar's theme from "Overture 1812." The legislator continues:

> Especially at your age, people are usually tempted to treat misfortune as something that happens to others. Everyone is immortal at twenty-one. But think how easily a disaster could strike. Chance happeneth to us all. If Cleopatra's nose had been half an inch longer, the history of the world would have changed, and if that driver in the opposing lane should be distracted for a split second, you will be hit head on. "Man knoweth not his time; as the birds are caught in the snare, so are the sons of men snared in an evil time, when it falleth suddenly upon them." When that evil time comes, you will want to tell others, "some day it will be you!" but they will not listen any more than you did. Wisdom begins when you see someone else suffering and think of the proverb—shall I say, the proverbial proverb?— "There but for the grace of God go I."
>
> *It could have been me:* that's what you should always say to yourself. Never send to know for whom the bell tolls. And ask not what others can do for you, ask what you can do for others.

A professor of French, compelled from lack of publications to represent his department at the ceremony, cringes at the line about Cleopatra, because for decades he has had his students learn French grammar by memorizing famous sayings. He knows that the original is: "*Le nez de Cléopâtre: s'il eût été plus court, tout la face de la terre aurait change.*" Pascal had asked what if the queen's nose had been shorter, not longer; and where did that "half an inch" come from? Was that the usual English translation, the correct version as given in Bartlett's? And was it necessary for the translator to give up the play on words in the original by substituting "history of the world" for "face of the world"?

For that matter, he thinks, could Donne's famous words allude to Pascal's aphorism "*Le moi est haïssable*"—"Self is hateful"? And did Pascal himself get that thought from somewhere? Could there be a chain of aphorisms going back to antiquity—maybe to some line in Ecclesiastes? "Chance happeneth to us all" is from Ecclesiastes, but what about "One's own anger is always righteous"—is that also Ecclesiastes, or maybe La Rochefoucauld, who must have borrowed from it? Come to think of it, Ecclesiastes itself reads like an anthology of earlier wisdom. Is *any* quotation original? Do great lines, like great thinkers, stand on the shoulders of giants?

An older parent, for whom this is his fourth child's graduation, winces at hearing Donne's line yet again, not to mention the number of errors in the speech. First of all, the words "Turn the other cheek" never occur in the Bible. There's no "ever" in "No man is an island." Is the speaker really ignorant that the words belong to John Donne, and if not, why does he just ascribe them to "a wise man"? Did he get his quotations from *The Speaker's Guide to the 2,548 World's Best Quotations*? He doesn't seem to know that "for whom the bell tolls" comes from the same Donne sermon! Maybe he thinks it's a proverb? Actually, maybe it *was* in Donne's day? Perhaps Donne expected his audience to know it, the way Shakespeare used common expressions we now assume were his invention? What anthologies did Shakespeare know?

For relief, the parent exchanges a knowing glance with his neighbor, whom he assumes is thinking what he is, but who is in fact congratulating himself: "That's from Hemingway, isn't it?"

His wife is ready to leap out of her seat when she hears her favorite quotation—"There but for the grace of God go I"—treated as an anonymous proverb, when its author is known and the original actually is: "There but for the grace of God goes John Bradford." The whole point is that Bradford was witnessing a man led to execution only shortly before he was himself martyred. Is this what a college education is about today? Can we get our money back?

Of course, she concedes, the line would *have* to be changed if it is to be quoted at all, because what sense would it make for anyone but John Bradford to say, "There but for the grace of God goes John Bradford?" No matter who says it, the point is "I." It's a quotation we must use *as if* it were our own words.

The man on her right remembers John F. Kennedy's inauguration and knows that the line should be "Ask not what your country can do for you." But he is a connoisseur of those countless debunking books exposing misquotations and misattributions, so he knows—probably the only one present who does—that the line really belongs to Oliver Wendell Holmes Jr., as modified by Kahlil Gibran in his book—title also cribbed by Kennedy—*The New Frontier.* So the quotation does not belong to Kennedy at all. People are always getting credit for someone else's words! And how about "Everyone is immortal at twenty-one": did the speaker invent that or is he alluding to something he hopes we haven't read or, on the contrary, expects some of us to know? How do you tell the quotable from the quote?

The class valedictorian, distracting herself from her nervousness, wonders how many concealed quotations she is missing. "Sweat of one's brow," that's probably from the Bible, along with "heap up wealth." And "Leave the world a better place than you found it"? It's a cliché, of course, but was it a quotation before it became a cliché? Or should we call it an idiom, and what exactly is the difference between a cliché and an idiom? "An eye for an eye and the whole world goes blind" is a quotation commenting on another quotation—it's two in one—and how many that we now take as one are really a compressed dialogue? Sometimes, perhaps, the thought being answered is so common it doesn't even have to be mentioned? Doesn't "Turn the other cheek" presume some once famous expression of contrary wisdom?

"Main chance," "tit for tat," "Water wears down a stone," "Dreams turn to dust," "Plenty makes you poor": why, it's almost as if we are constantly using expressions that were once quotations but are now remembered as such only by a few scholars, if at all. Who knows, perhaps everything we say draws on some invention of the collective human mind. Is language—words, gestures, tones, all of it—itself the residue of former quotations?

Maybe quotationality comes in degrees? Could it be that wishing to avoid even unconscious quotation is like trying to focus on one's unfocused thoughts? Didn't someone say, "Cursed be those who said our words before us?" Was Adam the only one able to speak without quoting?

Can one even think without the words of others?

Introduction

Verbal Gems and Treasuries

What man of sane mind would not prefer tiny gems
to giant boulders. As Pliny says, if one only looks
closely, the miracle of nature is greatest when seen at
its most minute; the intricacy of a spider or gnat is far
more impressive than the immensity of an elephant.
So, too, in the domain of literature, the smallest
things may possess the greatest intellectual value.
—Erasmus, Introduction to the Adages *(AE, 12)*

W. H. Auden described *poetry* as "memorable speech," a phrase that could elegantly and quotably define *quotation* as well.[1] Quotations are the lines that people remember—or are expected to remember. The various genres of quotation—wise sayings, aphorisms, maxims, proverbs, witticisms, heroic pro-

nouncements, adages, and many more—constitute the shortest literary forms. Their concision not only makes them easy
to memorize but also often confers considerable aesthetic
power. Pithy or succinct sayings stick with us when texts of
scholarly treatises have been long forgotten.

We sometimes think of quotations as extracts from larger
texts, but some quotations originated complete unto themselves. Anthologies may include these "unquoted quotations"
alongside lines drawn from longer works, but the two differ in
an important way. One is a work in its entirety, conceived and
presented as such. The other has been *made* into a separate work
by someone's act of selection. The former cannot be "taken out
of context"; the latter must be, often with a change of wording
that captures the sentiment while creating a more memorable
turn of phrase.

If epics and novels are by nature the longest literary
forms, while lyric poems and short stories are considerably
briefer, then quotations are the briefest of all. In each case, size
is more than incidental. The epic vision aspires to tell everything essential and so demands length. Even relatively short
epics, like *Beowulf* or *The Song of Igor's Campaign,* feel longer
than they are. Realist novels, which describe a personality's
gradual development, need time for small alterations to accumulate into real change of character. By contrast, short stories
typically aim at a purpose that precludes meaningful extension, such as a sudden epiphany illuminating a life.

Quotations demand extreme brevity. There are no long
maxims, bulky aphorisms, diffuse witticisms, or digressive
proverbs. Tombstones limit the length of epitaphs, and there
can be no famous last disquisitions. Only as a joke could
we imagine a shaggy-dog adage. Each genre of quotation ex-

ploits brevity in a unique way, but brevity is the soul of them all. Taken together, they constitute an important part of the world's literary heritage, oral and written.

Works short enough to be quotations are by no means all Western. The book we know in English as the *Analects* of Confucius unites diverse short pieces that may stand on their own. *Analects,* from the Greek *analekta,* means "selections," while the Chinese word it translates, *lunyu,* means "conversations," and indeed, the work contains accounts of conversations between Confucius and his followers or various rulers.[2] Numerous entries represent detachable and quotable bits of wisdom:

> The Master said, "A person who has no regard for what is distant will surely encounter sorrow close by."

> The Master said, "Without knowing what is ordained [by Heaven], one has no way to become a noble person. Without knowing the rites, one has no way to take one's stand. Without knowing words, one has no way to know other people."

> The Master said, "Zi, do you think of me as one who learns many things and remembers them all?" He replied, "Yes. But perhaps it is not so?" The Master said, "It is not. With me there is one that runs throughout it all." [or: "With me, there is one thread that runs right through it."] (SCT, 59, 63, 59)

As the *Analects* collect the wisdom of Confucius, the *Tao Te Ching* presents sayings attributed to Lao Tzu. These sayings appear as eighty-one "poems," which may not be poems in the usual sense at all. Rather than whole lyrics, they might just be groups of lines on a given topic placed together. In either case, the bits of extractable insight are brief.

Lao Tzu was by tradition a contemporary of Confucius. The wisdom of each sage disputes the other's. The two groups of sayings hardly seem to belong to the same genre, any more than epic and mock-epic do. Where Confucius strives to be rational, clear, and practical, Lao-Tzu cultivates the evocative, whimsical, enigmatic, and paradoxical:

> When the great way falls into disuse
> There are benevolence and rectitude . . .
> When the state is benighted
> There are loyal ministers.

> Exterminate learning and there will no longer be
>   worries.

> The way never acts yet nothing is left undone.

> One who knows does not speak; one who speaks
>   does not know.[3]

For obvious reasons, the wisdom of many traditions seems to be preserved in the sayings of real or legendary sages. Presumably, these sayings date to a time either before writing or when education was primarily oral. Sometimes, as at Delphi, the wisdom may be inscribed for all to see. Yet even the illiterate, or those with access to only a few books, can retain truths they have learned by heart.

The "seven sages" of ancient Greece offered the sort of wisdom that, like countless passages in the Bible or the Confu-

cian classics, inspired endless commentary and thought. As
the Talmud testifies, commentary invites ever more commentary. A single gnomic line can come to resonate with centuries
of subsequent wisdom.

No consensus fixed the list of seven sages. There were
seven sages the way there were (various lists of) seven wonders.
Like the number eighty-one, which guided the organization of
the *Tao Te Ching,* seven was traditional and magical. Nevertheless, the sayings of these seven sages, however identified,
formed a basis for Greek culture and were endlessly cited.
"Know thyself" (inscription at the Delphic oracle), "Nothing
to excess," "Not even the gods fight against necessity," "Know
the right moment," "Call no man happy until he is dead," "Remember the end": even today, all these still seem somehow to
contain the essence of Greek wisdom and make us ponder.[4]

Of course, the biblical Book of Proverbs contains countless detachable quotations, traditionally attributed in large part
to Solomon. We find similar bits of detachable wisdom in the
Psalms, attributed to David. The Bible also offers a sort of
counter-wisdom in Ecclesiastes and Job, which quote and
question the sort of pious assertions found in Proverbs. So we
read a dialogue of quotations, reminiscent of the encounters of
Lao Tzu with Confucius.

That sort of dialogue of wisdoms seems remarkably common. In ancient Greece, Diogenes the Cynic, Crates, and later
Menippus parodied traditional wisdom with their ironic
counter-wisdom. Diogenes' father was said to have "defaced
the coinage" of his city, and the Cynics made the accusation a
badge as they "defaced the coinage" of received wisdom. If
Solomon is thought of as the author of Ecclesiastes as well as of
many proverbs, he both defaces and coins traditional pious
sayings. William Blake, of course, composed his "Proverbs of

Hell" as counter-proverbial. Instead of "Nothing to excess," we read that "the road of excess leads to the palace of wisdom."[5] As with his poems of innocence and experience, Blake hoped to give voice to both sides of the human soul.

Numerous writers in European literature have contributed short works designed to stand on their own. The sardonic *Maxims* of La Rochefoucauld develop, in a psychological spirit, the sort of anti-proverbial wisdom spoken by Qoheleth in Ecclesiastes. La Rochefoucauld redirects us from knowledge to self-knowledge, from what we know to why we think we know it. Self-deception prompted by vanity serves as the endless theme of his maxims: "Whatever discoveries one has made in the realm of self-esteem, many uncharted regions still remain there"; "We all have sufficient fortitude to endure the misfortunes of others"; "Everyone complains of his memory, and no one complains of his judgment"; and, most famously, "Hypocrisy is a tribute which vice pays to virtue."[6] These maxims often take the form of condensed riddles. It is not immediately obvious exactly why people complain of their memory rather than their judgment, or in what sense hypocrisy is a tribute. To solve such riddles, we must identify in ourselves the thought processes that lead us to believe as we do, or, more accurately, to believe as we believe we do. Like many short literary works, these maxims do not give themselves away.[7]

Some lines are born quotations, some are made quotations, and some have "quotation" thrust upon them. These differences in origin raise questions that have bedeviled experts. If a quotation, as usually quoted and as found in anthologies, is discovered to differ from its source, is it necessarily a misquotation? If so, then most of what we know and quote consists of misquotations. If reference works should replace misquotations with the "correct" versions, as some have already undertaken to do, how will we decipher numerous allusions to the once familiar versions? Should the band change its name to "Blood and Toil, Sweat and Tears"? Or would such erasure of familiar versions, if successful, become a sort of Orwellian counterpart to Newspeak—Newquote?—erasing, along with supposed errors, a good deal of cultural memory?

For many reasons we shall explore, the question of correct and incorrect turns out to be a lot more complicated than it first appears. What if the version in the source is unquotable? We say, "Turn the other cheek," but no such words actually occur in the Sermon on the Mount, where we read: "If a man strike thee on one cheek, turn to him also the other." Should we intone, "As the Good Book says, 'Turn to him also the other'"? What if the whole point of a quotation depends on who said it, or when it was said, and experts determine it belongs to someone else or was said on a different occasion? What if the best-known user of a quotation turns out not to be its first user? "We have nothing to fear but fear itself," proclaimed Franklin Delano Roosevelt, as we all remember. But he was far from the first to express this idea. Montaigne confesses, "The thing I fear most is fear" (BFQ16, 145); Bacon advises that "nothing is terrible but fear itself" (BFQ16, 158); the Duke of Wellington recorded that "the only thing I am afraid of is fear" (BFQ16, 371); and there seems to be a source in Proverbs 3:25: "Be not afraid of sudden fear."[8] Was FDR, who mentioned no source, a plagiarist? Should we "dequote" him by ceasing to credit him with the famous line, and thereby strip the line of the context we all presume? As we shall see, John Kennedy's "Ask not what your country can do for you—ask what you can do for your country" (YBQ, 421) and Nathan

Hale's "I only regret that I have but one life to lose for my country" (YBQ, 331) also have earlier attestations. Should they, along with FDR, surrender their famous lines? If we were all credited according to our desert, who would escape dequoting?

It is pretty clear that Marie Antoinette did not say "Let them eat cake" or Louis IV "L'état c'est moi," so should quotation anthologies that profess strict accuracy leave them out? If not, how should they be treated? Some quotation researchers have decided that great words spoken by actors or actresses actually belong to the scriptwriters who wrote them, so should we stop speaking of Mae West's line "Why don't you come up some time?" (YBQ, 808) or Clint Eastwood's "Make my day" (YBQ, 267)? What happens when we are dealing with an influential translation, like Fitzgerald's "Rubaiyat of Omar Khayyam"? Whose moving finger, Fitzgerald's or Omar Khayyám's, wrote, "The moving finger writes, and having writ, / Moves on" (YBQ, 271)? What if a translation has, like the King James Bible, achieved such authority that referring to another version, even a more accurate one, makes allusions unrecognizable? Does it make sense to refer to "the guardian of my brother" rather than "my brother's keeper," and would anyone understand us if we did? Or should we ask the afflicted to recite that "Yahweh is my Shepherd, / I lack nothing"? That is how the Jerusalem Bible gives us the lines that are so famous I can rely on the reader silently referencing the King James version as I write the alternative.[9] And that is what any other version of such famous lines will always be, a mere alternative.

People love to cite "famous last words," and I shall devote a chapter to them. But a moment's reflection should persuade us that almost all examples depend less on factual reporting than on literary conventions. How does one verify last words? Sometimes the great last utterance seems almost, if not quite, impossible; or perhaps something resembling it was said—but on an earlier occasion. And what if, as with Thomas More, Rabelais, and Jesus in the New Testament, more than one set of "last words" has been attributed to the same person? They cannot all be final. Or is there some way in which they can be? After all, it cannot be that the compilers of the New Testament, let alone two millennia of readers, have failed to notice that Jesus speaks for the last time more than once. Instead of determining which version is original, perhaps we would do better to ask what such multiplicity tells us about how quotations live.[10]

Final utterances, epitaphs and supposed epitaphs, heroic pronouncements and inspiring homilies: all circulate both in speech and in writing. If the two versions differ, as they often do, which is to be preferred? Anthologies, of course, are written, rather than spoken, and so can hardly be considered neutral arbiters. One might as well ask a teacher whether the way to improve education is to raise teachers' salaries or a general whether we need a higher defense budget. What lies beyond personal preference or prejudice in choosing between written and oral versions of great quotations? Perhaps the complex ways in which oral and written genres interact require a definition that encompasses not just "memorable speech," but also memorable writing, and everything in between. For that matter, could an understanding of quotations as *both* oral and written help us to understand the texts of *all* literary works better?

Just as "myth" does not necessarily mean "lie," so "folklore" need not be a synonym for unsubstantiated belief. Does it make sense to ask what is the correct text of a joke? One can get a folk story or a joke wrong, but not because of historical evidence or authoritative textual editing. It would take a literalist, if not an idiot, to object that there is no documentary evidence for the words Herodotus attributes to Solon. One might as well object that Aesop had no good reason to think there really was a boy who cried wolf or a goose that laid golden eggs—if there ever was an Aesop at all. By the same token, which of the many versions of Aesop's fables, which changed from period to period in ways hard to trace, is the right one? If a quotation has evolved over centuries, should we even ask which version is correct? Beware lest you lose the substance while grasping for the shadow.

If we lack historical perspective, we may readily accept that the book of quotations arose recently, when John Bartlett invented it in 1855. Bartlett's name has become a brand, like Roget or Webster, and so no recent edition of "Bartlett's" bears the slightest resemblance to the 1855 version. Nevertheless, "Bartlett's" is the version with which all others compete.

Somehow, many have come to think of Bartlett's as the equivalent of Herodotus's *History:* the first work of its kind. But nothing could be further from the truth. Not only do anthologies extend into the remotest historical past, but they have been common in diverse cultures and over many eras. In the Middle Ages, learning often took the form of making one's own commonplace book of best quotations, a genre that still survives. Renaissance culture, so deeply concerned with fragments of the past, continued the tradition. One showed one's understanding of a book by the quotations one extracted from it, a process thought to resemble separating wheat from chaff or selecting gems from stones. Gems were gathered into "treasuries," a word we still use for collections of valuable short works.

Over the past decade or so, quotation anthologies have

exercised an ever-widening appeal. Bartlett's is by no means the only serious and comprehensive one around. The *Oxford Dictionary of Quotations,* the *Macmillan Dictionary of Quotations,* and, most recently, the *Yale Book of Quotations* all reflect real thinking, as do some anthologies devoted to particular topics, such as David and Hilary Crystal's *Words on Words,* the *Oxford Dictionary of Phrase, Saying, and Quotation,* and *History in Quotations.* As we shall see, recent anthologizers have even shown us how an anthology can acquire compelling narrative interest and, in the process, serve as a quasi-literary form.

I am always asked whether such books can possibly survive in the age of the Internet. The fact that, if anything, they are becoming more popular would seem to indicate that the question contains some mistaken presuppositions. It reminds me of the confident prediction back in the early 1980s that we were entering the "paperless society" or the assertion by experts of the 1950s that electricity would soon be "too cheap to meter."[11] Anthologizers themselves like to say, as the editors of the *Britannica* did in response to Wikipedia, that their printed books are more reliable. It does not take much Googling to see that this claim is largely correct, even if authoritative sources can also be less than scrupulous in ascribing wisdom to their heroes and idiocies to their enemies.

Might it not be that quotation anthologies have always encouraged the sort of reading we associate with the Internet? We do not just look up quotations, we browse for them. We "surf" Bartlett's, going from entry to entry, as association suggests. We can even open the book at random, which one cannot do on the Internet. Still more important, the best anthologies show genuine imagination. They are not just reference works, they are *books.* Unlike mere compendia of information, they demonstrate an active mind grappling with tradition and ephemera, with thoughts truly great and attitudes merely widely circulated. If well done, they can raise questions, whether aesthetic, social, or philosophical, we had not previously formulated.

Auden wrote: "The words of a dead man, / Are modified in the guts of the living."[12] We modify quotations and they modify us. As it digests quotations, language changes, along with the people who use it. In reply to a disparagement of quotation, Dr. Johnson insisted that "classical quotation is the *parole* of literary men all over the world" (WoW, 297). Anatole France frankly advised, "When a thing has been said and said well, have no scruple. Take it and copy it" (MDQ, 467). Yes, indeed, but do more. Copy many well-said things. Piece them together. Assimilate them. Make the process of reading them a way to form the mind and shape the soul. As anthologies can never be complete, we will never exhaust the ways quotations can enrich our lives.

I
The Market for Quotations

I
What Is an Anthology?

Books from Books

Amazon.com presently lists for sale several thousand books of quotations, not including those out of print or in other languages. Hundreds deal with the "wit and wisdom" of Oscar Wilde, Bernard Shaw, Mark Twain, Abraham Lincoln, and many other cultural figures. We may peruse Indian Wisdom, Great Thoughts of China, or a Treasury of Yiddish Quotations. Some collections console, others inspire; they may focus on the literary, the popular, or anywhere in between. Hackneyed profundity competes with platitudinous sarcasm. Many select from the Bible.

Various professions and fields have their competing anthologies of wisdom, insights, or rules of thumb. Fine collections of scientific quotations, philosophical quotations, religious quotations, mathematical quotations, and medical quotations can teach a lot. Divided into two sections, *Key Quotations in Sociology* allows us to look up important comments either by topic ("anomie," "Fordism," "moral panic") or thinker (Marx, Mead, Merton).[1] Publishers have presumably made back their investment in *A Dictionary of Economic Quotations* and *The Macmillan Book of Business and Economic Quotations.*[2] Every imaginable subdivision of society can boast its own books of identity-soothing words. Some day, historians will be able to use quotation anthologies to discover how people saw themselves.

Humorous, or supposedly humorous, quotations seem to be the most numerous of all. There is a laugh for every occasion, and books of insulting comments endlessly repeat the same material. One rapidly reaches a point of diminishing returns as one consults the *Cassell Dictionary of Insulting Quotations, The Mammoth Book of Zingers, Quips, and One-Liners* (with a picture of Oscar Wilde on the cover), *The Nasty Quote Book, Poisonous Quotes, Fighting Words, Put-Downs,* and *Viva la Repartee.*[3] Misanthropy, misogyny, and misandry seem to enjoy insatiable demand. Cynicism never goes out of style. If you exhaust *The Cynic's Lexicon,* try *The Portable Curmudgeon.*[4]

It takes little effort to find anthologies devoted to every religious, cultural, or political movement. Some are carefully done, others slapped together. Many limit themselves to the twentieth century and soon, one supposes, to the twenty-first. A few collections represent significant intellectual achievements or notable displays of imagination, even if most reflect little more than someone's discovery of a new market niche or a propagandist's desire to circulate the equivalent of bumper stickers. No one ever lost money selling the thoughts of others.

Organizations known for scholarly respectability have recognized that their names ensure profitability for a volume of quotations. American Heritage, Yale University Press, Oxford, Cassell, and the New York Public Library have all used their reputations in this way, and why not? With so many competing and shoddy goods, a respectable brand does in fact mean something. Many books of quotations select from others, and some publishers, like Oxford University Press, use a pooled data base to be ready for an anthology as soon as a new demand or idea arises. Is there some topic to which an "Oxford Book of" has not been dedicated? Along with general anthologies, Oxford collections include volumes devoted to proverbs, scientific quotations, legal quotations, biographical quotations, humorous remarks, political pronouncements, aphorisms, nursery rhymes, and allusions.

Yale University Press recently published not only a volume of Bedouin proverbs, but also a curious collection of quotations about espionage.[5] *The Literary Spy,* compiled by former CIA speechwriter and analyst Charles E. Lathrop, overtly discusses the covert and so reads like a collection of open secrets. Other anthologies instruct readers; this one takes them into its confidence. Much like an intelligence report, each section includes data (in this case, selected quotations) and analysis. In the section on "Nut Cases and Conspiracy," for instance, we unearth Prof. John P. Roche's suggestion that "whenever an event can be explained either by conspiracy or idiocy, choose idiocy" (*Literary Spy,* 267), as well as this commentary by "The Literary Spy"—that is, by Lathrop himself: "The course of human events is better explained by idiocy than by conspiracy, by stumbling than by planning, by accident than by design" (*Literary Spy,* 264). Yet the book is itself designed with exquisite care.

Volumes of quotations can almost amount to a short course on a given topic. The anthology compiled by Mortimer

Adler and Charles Van Doren, the *Great Treasury of Western Thought,* creates a virtual dialogue among the most important ideas in the history of philosophy, politics, and psychology.[6]

History in Quotations, the work of specialists from a variety of fields, can be seen either as a reference book tweaked into a narrative or a narrative made up of suitably presented quotations. Instead of being told what Galileo, Robespierre, and Lenin thought, we encounter, almost hear, their very words. Reading through particular chapters of this magnificent collection, introduced by Simon Schama, one can study topics as various as the French Revolution, the Scientific Revolution, and the Russian Revolution; civilizations from antiquity to the present; and cultures from China to Peru, to give just a sampling of the contents. Each chapter presents quotations in chronological order. Building upon each other and glossed by notes, they transform this anthology into a compelling narrative history.

For a quick survey of the development of the social sciences, one may consult a true classic, *The Macmillan Book of Social Science Quotations.* The editors, David Sills and (the great) Robert Merton, relied on the expertise of prominent consultants (Daniel Bell, Lewis Coser, Peter Gay, Dell Hymes, Edmund Leach, R. R. Palmer, Herbert Simon, Neil Smelser, Lawrence Stone, and about three hundred others) as well as their own considerable knowledge. Evidently, these thinkers considered the anthology of quotations a significant form.

Very different but extremely popular are anthologies of exquisitely stupid remarks. Collections of "the dumbest things ever said" sell well enough to beget sequel after sequel (more dumb things, even dumber things, and so on).[7] Since stupidity is endless, it is only surprising how many selections are considered dumb simply because they express the sentiments of a foreign enemy or the opposite political party. Unwittingly, these selections testify to the narrow-mindedness of the anthologizer. How could anyone be so dumb as to believe what Democrats (or Republicans) believe!

Recently, several editors have achieved success with collections of quotations that were *not* said, which, perhaps, should include (in a postmodern or Rabelaisian spirit) advertisements for anthologies never actually compiled. One could assemble an interesting volume of quotations simply by selecting the most overstated claims in the generally slapdash prefaces to commonly available anthologies. How about an Oxford Book of Blurbs?

Volumes of quotations clearly have an appeal that goes beyond mere reference. We find excuses to buy or compile them. Periodicals review them. In one book review, George Orwell described the author as "no more able to resist a quotation than some people are to refuse a drink" (MDQ, 478), but when it comes to anthologies of famous remarks, it is the reviewers who become quotaholics. They cannot resist quoting line after favorite line and so turning their reviews into mini-anthologies of their own. They accept the invitations, which such collections extend to everyone, to season their conversation and prose with borrowed wit.

Despite all this interest, we find few serious studies of quotations (let alone of anthologies of quotations) as a form. Merton wrote what is probably the best book ever about quotations, which I shall refer to more than once, *On the Shoulders of Giants: A Shandean Postscript.* But Merton's effort is unusual. It is also sociological rather than literary. Although anthologies are filled with lines from the great thinkers, and have sometimes been compiled by writers as significant as Erasmus, Tolstoy, and Auden, literary critics have largely overlooked the topic.

Before Bartlett's

Notwithstanding common claims to the contrary, anthologies of quotations have a long history. The most authoritative current compilers of quotations constitute a sort of club and, like poets awarding each other prizes, frequently cite each other. One of the more prominent members, Suzy Platt, has asserted: "Quotation books, surprisingly enough, are a rather recent invention. The classic *Bartlett's Familiar Quotations* started the tradition in this country and was begun in 1855 by the owner of the University Book Store in Cambridge, Massachusetts. Burton Stevenson's massive *Home Book of Quotations* started in 1934, and the dignified *Oxford Dictionary of Quotations* did not appear until 1941" (RQ, xvii). Such carelessness can only make one question the depth of Platt's sense of history. As we shall see, quotation books are anything but a recent invention, and even in the English-speaking world, they enjoyed centuries of appeal before Bartlett's, Stevenson's, and the Oxford.

Quotation books in fact go back to antiquity and there have been equivalents of Bartlett's in many ages and cultures. Cultures are constantly compiling collections of their wisdom. Those without writing rely on memorization, and those who have recently acquired writing usually hasten to record accumulated memorable wisdom. Once one understands the reasons that such anthologies are assembled, it becomes surprising when a culture does *not* offer an example of some sort.

Platt also misleads in suggesting that between 1855 and 1941 the form developed slowly. Between Bartlett's and the Oxford, more than Stevenson's appeared. First published in 1907, *Benham's Book of Quotations, Proverbs, and Household Words* circulated widely. It went through several editions and, after a substantial revision and enlargement, was renamed *Putnam's Complete Book of Quotations, Proverbs and Household Words: A Collection of Quotations from British and American Authors, with Many Thousands of Proverbs, Familiar Phrases and Sayings, from All Sources, including Hebrew, Arabic, Greek, Latin, French, German, Italian, Spanish and Other Languages,* edited by W. Gurney Benham and published by G. P. Putnam's Sons (New York, 1926).

Kate Louise Roberts, the compiler of the quite substantial *Hoyt's New Cyclopedia of Practical Quotations* (1922 and several editions thereafter) boasts: "It may be claimed for this work, without fear of contradiction, that no other of its kind contains so full an array of material under topics; none with such a representation of modern writers and speakers; no other includes such a record of modern war phrases, songs and poems; nowhere else are kindred thoughts and expressions so closely connected by cross references that they may be compared, and in no other collection of quotations have the nerves and arteries of the contents been laid open so plainly through so comprehensive and complete a concordance."[8] When an editor proclaims superiority to rivals, she affirms their existence as well as a readership for whom these rivals are relatively familiar. Such boasts imply a recognized genre, books "of its kind." The date of Roberts's introduction to the 1940 edition perhaps explains its stress on military quotations and "stirring lines" (Hoyt's, vii), but it is not the events of the day that account for her pride in how many "literary gems" she has included and how comprehensive her collection is. Such claims of bigger and better, like the boasts of "new and improved" on detergent boxes, reflect the genre's established rules.

Roberts promoted her book as a classic edited to match more closely the tastes of her day. Her preface begins: "To Amalthaea, the nurse of his infancy, Zeus gave a magic horn of plenty, which by his grace was over-brimming no matter what was taken from it. This *new edition* of a standard work, like the famous cornucopia, contains a freshened and replenished store" that is a "garnering of this rich harvest of fruits culled from the vast fields of literature" (Hoyt's, vii).

Anthony W. Shipps's *The Quote Sleuth: A Manual for the Tracer of Lost Quotations* mentions several "older collections" including two by Samuel Austin Alliborne, one devoted to *Poetical Quotations from Chaucer to Tennyson* (1873) and the other to *Prose Quotations from Socrates to Macauley* (1875).[9] For that matter, the *Oxford English Dictionary* is itself a kind of quotation anthology, probably containing more quotations than any other publication ever. The *Oxford Companion to the English Language* (1992) tells us that by the time the first edition of the OED was completed in 1928, its twelve volumes printed over two million quotations, out of five million gathered for the project (OCEL, 737). Interestingly enough, the subentry in the *Oxford Companion to the English Language* on "books of quotations" begins not with Bartlett's but with the much later *Oxford Dictionary of Quotations* (1941) and then surveys subsequent anthologies, as if the publisher of this *Companion* was tacitly omitting upstarts like Bartlett's that had the temerity to appear earlier (OECL, 837).

John Bartlett himself had many precedents to draw upon, including *A Complete Dictionary of Poetical Quotations: Comprising the Most Excellent and Appropriate Passages in the Old*

British Poets; with Choice and Copious Selections from the Best Modern British and American Poets, edited by Sarah Josepha Hale, published a few years before the first edition of Bartlett's (1849, with revisions appearing until 1883). Incorporating the equivalent of advertising hype into a book's title was conventional; burgeoning comprehensiveness counted both in naming and editing these works. Hale's volume announces itself as "the only complete work of the kind in the English language," although how an anthology of quotations could ever be complete is not explained.[10]

Hale informs us that she continues the work of John F. Addington, whose labors were "incomplete" and whose selections "were not always in accordance with the present standard of public taste. The old dramatic poets wrote according to their light, which was often reflected through a foul medium, and revealed much that is now considered, and justly, too, as coarse and indelicate" (Hale, ii). Modern anthologizers sometimes make the reverse claim, professing to correct the delicacy of predecessors while honoring the more enlightened, liberated, and foul standard of taste today.

As we might suspect by now, neither Hale nor Addington came up with the idea of a quotation anthology. Shipps lists several earlier ones, including a four-volume 1777 revision of a 1737 anthology, *The Beauties of English Drama;* a 1702 collection, Edward Bysshe's *The Art of English Poetry;* Thomas Hayward's *The British Muse: or, A Collection of Thoughts Moral, Natural, and Sublime, of Our English Poets, Who Flourished in the Sixteenth and Seventeenth Centuries* (three volumes published in 1738 and republished with a different title in 1740); and a four-volume collection of 1761, *A Poetical Dictionary; or, The Beauties of the English Poets, Alphabetically Displayed.* (See

Shipps, 125–127.) The first edition of the Oxford mentions vaguely that "small dictionaries of quotations have been published for many years—in 1799 D. E. Macdonald brought out a *Dictionary of Quotations chiefly from Latin and French translated into English.*"[11] Of course, England and America did not produce the only examples.

In short, to say that Bartlett invented the form is like proclaiming Julia Child the inventor of the cookbook or Thomas Edison the inventor of inventions. Since antiquity, various people—well known, formerly well known, or simply obscure—have composed collections, based on diverse principles, intended for various audiences, and compiled for heterogeneous purposes. Some of these collections are themselves literary classics.

The form was particularly common in the Middle Ages and Renaissance, when the expense of books, the primacy of rhetoric-based education, and a flourishing interest in the works of antiquity fed the appetite for such collections. The invention of the printing press only spread the form further. Significantly, the first book printed in England (by Caxton, the first English printer) was *The dictes or sayengis of the philosophhres.* Evidently perceiving a market for such collections, Caxton the next year brought out *The moral prouerbes of Cristyne,* a translation of a fifteenth-century French volume of wise sayings.[12]

Erasmus

Caxton was well acquainted with the most important collection of the past millennium or more, Erasmus's *Adages.* One of the most influential books of the Renaissance, reprinted, anthologized, plagiarized, and updated countless times, the *Adages* constantly grew. The first edition, entitled *A Collection of Paroemiae or Adages, Old and Most Celebrated, Made by Desyderius Herasmus Roterodamus, a Work Both New and Wonderfully Useful for Conferring Beauty and Distinction on All Kinds of Speech and Writing* (1500), contained 818 entries. Each entry contained a classical saying, adage, or proverb elucidated by an essay.

Erasmus kept expanding the work edition by edition so that by 1536 it had 4,151 entries. As Erasmus himself remarked, he did not seem able to stop enlarging his book, which became for him a sort of quotational Sisyphus. In Erasmus's satire *The Praise of Folly,* the goddess Folly, after a volley of proverbs, concludes: "But enough of quoting proverbs, I don't want you to imagine that I've been plundering the notebooks of my friend Erasmus."[13] Holbein illustrated Folly's reference to her friend and author with a portrait printed in the margins showing Erasmus collecting his sayings—as if the act of collecting continues as long as the work itself is read.

We shall have occasion to examine Erasmus's collection, its sources, and its influences, in greater detail, but here it is worth noting that Erasmus himself drew on numerous ancient and medieval collections. Collecting the words of the great, as we shall see, was a recognized form of learning. Even before the Greeks and Romans, the biblical Book of Proverbs collects not only wise sayings but also collections of wise sayings. It is a book of books, and it reflects wisdom compiled previously throughout the Middle East. For that matter, the book often called "the oldest book in the world," *The Precepts of Ptahhotep,* collects still earlier bits of wisdom.[14]

So long as there has been writing, people have collected

quotations. One is almost tempted to say that writing began so as to preserve the words of others.

Museum of Utterances

The impulse to collect seems universal. We all collect, or have collected, something. And even when we stop collecting things (if ever), we still collect memories. Indeed, it may well be that identity consists in the experiences, verbal or behavioral, that we remember.

Sometimes cultures institutionalize the collecting impulse. The Renaissance, which produced so many anthologies of quotations, also saw the birth of the modern museum. Once-famous figures like Ulisse Aldrovandi (1522–1605) and Athanasius Kircher (1502–1680) sought to offer a summary of nature in one place. In her excellent book *Possessing Nature: Museums, Collecting, and Scientific Culture in Early Modern Italy,* Paula Findlen notes that in Italy "collecting [of this sort] first became a widespread practice, among an elite desirous to know the past, in all its forms, through the possession of its remnants."[15]

Today, we have museums of just about everything. Visiting another city typically includes viewing its collections. In fact, many people make a sort of collection of the museums they have visited around the world. Perhaps the impulse to collect reflects a desire to arrest time by preserving pieces of the past. Or, on the contrary, it may reach out to the future by providing material for new, creative combinations. One way or another, all museums exhibit time.

An anthology of quotations is a museum of utterances. It collects and displays masterpieces of phrase and thought in a small space. Unlike art museums, of course, anthologies of short literary works have no unique original that leaves only mere substitutes for rivals. Verbal art is infinitely reproducible with no copy more genuine than the others. There is only one statue of David and one original of the Mona Lisa, but everyone who has a copy of *Hamlet* has *Hamlet,* and not a mere reproduction. To be sure, there may be only one manuscript of a great literary work, but the work itself exists each time it is published.

For this reason, and many others, it is much easier to own a museum of great verbal artworks than a collection of great paintings. At Barnes and Noble, such museums are always for sale. They are also portable. Even without an electronic reader, one can carry the great sayings and witticisms of the world wherever one goes.

To be sure, anyone with enough space can, theoretically, own a vast library of the world's great books. One can also go to library stacks or good used book stores to browse. But a good anthology of quotations, as Erasmus and Caxton knew, already contains many excellent works. One cannot quickly browse through a major library's collection of European novels, but great aphorisms invite us to skip from one to another. Elias Cannetti observed aphoristically, "The great writers of aphorisms read as if they had all known each other well" (OBA, 364). Intellectually speaking, many did, but we can easily introduce the others to each other. We can make one aphorist speak to, provoke, or answer another. We can "draw dotted lines" extending the thought of one aphorist until it intersects with that of another, and then imagine what dialogue would ensue.[16]

Collectors of anything soon learn that to understand, one has to classify. They also learn that there is never a single correct classification system. Every person is his own Linnaeus. As we accumulate short works of verbal art, we come to resemble those botanists of the Age of Discovery flooded with samples from new places. Old classification systems break down, but that is all to the good because devising new ones makes us think of new relationships.

The more quotations one knows, and the more small bits of wisdom one ponders, the more thought can be made to speak to thought. Wisdom grows by interrogating other wisdom, the way one's self-knowledge grows by reflecting on earlier things one has told oneself.

The process is endless, because quotations resemble language as J. A. H. Murray described it: they have "a well-defined center but no discernible circumference" (WoW, 126). It can be hard to tell what *isn't* a quotation. To understand why, we need to consider quotationality itself.

II
Quotationality and Former Quotations

"Blessed are the peacemakers; theirs is the kingdom
of heaven," said Betsy, vaguely recollecting she had
heard some similar saying from someone.
—*Tolstoy,* Anna Karenina *(Part II, ch. 4)*

Aura

Sometimes we do not cite specific words but rather conjure the *aura* of a quotation. In such cases, an utterance displays what might be called "quotationality" without actually quoting anything specific. Quotationality comes in degrees.

Quotationality confers upon phrases a degree of otherness. Creating a vague feeling that something is being cited, such phrases appear in stories ranging from everyday anecdotes to great novels. They also figure prominently in thought and in inner speech, while playing an important role in the life of language itself. A language's partial assimilation of foreign words and phrases, its development of clichés and idioms, and its deployment of a host of other quotational phenomena often make it hard to say where one speaker's words end and another's begin. We make the most of this ambiguity as we orient ourselves in a linguistic world that is always shared. Even in our dreams, we hear the words of others. Each of us lives and thinks in dialogue with utterances that either have been, or sound as if they could have been, said before.

Quotationality defines us. We are what we quote.

The Insufficiency of Quotation Marks

At one extreme of a continuum, one is clearly quoting: unambiguously citing another's words *as* another's words. At the other, one is just saying what one means: speaking directly with no attempt to invoke anyone else's utterances. A great deal of what we say, write, or read partakes of both extremes.[1]

In between the extremes, we find numerous quotational phenomena, such as paraphrase, indirect discourse, or "free indirect discourse." Sometimes speakers and writers slide up and down the scale of quotedness, as they both quote and comment on the words quoted at once. Mikhail Bakhtin famously defined a category of "double-voiced words" that are simultaneously speech and quoted speech.

Consider the following passage from Tolstoy's *Anna Karenina,* in which Anna, after having met and flirted with her future lover Vronsky, is reading an English novel on the train returning to Petersburg:

The hero of the novel had almost attained his English happiness, a baronetcy and an estate, and Anna
was feeling a desire to go with him to the estate,
when she suddenly felt that *he* ought to feel ashamed,
and that she was ashamed of the same thing. But
what had he to be ashamed of? "What have I to be
ashamed of?" she asked herself in injured surprise.
She laid down the book and sank against the back
of the chair, tightly gripping the paper cutter in
both hands. There was nothing. She went over all
her Moscow recollections. All were good, pleasant.
She remembered the ball, remembered Vronsky
and his face of slavish adoration, remembered her
conduct with him: there was nothing shameful.
And for all that, at the same point in her memories,
the feeling of shame was intensified, as though
some inner voice, just at the point when she thought
of Vronsky, were saying to her "Warm, very warm,
hot." "Well, what is it?" she said to herself resolutely,
shifting her seat in the lounge. "What does it
mean? Am I afraid to look it straight in the face?
Why, what is it? Can it be that between me and this
officer boy there exist, or can exist, any other rela-
tions than such as are common with every acquain-
tance?" She laughed contemptuously and took up
her book again; but now she was definitely unable
to follow what she read. (AK, 107)

Who says "But what had he to be ashamed of?" or "All were
good, pleasant"? Although the narration begins and remains
in the third person, by the end of the first sentence, we are

clearly following Anna's thoughts in Anna's words: that is why the reference to "he" does not need to be explained. In inner speech, pronouns without antecedents pose no problem because we know to whom we are referring as another might not. Their presence in a narrative therefore often indicates inner speech.

We hear Anna asking what *he* (Vronsky) had to be ashamed of, but the very fact that she is asking this question, while telling herself that "there was nothing shameful," betrays her own shame. She is denying an accusation that *might* be made, and which her own feelings would prompt. With each repetition to herself that "there was nothing" we detect her detecting, and trying not to detect, that there was something. The line between the narrator's words and Anna's has been blurred.

So gradually do we slide into Anna's voice that it is sometimes possible to move the quotation marks without significantly distorting the meaning. We could write, "But what had he to be ashamed of? What have I to be ashamed of?" as we could not if the first of these two questions were not already largely Anna's in effect. Then why not rephrase the entire passage in the first person and put it all in quotation marks? Because we do not hear *only* Anna's voice. We also hear the tonalities of the author's implicit commentary at the same time. With or without quotation marks, we sense both Anna speaking to herself and the author commenting on that inner speech. The irony possible in paraphrase infects even the direct quotations.

In places, the author rephrases Anna's thoughts. He quotes them in a way that indicates his own attitude along with hers. In the reference to the children's game—"warm, very warm, hot"—we are hearing the substance, not the very words Anna thinks ("it is *as if* some inner voice"). Throughout the whole passage, we sense the author almost teasing the heroine in the quotations and half-quotations tracing her thoughts.

We also sense authorial presence in his notation of what she expresses nonverbally, in the mention of how she shifts her position. The observation that "now she was definitely unable to follow what she read" could be from either Anna or the author, and it is in fact from both. She is telling herself she can no longer follow the book, and the author is commenting ironically on a symptom of her attempted self-deception. If she really felt she had nothing to be ashamed of, she could resume reading.

In all these ways, which do not exhaust the possibilities of quotationality, the passage is "double-voiced," both narration and quotation at the same time.

Passages like these are the trademark of the realist novel. They depend on the fact that quotationality comes in degrees, and so the author can choose how much to use at any given point. They also depend on the possibility of quoting from more than one voice at the same time. Perhaps we, too, when imagining how other people think about actions we dislike, combine their presumed words with our ironic responses.

Quotation marks are either present or absent, and so they are altogether too crude an instrument to register degrees, and complex kinds, of quotationality.

Quoting Quoting

In everyday life, we also "double-voice" our words: we often say something in the accent, frequently exaggerated, that another might use to say it. That is, we rely on quotationality without having a specific quotation in mind.

One may be more or less aware of making a statement, to oneself or others, that sounds like it *could be* a quotation. "Could be" is a specific quality we can sense, and often do.

In George Eliot's *Middlemarch*, for instance, Caleb Garth loves the very feel of biblical quotation as such. "It was one of Caleb's uniquenesses, that in his difficulty of finding speech for his thought, he caught, as it were, snatches of diction which he associated with various points of view or states of mind; and whenever he had a feeling of awe, he was haunted by a sense of Biblical phraseology, though he could hardly have given a strict quotation."[2] Such "snatches of diction . . . associated with various points of view or states of mind" carry quotationality so as to evoke what another voice of a certain sort *might* have said. Caleb Garth quotes not any particular quotation but the *elements* of such quotations, "Biblical phraseology." Or perhaps he is quoting the very act of quoting the Bible. In many ways, quotationality shadows his words.

Quoting with a Wink

If one listens carefully to the conversations of daily life, one may be struck by the sheer number of quotations of one sort or another. Some are barely conscious, and many remain unmarked as quotations, indicated neither by raised fingers making punctuation marks in the air nor by a quotatory tone of voice.

In fact, some quotations are meant to be heard precisely *as* unmarked: they are spoken or written with no clear clue to their status so that most will miss them and only the properly educated will recognize them for what they are. The speaker or writer shares a secret with one part of his or her audience at the expense of the rest. Those who do understand form a special bond of shared superiority. I refer to this kind of quotation without quotation marks—quotations whose quotationality is hidden—as quoting with a wink.

For obvious reasons, such "quotations with a wink" are especially common among academics. I often feel the temptation to use them. Recently, I happened to come across the following passage in Anthony Grafton's celebrated and whimsical study *The Footnote:*

> Rather like the modern scholar who addresses the limited audience that really matters in a code that the larger public cannot break, de Thou provided the Republic of Letters with a critical apparatus that proved the reliability, the *fides,* of his unannotated text. Moreover, his library became a way station where all the vastly erudite travelers of the Republic of Letters stopped on their way from Hamburg to Madrid or London to Rome in order to read the newest books and swap the newest gossip. In this museum created to show how late Renaissance history at its best had been written, where the librarians, the learned brothers Dupuy, pointed morals and adorned tales about scholars and scholarship, everyone could see how de Thou had worked.[3]

If we should be fortunate enough to belong to "the limited audience that really matters" to Grafton, we erudite travelers may recognize "pointed morals and adorned tales" as a near (but unreferenced) quotation from Samuel Johnson's "The Vanity of Human Wishes" about Charles XII of Sweden: "He left the name, at which the world grew pale, / To point a moral or adorn a tale."[4] If we do not belong to the audience that matters, we will probably not even know we have missed something.

Of course, "pointed morals and adorned tales" is poetic enough that some may guess that *something* is being quoted with a wink, even if they do not know what. They may recognize their exclusion from the limited audience. As there are in-jokes, there are "in-quotes," which are always at someone else's expense. Overuse of them runs the risk of snobbery or mere preciousness.

When one quotes with a wink, the logic of clubs operates. Those excluded may respond, like countless journalists forced to endure academic speech, by mocking the highfalutin' and needless display of erudition. Or, quite the contrary, when people do unexpectedly detect a hidden quotation, they may respond with Groucho-like disappointment: any quotation I recognize isn't worth knowing.

To preclude such reactions, quotes with a wink are often disguised so as not to look like quotes at all. While Grafton has preserved some of Johnson's style, what is left hints only minimally at a literary source.

As the smallest of clubs, families often have their favorite quotations-with-a-wink. They repeat them in order to evoke the shared experience that makes them a family distinct from all others. As a couple grows weepy hearing "our song," we may share a memory associated with one of our quotes. It may be a verbal tic habitual to one family member or, often enough, a shared joke. I once knew an aging wife and husband whose children often heard one of them repeat: "When one of us dies, I'm going to Paris." Or the quotation may have been something one of the family overheard and shared with the others. That same wife once overheard someone seriously say, "My psychiatrist says that religion is only for people who need to be told what to believe." Now her relatives only have to intone "my psychiatrist says" to invoke the all-too-common practice of an authority mandating skepticism of other authority. In this case, quoting with a wink efficiently recalls deeply shared values otherwise too laborious to explain.

Just as certain quotations can be a badge of membership, others can be badges of *non*-membership. We are not one of those people, and so we do not use such ignorant, vulgar, or insensitive phrases, except ironically. Nobody like us still says "too many chiefs," which is why younger people no longer even recognize the saying. For older people, the phrase belongs to the quotations we do not use, but younger people simply don't use it.

Unrecognized Quotations

Sometimes phrases we have read or heard become so thoroughly assimilated into our way of speaking or thinking that we no longer recognize them as anything but our own. In such cases, we would be surprised to discover that someone assumed we were quoting. We might be distressed to learn that a listener had actually detected the words of another when we were not intending anything of the sort. The fact that such assimilation happens to us all allows plagiarists a frequently used defense.

Phrases we once learned as quotations are now just a part of our vocabulary. We may never have known their source, and we do not even notice that we are using them. As Molière's Monsieur Jourdain was amazed to discover that all his life he had been speaking prose, we may be equally surprised to learn that we are constantly speaking in quotes. It's Greek to me, when in Rome, call a spade a spade, strange bedfellows, play fast and loose, cold comfort, kill with kindness, more sinned against than sinning, dead as a doornail, foregone conclusion, a multitude of sins, heart of gold, laid it on with a trowel (or thick), melted into thin air, neither rhyme nor reason, time is money: none of these seem like quotations from anyone anymore.

I have attended meetings where quotations, not recognized as such, occur in practically every sentence. It's all a case of sour grapes and bait and switch, she shed crocodile tears, we'll cross that bridge before we count our chickens, garbage in garbage out, question authority, a flea in my ear, done to a T, plain as the nose on his face, six of one and half a dozen of the other, one man's meat, all that glitters, out of the mouths of babes, easy come easy go, too many cooks, when the going gets tough, the grass is always greener, cry wolf, a word to the wise, set a thief, you can't tell a book by its cover, you can't win them all, no free lunch, everybody wants to get into the act: I invite my readers to watch for such expressions. I suspect they will hear, and discover themselves using, many more than they expect, and that very rapidly these expressions will cease to be perceptible at all. You might as well try to notice breathing. Some common quotations are proverbs; others are catchphrases from radio, television, or film; and many come from Shakespeare, Rabelais, Pope, Franklin, or the Bible. Most are phrases we know come from somewhere without knowing or caring where. Explicitly or implicitly, we say, "As they say," and we live surrounded by "they."

Advertisers constantly attribute remarks to that all-speaking "they." They put quotation marks around the most unquotable phrases as if to show what "they" say. Not so long ago I saw, in the local paper, store windows, or on the side of delivery trucks, in quotation marks: "Chicago's best pizza," "Famous for over one hundred years," "No one beats our prices!" and "It's the sauce!" As the saying goes, "self-praise is no recommendation," and so those intent on self-promotion are most successful when they allude to the positive statements supposedly made by nameless hordes of satisfied customers.

Quoted Style Sounding Like Quoted Words

In the middle of the continuum between direct speech and clear quotation, quotationality may sound like quotation with a wink even when it is not. In Dostoevsky's *The Idiot,* for example, Adelaida understandably mistakes a comment by Kolya as a quotation she cannot identify:

> "And it's not the thing for people of the best society to be too much interested in literature," added Kolya. "Ask Yevgeny Pavlovich. It's more correct to be keen on a yellow char-a-banc with red wheels."
>
> "You are talking in quotations again, Kolya," observed Adelaida.
>
> "But he never speaks except in quotations," chimed in Yevgeny Pavlovich, "he takes whole phrases out of the reviews. I've long had the pleasure of knowing Nikolai Ardalionovich's [Kolya's] conversation, but this time he is not talking in quotations. Nikolai Ardalionovich is plainly alluding to my yellow char-a-banc with red wheels."[5]

Kolya talks in quotation because, like all good young Russian rebels against authority, he worships his nihilist mentors and memorizes their antiauthoritarian words. Dostoevsky typically uses quotation to mock the radicals forming the herd of independent minds. "Yellow char-a-banc with red wheels" is just the sort of phrase a nihilist critic would use to satirize the shallowness of the rich, and so it sounds *as if* Kolya is quoting when he is not. Or rather, he is quoting not the specific words of the nihilist critics but their style and attitudes. That is why Adelaida detects a hidden quotation when in fact she is hearing an example of quotationality without a specific quotation.

Such quotationality of style appears often in everyday conversation. For irony or borrowed authority, we imitate the way advertisers, lawyers, or doctors speak. We love to use unnecessary acronyms or technical phrases. Like learned quotations, they indicate who belongs and who does not. Or we use the slang of teenagers to indicate we are saying what they would say. "It's awesome." "That's totally random." "It's really lame." In the same way, novelists often mock the bureaucratese, legalese, or journalese of their characters' speech. They repeat a character's phrases to evoke the style they exemplify and the values that style betrays. They quote it as *typical.*

When we tell stories about others, we may employ a similar irony of quotation, by mocking the way they speak. To do so, we may use some of their actual words. But an imitation sometimes proves all the more effective if it sounds as if it just *might* be an actual quotation or near quotation. In that case, we provoke the audience of our imitation to ask, did he really say that? Then the very fact that the audience regards our absurd exaggeration as just possible itself convicts the one imitated.

In such cases and others, we exploit the fact that certain words and syntactic constructions "remember," and so convey, the contexts and genres in which they typically appear.[6] Thees and thous, combined with a vocabulary we have heard in prayer, convey a sense of the biblical or, occasionally, of Quakers. We recognize other constructions and words as "poetic." Where are the poems of yesteryear? The use of the vocative— O hands!—almost always feels like some sort of quotation. So does the third-person imperative without a contraction: compare "let us pause" with "let's go," the first of which sounds quotational while the second does not. "Let us pray," which is a quotation, would cease to sound like one if spoken as "Let's pray." As rhetoricians from Aristotle on have argued, mastery of such language—of what I have been calling quotationality— significantly affects the meaning and power of speech.

Your Inner Bartlett's

Schoolchildren are taught to distinguish between reciting a text and retelling it "in one's own words." In much the same way, Bakhtin argues, the creation of a self involves transforming authoritative but alien voices into voices that we sense as our own. We are what we have deitalicized. This process continues throughout life. We think by orchestrating utterances to which quotation marks cling more or less securely. In our inner dialogues, phrases still felt to be another's interact with those we have made "half ours and half someone else's" (Bakhtin, 345).

We might say that, to the extent a style or set of words remains unassimilated, it has quotationality. Even our own way of speaking at an earlier time of life can come to sound like the voice of another, to the point where we are abashed to discover that we actually did use a given phrase without irony. What writer has not been embarrassed by a sample of his or her earlier prose?

We sense a continuum of quotationality in ourselves. Alienation or wisdom may derive from hearing quotation marks around one's own characteristic words. Do I really say that? At war with ourselves, we may at times experience our own most authentic utterances as if someone else were mocking them. Or as we acquire new self-insight, and recognize our self as something slowly changing, we may become keen enough to sense quotation marks in the process of emerging. We may see their incipient form around words that only recently expressed our most fervent beliefs. Now those words sound a bit naïve, as if, thank God, they belong to some earlier self, not the wiser one we are now.

As we grow, we learn to see how we might look and hear how we might sound. Wisdom and quotation develop in tandem.

Former Quotations

Quotationality shapes language itself. Our speech and writing contain countless quotations, possible quotations, allusions to quotations, and suggestions of quotation.

The undigested is quoted, the assimilated is not. We often use quotation marks when words are borrowed or extracted—in that sense, quoted—from an unfamiliar context. We may do so because we want our readers to recall that context—as if to say, this is the word connoisseurs or Frenchmen use—or we may just want to indicate our awareness that the source of the extraction may still be unknown to our readers. They may not have yet have made it their own. We put quotation marks around unfamiliar technical terms, nontechnical terms used in a technical sense, and slang that may be unfamiliar to our readers. We do not use quotation marks around such terms when our readers have already come to know them—technical terms in a technical journal are just part of the language—or even after our first mention of them. As the sense of foreignness is lost, so are quotationality and the punctuation that marks it.

Languages constantly assimilate new or alien words, both of which, so long as they are sensed as partly new or alien, feel like a kind of quotation. Borrowed words may be italicized to mark their foreignness and lose their italics somewhere on the way to being like any other words. We may italicize *pro bono,* but not champagne. It is much like the process by which foreign foods are introduced into our cuisine. First they are unheard of, then they can be consumed in foreign restaurants and purchased in specialty aisles or stores. Those special milieus serve as quotation marks of a sort. When I was growing up, pizza, egg rolls, and bagels were all foreign, not served at home unless one belonged to the appropriate ethnic group. I first encountered falafel at college. When I was growing up, we had spaghetti and macaroni, but not pasta. As Joseph Epstein has observed, the use of the term "pasta" was a form of snobbery until, at last, it was used to label supermarket displays.[7] Sushi, which now appears in airport kiosks alongside bagels and Caesar salad, was unheard of.

No one today would think of kielbasa and yogurt as foreign dishes or foreign words. Language and diet undergo Dannonization. One cannot call a pizza bagel or a chili dog fusion cuisine. By insensible gradations what was once a term or dish belonging to some person, group, or epoch becomes wholly our own. How many people know who the Stroganoff of beef Stroganoff was, and why is it "Stroganoff," instead of "Stroganov," as Russian names are usually rendered? Foreignness at last becomes nothing more than an etymological fact.

In daily life, we constantly communicate concepts, attitudes, or definitions of circumstances in fixed phrases derived (but no longer felt to be derived) from proverbs, adages, or sayings. When awareness of this derivation is entirely lost, these phrases have become what might be called *former quotations,* the way yogurt is a formerly foreign food. Their source is now nothing more than a historical fact about the phrase and does not affect its usage in the present.

In much the same way, proprietary words—words *belonging* to someone and often copyrighted—become everyone's. What was once a brand becomes the category, as we use the word "Kleenex" to mean a kind of tissue, no matter who makes it. In Russian, the word "lightning" (the first available brand of zippers) now simply means both lightning and zipper. At one point, "Frigidaire" (the General Motors brand) was a synonym for "refrigerator," as, in some parts of the United States today, "Coke" means any carbonated soft drink. Time and again, words and phrases coined by someone and entering a language at some point become everyone's and dateless.

The jargon of special disciplines consists in large part of terms and phrases that were invented at one time but now appear to be part of the discipline's anonymous language. From there, these phrases may enter common speech. Neologisms sound like quotations until they no longer sound like neologisms at all. "Sociology," a coinage of Auguste Comte, was once a quotation from him, as "folklore" was once a quotation from William Thoms, but they are quotations no longer. We are even surprised that they ever could have been, although, upon reflection, we may suppose that *someone* must have coined them.

Who coined the word "biology"? (It was apparently the German naturalist Gottfried Reinhold.) How about "DNA," "oxygen," and "vestigial organ"? No one but a few specialists know, and that is precisely the point: it would be absurd to say "biology, to use Reinhold's term." To say "sociology as Comte coined the term" would mislead because it would suggest one had in mind not "sociology" but some special kind of sociology.

In fact, one good sign that a word has lost its source or sense of quotedness is that providing the name of the originator misleads or confuses. Former quotations stand on their own; that is why they are *former* quotations. Sills and Merton observe that "many concepts-and-phrasings—such as charisma, stereotype, opportunity costs, significant others, self-fulfilling prophecy, and double-bind—have entered the vernacular with little awareness of their sources in the social sciences."[8] I wonder how many people who read this observation recall that it was Merton himself who coined the now anonymous term "self-fulfilling prophecy." These concepts-and-phrasings have lost not only their author, but also the parent discipline in which they originated. "Self-fulfilling prophecy" turned out to be a self-orphaning neologism.

Literature has provided many words that are now former quotations. We don't put inverted commas around "pandemonium" and "chortle," any more than we think of the *Iliad* when someone hectors. Many words and phrases represent quotational residue. Since all words must have come from somewhere, and all words of foreign origin must have felt foreign at some time, could it be that most of language consists of former quotations?

Former Quotations and Slogans

Sometimes foreign phrases are assimilated into the English language without changing their foreign form. Once this happens, these phrases, and not some translation of them, *are*

English. As they are no longer quotations, they are no longer
foreign, even if they contain marks not normally used in
English—like é, è, and ç. One can neither provide their origin
nor translate them without distorting their meaning. They are
already just part of our language.

A femme fatale is not a fatal woman. The English for
"laissez faire" (a term coined by Quesnay) is "laissez faire." The
English title of Victor Hugo's novel is "Les Misérables."
It would sound awkward, and convey not quite what one
means, to translate "enfants terribles," "éminence grise," "coup
d'état," "comme ci, comme ça," "bona fide," "carpe diem," "mea
culpa," or "deus ex machina" into some combination of English words, just as there is no other phrase in English for "à la
carte" or "déjà vu" (except, perhaps, "a la carte" and "deja vu").
I have seen frozen food labeled as "beef with au jus," which
means that this formerly French phrase now functions as a
single English noun, like bonbon. Such phrases (regardless of
the context of their origin) *are* English even when we also recognize them as carrying some aura of foreignness. Thus the
joke about the sneezing American in Germany who replies to
"Gesundheit" with "I'm so glad you speak English!"

Even the aura of foreignness is sometimes lost. "I.e.,"
"e.g.," "P.M.," and "A.D."—or is it now "PM" and "AD"?—may
have once been abbreviations, but they are now complete
words used by people who neither know nor care what they
might once have abbreviated. Does anyone sense "etc." (or "et-
cetera" or "et cetera"?) as foreign? How many people use the
terms "habeas corpus," "alter ego," "ex post facto," "ad homi-
nem," or "per capita" without any feeling at all they have been
quoting from the Latin? At my own university, each tenure
case is reviewed by an "ad hoc committee" not by an "'ad hoc'
committee." In many style sheets, using italics or quotation

marks for such words is improper. Latin becomes English, as quotations become former quotations.

No matter who coined the term "greenhouse effect," it would be hard to talk about "global warming" without it. Whether we are speaking of former quotations or quotations assumed to be universally known (even if their precise origin is not), we would find it difficult to think as we do without quotations.

Erasmus "insists on the literal meaning of the Greek term *paroemia* as 'a road that travels everywhere' and of the Latin *adagium* as 'something passed around'" (AE, xxix). In doing so, he was trying to reverse the process of assimilation or recall an earlier stage of it—to add quotation marks that had been lost. Whenever we argue by etymology—or false etymology—we are doing, or think we are doing, much the same thing.

To speak a language and belong to a culture involve recognizing that a given phrase is a *live* quotation—a phrase expressing a current attitude—and even recognizing when a once-live quotation *was* current. "A woman without a man is like a fish without a bicycle"; "Spaceship Earth"; "One nuclear bomb can ruin your whole day"; "Mr. Gorbachev, tear down this wall"; "Never again!"; and "change we can believe in"—all of these phrases are part of American culture and language. We know them and more or less when they came to be widely used. As "liberty, equality, fraternity" was to the era following the French revolution, so "a house divided," "the war to end all wars," "Give peace a chance," and "vast right-wing conspiracy" have been subsequently. Let them eat quotes! Some of these quotations become slogans—a slogan is a particular kind of quotation—and, after the slogan ceases to be used, it may serve as a kind of monument to the age that coined it. "At length the Man perceives it die away," and merge with speech to be just what we say.

New Clichés

Timeless anonymity is one thing, the sense of timeless anonymity quite another. Likewise, we may sense recent coinage when coinage is not recent. The sense of antiquity or novelty is itself *part* of a quotation or phrase whether or not that sense accurately reflects historical fact, much as assumed but inaccurate etymology shapes the meaning of a word. I remember somewhere a false medieval etymology of "Tartars" as people who have come straight from Tartarus, hell.

Proverbs, whenever they are coined, typically carry marks of agedness or timelessness. What may sound like hoary wisdom may in fact have been unknown a century ago, and we easily mistake indubitability for antiquity. Fred Shapiro, the editor of the *Yale Book of Quotations,* correctly disputes the notion that proverbs "are purely antiquarian sayings that are no longer coined in modern times. Nothing could be further from the truth. Modern proverbs proliferate constantly and are among our most colorful and popular expressions" (YBQ, xxi). The Yale collection therefore includes a section on "Modern Proverbs," defined as those coined since 1900. These include not only some that sound recent—"Shit happens," "Been there, done that," "When you're hot, you're hot," and "Garbage in, garbage out"—but also some that seem centuries older: "Curiosity killed the cat," "Some things are better left unsaid," "It takes one to know one," "Elephants never forget," "Don't burn your bridges," and "Opposites attract" (YBQ, 525–530). Since there have been cats, bridges, and opposites longer than there has been an England, these new coinages seem old.

Proverbiality by its nature includes the attribution of great age unless there is contrary evidence, such as memory of the time of coinage or mention of some relatively new invention. For "What you see is what you get" to achieve a sense of great age, it would need to lose the memory of its connection with computer technology.[9]

In much the same way, objects of daily life often seem older than they are. Henry Petroski's book, *The Evolution of Useful Things: How Everyday Artifacts—From Forks and Pins to Paper Clips and Zippers—Came to Be as They Are,* surprises us as it constantly shows the recent origin of objects we take for granted.[10] We mistakenly assume them to be old because their present shape required no great recent technology. We did not need relativity, quantum physics, or even advanced chemistry to produce forks or paper clips as we know them, so they seem to have been there beyond memory, a sort of material equivalent to the proverb.

Proverbs carry what might be called marks of agedness. Certain ideas (various forms of communism?) may carry marks of up-to-dateness. Forgers, plagiarists, and salesmen know how to exploit such marks.

Again, we may speak of a continuum: there is a continuum between phrases that seem to belong to today and those that seem timeless. For that matter, we may discern a continuum extending from phrases that seem authored by a specific person to those that seem to lack a particular author. I stress "seem" because I am describing *an attribute of the phrase—* how it sounds to us—and not an empirical fact about its origin. The two are easily confused.

Phrases that seem timeless and unauthored may in fact have been written or put into circulation recently by someone identifiable. The first known usage of "Elephants never forget" apparently belongs to the comic story writer Saki in 1904 (YBQ, 527). But such phrases may nevertheless function *as* timeless. Timelessness is part of them, not a fact about their origin. It is entirely possible, as Sam Goldwyn once advised, to coin some new clichés.

Hathifying

In between the authored and the authorless, or between the new and the timeless, we may place those expressions that seem as if they *might* have been coined by someone and *might* be more or less recent. Again, I am speaking of an attribute of the expression, not a historical fact about its origin.

As collectors of proverbs can attest, no one has discovered a clear way to distinguish anonymous proverbs from sayings that were composed by someone. Phrases come and ago, seem oral or written, gain or lose an author. The *Concise Oxford Dictionary of Proverbs* (third edition) includes quotations whose author is known, but only if "the origins of the quotations are no longer popularly remembered" (ix). They are right to do so, because the *sense* of anonymity may be a part of a saying irrespective of whether it in fact lacks a known author. For that matter, the same saying may be anonymous to one group while another knows, or ascribes to it, an author.

Erasmus realized the impossibility of drawing a clear line between proverbs and numerous similar phenomena, such as quotations, metaphorical expressions, figures of speech, adages, apothegms, and others. His anthology includes the authored and the authorless, the oral and the written, the popular and the learned. In much the same spirit, the Yale collection lists as proverbs "Don't stick your neck out," "It takes one to know one," "Don't push your luck," and "The truth hurts," although, depending on one's criteria, they might be sayings or just common expressions of some sort.

Phrases, fixed expressions, proverbs, quotations: all these and more belong to "the stock of figurative language" (ODPSQ, xiv). How interesting it would be to trace the progress of expressions as they move along the continuum from new and authored to timeless and anonymous! As a matter of fact, that is just what Elizabeth Knowles and Susan Ratcliffe do in their illuminating and conceptually imaginative collection, the *Oxford Dictionary of Phrase, Saying and Quotation*. This volume's premise is that, if we think of a quotation as having a particular author, a proverb as general wisdom that could have been coined at almost any time, and a phrase as a common way of saying something, then the three slide into each other not only because it is impossible to draw clear lines between them but also because over time a member of one category becomes or generates a member of one of the other two. The same expression may exist, perhaps with different wording, as phrase, proverb or saying, and quotation. Thus we have the quotation "One more such victory, and we are lost," and we have the (much more commonly known) phrase "Pyrrhic victory." The familiar phrase derives from the less familiar quotation and is used by people who know neither the quotation nor the story from which the phrase is derived.

Most of us who use the phrase "weasel words" are aware that it involves being deceptive. (Is a weasel deceptive? Why not refer to an animal that practices camouflage?) But very few, I think, are aware that the term was put in currency by Theodore Roosevelt, who explained it as alluding to a specific practice of weasels: "One of our defects as a nation is a tendency to use what have been called 'weasel words.' When a weasel sucks eggs the meat is sucked out of the egg. If you use

a 'weasel word' after another, there is nothing left of the other"
(ODPSQ, 251). By Roosevelt's account, then, the weasel word
is not the misleading word itself but the word that makes it
misleading. But with this explanation forgotten except by quotation experts, a weasel word is (in the sense of "is now," not "is
as it was coined") simply one used in a misleading way. What
we call this phrase's real meaning depends on what the meaning of the word "is" is.

Consider this dictionary's entry about "change" (ODPSQ,
68–71). Like other entries, this one is divided into sections
devoted to "proverbs or sayings," "phrases," and "quotations."
Versions of the same expression appear in all three. "The leopard does not change its spots" is a proverb used in English as
early as the mid-sixteenth century. We also have the phrase
"change one's skin." Both probably derive from the biblical
quotation, in the book of Jeremiah: "Can the Ethiopian change
his skin, or the leopard his spots?" The first two are not misquotations of the third; rather, we have a proverb, a phrase,
and a quotation all related to each other.

"Variety is the spice of life" is a proverb we have all heard,
and it makes no difference that very few of us can connect it
with Cowper's lines: "Variety is the spice of life, / That gives it
all its flavor" (ODPSQ, 69). We have the phrase "new wine in
old bottles" and the proverb (dating from the early twentieth
century) "You can't put new wine in old bottles," both ultimately derived from the verse in Matthew: "Neither do men
put new wine in old bottles; else the bottles break, and the
wine runneth out, and the bottles perish" (ODPSQ, 69).

If we check the Knowles and Ratcliffe book's cross-
references, we find that Shakespeare's line "The Devil can cite
Scripture for his purpose" (ODPSQ, 42, from *The Merchant of
Venice*) relates to the proverbial, but not identical, "The devil

can quote Scripture for his own ends," which in turn alludes to the biblical story of the temptation.

In *The Mourning Bride* (1697), Congreve wrote: "Heaven has no rage, like love to hatred turned, / Nor hell a fury, like a woman scorned" (ODPSQ, 382); and we also have the unappealing proverb (or in other volumes, the cliché): "Hell hath no fury like a woman scorned" (ODPSQ, 494). Interestingly enough, as Congreve's line lost its author and became a proverb, it transformed "has" to "hath," evidently as a mark of agedness—a common process I like to call "hathifying."

None of these differing versions are errors. Rather, they illustrate the life of quotations as they move along the continuum from having strong quotation marks to none.

Becoming a Cliché

In the beginning was the Word—in the end just the Cliché.

—*Stanislaw Lec*[11]

What distinguishes a quotation, proverb, saying, or phrase from a cliché? "Hell hath no fury" and "weasel words," which we have seen as both a quotation and a phrase, also appear in James Rogers's *Dictionary of Clichés.* Rogers understands quite well that one man's saying is another man's cliché. For that matter, the same person may find it impossible to draw a clear distinction and may *use* the phrase variously on different occasions. "Since proverbs represent the distilled wisdom from decades or centuries of human experience, it is small wonder that many of them become fixtures of the language," and thus clichés.[12]

For reasons we have seen, Rogers errs in suggesting that proverbs are necessarily old: he mistakes marks of agedness for age. But he has a point when he distinguishes a cliché from a proverb not by any particular choice of words but by the frequency of use. "If a proverb still gets heavy duty in the language, it ranks as a cliché" (Rogers, vii). At some point, though not one clearly marked, a phrase is used often enough to qualify as a cliché. Perhaps it may later be used less frequently and again become a proverb, or perhaps it may even cross the hazy boundary many times.

If frequency of use distinguishes the proverb from the cliché, then what is a proverb to some social groups or nationalities may be a cliché to another. And a cliché, like a quotation from a particular person, may turn into a proverb when no one remembers if anyone used it before a certain time. It may be cited *as* a proverb. Thus reference works sometimes leave it ambiguous whether the "earliest known usage" of a phrase marks its coiner or simply the first person on record to employ it. How many of the proverbs or sayings recorded by John Heywood (whose collection we will examine later) are his?

A quotation may function as a cliché when most people have lost the sense of an origin. We think of "conventional wisdom" as a cliché because most of us do not know that the phrase was coined by John Kenneth Galbraith as recently as 1958. Few of us are aware that the phrase "keeping up with the Joneses" comes from a comic strip of that title that ran from 1913 to 1932 (and still fewer remember the cartoonist who coined the phrase). Those who refer to "the blind leading the blind" are mostly the forgetful speaking to the forgetful—since they forget, if they ever knew, that they are using a phrase from the Gospel According to Matthew.[13]

Indeed, when the speaker does not know the source and

uses a phrase just because its familiarity makes it readily understood, it would be wrong to say that he or she is quoting
anyone. However the fixed expression originated, the speaker
is not using it *as* a quotation unless he or she means to evoke
another speaker or utterance. An anecdote or joke may have
first been made up by someone, but usually when we tell it
we are not quoting anyone, just retelling a story we have heard
somewhere or trying to make someone laugh.

In terms of function or purpose, one could say that it is
not the words, and not even the frequency of use, that makes a
cliché. It is the intent of the user. Is the point to substitute a
prepackaged generalization for a questioning engagement
with a particular situation? People use clichés to shut down
diversity of judgment. When we want to open a question, we
use a quotation, because in most cases a quotation easily allows for an answer. It reminds us of wisdom that might have
been overlooked, where a cliché would present the matter
as settled. Of course, it is not we, but others, who appeal to
clichés.

Cliché and Idiom

However one classes such expressions, knowing them is part
of belonging to a particular culture and speech community.
We would not be surprised, I imagine, to discover that the
English—despite their apparent mastery of our language—say
neither "shit or get off the pot" nor "three strikes and you're
out." On the other hand, Americans have no clear idea of what
is meant by a sticky wicket, not to mention still less familiar
phrases used by those outlanders, the English, Scots, Irish, and
Australians. Learning a language involves mastering not just
grammar and vocabulary, but also a set of expressions of vari-

ous sorts, from quotations to proverbs and sayings to clichés. Such knowledge demonstrates not only cultural literacy but also true mastery of a language. If we encountered someone who regarded "better half," "bats in the belfry," or "born with a silver spoon in his mouth" as striking turns of phrase, we might well doubt that he or she is a native speaker.

Beyond the cliché is the idiom, and again there is no clear line between the two. The difference might be that in a cliché we still sense the turn of phrase *as* a turn of phrase, however hackneyed, and we sense whatever image is used *as* an image, however faded. In the idiom, by contrast, we no longer do. An idiom is just the way one says it. But losing the sense of image or phrase is evidently a matter of degree. Is "train of thought" an idiom or a cliché? Most people are surprised that, like "conventional wisdom," it has an author. Thomas Hobbes offered it with the following definition: "By *Consequence,* or TRAIN of thoughts, I understand that succession of one thought to another, which is called, to distinguish it from discourse in words, *mental discourse*" (from *Leviathan,* as cited in Rogers, *Dictionary of Clichés,* 322). Even highly educated users rarely suspect that the phrase had a known coiner, nor do they think of any particular image. Who thinks of a train? Train in what sense? In Hobbes's usage, this is evidently not a choo-choo train. For most users, the phrase is now an imageless idiom (although it is also included by Rogers as a cliché).

OBI, Extended

Some may be surprised to discover, as I was in researching this book, that many idioms or phrases that seem to be just "how one says it" can be attributed to specific authors or have evolved from well-known proverbs. Erasmus traces, to specific Greek and Latin sources, clichés—or are they idioms?—like "to have one foot in the grave," "to be in the same boat," and "to put the cart before the horse." Let us add that "least (or lesser) of evils" goes back to Aristotle, "broke the mold" to Ariosto (YBQ, 25), and "noble savage" to Dryden (HiQ, 483).

A great deal may be understood once we acknowledge the impossibility of drawing clear lines between quotations, proverbs, sayings, clichés, and idioms. The slippery slope of popular usage accommodates a continual shifting of perception. A quotation whose author is forgotten becomes a saying; a saying used too often becomes a cliché; and an idiom is a cliché taught in a grammar.

Expressions may be authored, may lose an author, or may acquire an author. Witticisms have many fathers, while a proverb is an orphan. Between phrases felt to belong to some specific person and those inherently the product of a whole people lie those that are used with the sense they *may* have an author. The phrases that "may have an author" are related to a distinct group sensed as having a specific author who is unknown: the master we call Anonymous.

A process that Sills and Merton have abbreviated OBI—obliteration by incorporation—is not only quite common but also an essential element in the dynamic life of quotations (Sills and Merton, xvi). The words of someone become the words of no one: the source is obliterated by the quotation's incorporation into common discourse. A proverb appears to arise anonymously from the timeless essence and wisdom of the people. Losing a date of origin, no less than losing an author, belongs to the very nature of quotationality. Sensing a

"Russian proverb" or a "Yiddish saying" is quite different from sensing a Russian statement coined at the time of Peter the Great or a Yiddish response to the Enlightenment. When the time of origin has faded away, a record of an age becomes a testimony to the timeless spirit of a people.

All these processes resemble those that characterize the history of language. For example, it is common for expressions to weaken: not so long ago, a phrase like "traffic from hell" was new. It still conjured up images of an eternal bumper-to-bumper or Sisyphus at last reaching the next exit to find it, too, closed for repair. Now, the phrase means little more than bad traffic. The same happened with the word "terrible." Young people say "awesome" when all they mean is "yes" or, ironically, that something is so common as to be boring.

Articles arose in French by a similar process of weakening, as stressing something as "*that* something" became more and more common and so lost its force. At last, every noun in French required an article. As linguists say, the usage was "grammaticalized."[14] Grammaticalization lies at the extreme end of the continuum, beyond proverb, proverbial expression, cliché, and idiom.

The absence of unambiguous boundaries along the continuum from grammar and idiom to saying and quotation shows either that quotations are a part of a language or that the boundaries of "the language" are fluid. I think Wittgenstein is correct when he writes that language has no single essence or boundary, although "we can draw a boundary—for a special purpose." "New types of language . . . come into existence, and others become obsolete and get forgotten."[15]

The same expression may be quotation, saying, cliché, idiom, or grammar at different times and for different groups.

Whether a given expression is part of language or just part of speech depends on how or for what purpose one chooses to define these two terms.[16]

Second-Order Knowledge

Some quotations include the sense that they are known by almost everyone. We look for an explanation when someone does *not* know them. People my age know, as my daughter does not, important lines from the Watergate hearings, the Vietnam War era, and the Civil Rights struggle. And people my age also know that other people of our age know them.

In other cases, the assumption that a quotation is shared knowledge marks not a generation but a people. We might well wonder whether someone who had never heard the phrase "I have a dream" could possibly be an American. Try to solve a British crossword puzzle and you will soon realize how many phrases assumed by one culture are unknown to the other. Is it characteristic of Americans, or just Americans above a certain age, to know "four score and seven years ago"; "government of the people, by the people, for the people"; "We hold these truths to be self-evident"; and "Give me liberty or give me death"?

This argument also works in the negative: at times, belonging to a given culture or speech community entails *not* knowing certain quotations. Here I do not mean not using them, as a sort of badge, but actually not knowing them. An apocryphal anecdote about World War II describes an American outpost afraid it is being infiltrated by well-trained German spies. The commander orders that suspects be asked to recite the second stanza of *The Star-Spangled Banner;* if the suspect can do it, he is shot. The point is that only a native speaker would know when something is *not* generally known. This second-order knowledge requires experience in the culture not easily obtained without living in it. Mastery of a language involves specific ignorance, and it is possible to specify which ignorance characterizes such mastery.

"Known to everyone in the group," or "not known to anyone but specialists," may itself be an attribute of a quotation. In this respect, it resembles the sense of a time of origin. As we shall see, quotationality may also entail other supposed facts that at first appear to be information about a quotation but, upon closer reflection, turn out to be attributes of it.

If quotations as a group have vague boundaries, and if quotations include intrinsic attributes beyond their words, then the nature of quotations is more complex than we might have supposed. What *is* a quotation?

II
The Nature of Quotations

III
What Is a Quotation?

All taxa [classificatory units] show relationships on
all sides like the countries on a map of the world.
—*Carl Linneaus,* Philosofia Botanica *(1751),*
aphorism 77 (ODSQ, 390)

Table of Discontents

What is a quotation? And how does it differ from an aphorism, a proverb, or a saying? What defines each short form and its relation to the others?

From Erasmus to the present, anthologizers have tried to draw lines on the sea, only to recognize that no firm boundaries are to be had. They lament in unison, or quote each other quoting each other, that consistent adherence to any proposed criteria is impossible. Interesting material always lies just beyond any boundary, and, once that material is accepted, the new boundary invites the same process of expansion. Consider "aphorisms." Used in its broad sense, the term frequently designates all remarks of literary value. Used in a narrow sense, it names a particular type of such remarks. But what type? In his preface to the *Oxford Book of Aphorisms,* John Gross begins with a good working set of criteria, only to conclude—wisely enough—not to observe them too conscientiously. To do so would mean to exclude too much: "When I began making the present selection I considered limiting myself to what might be called the aphorism pure and simple. . . . But it was soon borne in on me that to read a series of such pronouncements in unbroken succession would be to diminish their value. . . . And in any case few aphorists have themselves been willing to submit to such a self-denying ordinance. It seemed to make better sense, on reflection, to interpret the idea of aphoristic writing more loosely."[1] What Gross says about aphorisms "pure and simple" is also true of aphorisms in the broader sense and of quotations generally. So what should one look for in compiling a general anthology of "aphorisms" or "quotations"?

As might be expected, answers vary according to cultural needs and interests. In her preface to the sixth edition (2004) of the *Oxford Dictionary of Quotations,* Elizabeth Knowles reflects on the change in criteria distinguishing each edition from its predecessors. The first edition (1941) relied primarily on high literature, mostly in English, and most of that British. It aimed to be "a dictionary of quotations that would have a primarily literary base, and which would include quotations from major writers likely to be quoted in English by the literate and cultured person" (ODQ, xii). Tellingly, the volume featured a separate section called simply "Foreign Quotations."

That section did *not* include the Bible, which was evidently too familiar to be thought of as "foreign." The Good Book had a section of its own. So did the Book of Common Prayer. "Opening the pages," writes Knowles, "is rather like walking into a traditional study lined with leather-bound volumes" (xiii).

Over the years, Oxford editors debated the suitability of advertising, song lyrics, the opening lines of hymns, and Latin prayers. Durability also proved a puzzling criterion. Are recent phrases, known only for a short time, quotations? If so, are they still quotations a generation after they have ceased to be well known? Whether we have suitability or durability in mind, do anthologizers go too far when they include lines from an episode of *The Simpsons?* Is "Eat my shorts!" a quotation? If so, what about its equivalents in 1950, 1900, or 1870? How about new words or phrases whose author is anonymous or collective? Is a book title a quotation?

Because editors have differed on what a quotation is, they have sometimes arrived at baffling organizations of material. Benham's collection, for instance, begins with 409 pages of British and American authors, then proceeds to 23 pages from the Bible, and 2 from the Book of Common Prayer. It also includes sections of very different length on Greek quotations (5 pages), Latin quotations (207 pages), modern languages (French gets 21 pages, Spanish and Dutch together add a page), and proverbs (164 pages). Oddest of all is a section called "Waifs and Strays," an omnium-gatherum in which 33 pages are divided into several subsections. Four are devoted to periods of English writing, followed by subsections, in no discernible order, including "London Street Sayings," "Forensic," "Phrases and Household Words," "Book Inscriptions," "Bell Inscriptions," and "The Koran."[2]

It is easy to see why reference works eventually combined everything in one alphabetic sequence. The second edition of the Oxford incorporates previously separate sections into the alphabetic sequence. Henceforth, Montaigne would appear not under "Foreign Quotations" but under M, nursery rhymes would be placed under N, and the Bible would be become just another B. But it may be surprising that recently Oxford and other publishers have reverted in their table of contents to the "waifs and strays" type of listing. Why?

For one thing, an interesting table of contents makes a collection more enticing. As numerous volumes compete for limited display space, publishers find more and more categories to include and, often enough, call attention to the fact by putting them in separate sections singled out in an initial list. The sixth edition of the Oxford lists "special categories" of advertising slogans; borrowed titles; catchphrases; closing lines; epitaphs; film lines; film titles; last words; military sayings, slogans, and songs; misquotations; mottoes; newspaper headlines and leaders; official advice; opening lines; political slogans and songs; prayers; sayings; slogans; songs, spirituals, and shanties; taglines for films; telegrams; and toasts. Its more recent competitor, the *Yale Book of Quotations* (2006), includes "special sections" on advertising slogans; anonymous; anonymous (Latin); ballads; film lines; folk and anonymous songs; modern proverbs; nursery rhymes; political slogans; proverbs; radio catchphrases; sayings; and television catchphrases. How long until we get a Lake Wobegon listing in which *everything* is special?

None of these categories were treated as quotations a few decades ago, whether by Bartlett's, Oxford, or others. The definition of a quotation has been repeatedly expanded. We have come a long way from that traditional study with its leather-bound volumes.

Nonverbal Quotation

Perhaps we could expand the territory still more? Quotations need not be verbal at all. We speak of musical quotations, when one composition cites a well-known passage from another, and of artistic quotations, when one painting repeats a well-known image from another. Mimicry quotes gestures, usually to make fun of them. At the beginning of Dickens's *Pickwick Papers,* the heroes are terrified by a reenacted (or quoted) battle.

My primary concern is verbal quotation. But it would still help to grasp how quotation in general—regardless of what is quoted—works. Quotation is everywhere. Anything that can convey meaning, whether consciously or unconsciously, can be quoted. In other words, everything people do is quotable.

As there is mimicry, quotation of a gesture, there is also what might be called "topicry," quotation of a place. Towns, farms, villages, and any other place people construct can be quoted. In Colonial Williamsburg and several other "historical re-creations," quotation of place includes quotation of actions characteristic of the place. As one walks through the quoted colonial town, one can watch a "blacksmith" at work or, inevitably, pay modern currency to eat the food of the past (not *too* authentic, please!). The use of today's money, not to mention modern hygienic standards, testifies that quotation, rather than original action, is taking place. Wherever quoting is found, some elements imitate what is quoted while others testify to the act of quoting. To understand an act of quoting, one must be able to recognize both.

Historical re-creations include reproductions of Tudor life at Kentwell in Suffolk—their website proudly proclaims that "it has taken 30 years to go back 500 years"—as well as numerous "historic" farms, old Western towns, and medieval sites that seem closer to images from Walter Scott than to anything medieval. At quoted jousts, controlled mayhem safely imitates real mayhem.[3] In Sterne's *Tristram Shandy,* a novel that deals constantly with quoted words, gestures, and behavior, Uncle Toby and Corporal Trim perfectly reproduce the battlefield at which Toby received his wound. It is a quoted location.

The Chicago Botanical Garden includes an English Walled Garden that in turn comprises six smaller English gardens highlighting "contributions of English garden design through the centuries." The CBG also displays Sansho-Eno, the Garden of the Three Islands, which reproduces a Japanese garden complete with "the Shoin Building, a recreation of a 17th century samurai's retreat." As if they were gardeners themselves, "visitors are encouraged to sit and rake patterns in a tabletop garden" and, just like the real Japanese of the past, "listen to Japanese tales" (CBG website). By imitation, they may learn, oddly enough, the Japanese art of understatement.

A couple of decades ago, I found myself with an hour to kill in a town where I was giving a lecture. I wandered into a museum. Having entered at the exhibit's middle, I was delighted to discover from the first few displays that it dealt with my favorite topic, time. I learned about diverse calendrical systems: lunar calendars, solar calendars, mixed calendars, several ways of handling the fact that a solar year does not divide into an equal number of months or a round number of days, intracalendrical days, ten-day weeks, leap-years and their analogues, and so on. But when I worked my way around to the entrance, I discovered that I had not been viewing an exhibit about time measurement after all. Rather, it was an exhibit of particularly effective museum exhibits, of which the time-measurement display was one. Without knowing it, I had been viewing a *quoted* exhibit. Having entered in the middle I had missed the explanatory plaque that served as the functional equivalent of quotation marks.

At one time, young men wore James Dean haircuts to make a statement that quoted the hero's image in *Rebel Without a Cause*. Literary historians report that young people committed suicide to imitate Goethe's Werther or the Russian writer Karamzin's "poor Liza." They were not just inspired by literary heroes, but dying in allusion to them. In *The Brothers Karamazov*, the narrator compares Dmitri's mother, Adelaida Miusova, to a woman belonging to the last "romantic" generation "who after nine years of an enigmatic passion for a gentleman, whom she might easily have married at any moment, invented insuperable obstacles to their union, and ended by throwing herself one stormy night into a rather deep and rapid river from a high bank, almost a precipice, and so perished entirely to satisfy her own caprice, and to be like Shakespeare's Ophelia. . . . This is a fact, and probably there have been not a few in the last two or three generations." This woman chose her actions in what the narrator calls "an echo of alien ideas," a sort of performance, designed to be seen as such. In much the same way, the narrator explains, Adelaida imitated the ideas, phrases, and actions of the next generation. She wound up marrying that buffoon, Fyodor Pavlovich Karamazov, in order to "show her feminine independence," to "override class distinctions," and to defy "the despotism of her family," all familiar expressions indicating that her actions were quoted.[4]

Presumably, people like Adelaida think of their quoted actions as signs of belonging to a superior group, in much the way that scholars who exchange obscure lines of verse compliment each other on their erudition. To Dostoevsky, of course, such living sacrifices authenticity.

Quoted actions can combine to make a quoted life.

What Must a Quotation Have?

> The first step in wisdom is to know the things themselves. This notion consists in having a true idea of the objects; objects are distinguished and known by classifying them methodically and giving them appropriate names.
>
> —*Linnaeus*[5]

So what is, and what is not, quotation? Mere imitation or repetition of someone else's words or actions do not suffice. Parrots and shadows do not quote.

A quotation repeats the words (or actions or other defining features) of another *as* the words of another. A performance of Chekhov's play *The Seagull* is not a quotation of it. (Of course, one could quote a performance—say, by reenacting it not in order to present the play but to show a classic performance, like the Joffrey Ballet reproduction of *The Rite of Spring* "in its original form, as given in Paris by Sergei Diaghilev's Ballets Russes on May 29, 1913.")[6] Neither are the speech acts that philosophers call "performative" quotations. These performatives demand a precise set of words and actions to accomplish something: for example, marrying a couple by saying "I now pronounce you man and wife" in the right circumstances. Although they repeat words said countless times before, performatives do not quote those words. They *use* them.

Of course, one could quote or mimic a minister marrying people. For instance, one might instruct a new justice of the peace by quoting the marriage formula. But that is very different from actually marrying people. In performing a marriage, the minister is not pointing to some other occasion in which the prescribed words were used, but using them yet again.

To be precise: whether they quote words, actions, or places, quotations must do two things. First, they must more or less reproduce an original, as a verbal quotation recognizably reproduces words. Second, they must do so precisely as a reenactment, intended to be perceived as such. They must point to another, similar action.[7]

The first criterion distinguishes a quoted place from a symbol or monument. The Washington Monument resembles neither George Washington nor Mount Vernon. It does not reproduce anything about them.

The second criterion distinguishes quotation from mere repetition. It shows us that one cannot understand quotation in terms of form alone. One must also consider *purpose.*

If one just happens to repeat words that have been used before—and how can we avoid doing so?—one is not quoting them, because one's purpose does not include repetition. A listener who mistakenly imagined that a speaker was trying to repeat someone else's words would misunderstand them.

Not every hackneyed expression is a quotation. When I ask, as we all often do, "What time is it?" I am not expecting someone to compliment me for repeating a Chekhov character's question, but asking the hour. We all use words and phrases that we and others have used countless times before.

When I say, "I love you," I mean to avow love, not to quote an avowal. If repetition without a purpose to repeat were enough to make a quotation, the term would lose all distinctive meaning.

With nonverbal quotations as well, the quoted event or place must be offered as a re-enactment. Again, purpose, as well as formal similarity, is essential for quotation.

For reasons that will become clear, I would like to clarify terms as I shall use them. From now on, I will refer to actions or words that meet these two criteria—formal repetition and re-enactment—as *citations,* rather than quotations. I shall call verbal citations "extracts." That is because I want to reserve the term "quotation" for a set of short literary works. This book is mostly concerned with that kind of quotation.

Some quotations are also extracts, some extracts are also quotations. But even when examples coincide, the two concepts must not be confused. So let us ask again, what is a quotation?

Quotation and Extract

Aphorisms, witticisms, maxims, proverbs, wise sayings, and many other short literary forms are all types of quotation, as I shall henceforth use the term. A quotation in this sense is the sort of thing that could find its way into an anthology of quotations.

To be sure, the expression "a quotation" is used in more than one way. In addition to naming the sort of expression we associate with Shakespeare, Franklin, and Pope, it may also refer to any set of words marked as taken from a larger text. When one scholar reproduces the published comments of another, the reproduced words are surely a quotation in one sense—an extract—but not in the sense I have in mind. They are not a candidate for the next edition of Bartlett's.

To be sure, instead of defining "extracts" as sets of cited words and "quotations" as short literary works such as adages or aphorisms, it would also be possible to distinguish between a quotation and a Quotation or a quotation and a "quotation." But I have found it more convenient to use two different words, rather than two typographic variants of the same word, because, as I shall try to show, many confusions are clarified if one stresses that one is dealing with two quite different things.

Quotability and Literariness

Not everything that can be extracted appears in anthologies of quotations, in commonplace books, or on the back of Celestial Seasonings boxes. Only certain sorts of extracts become quotations. They differ in a variety of ways that make them pass from mouth to mouth or text to text.

Quotations in anthologies must be brief. No one goes to the *Oxford Dictionary of Quotations* to find the first book of *Paradise Lost* or Part III of *War and Peace.* We leave it to other sorts of anthologies to collect somewhat longer passages (the *Viking Portable Enlightenment Reader*) or still longer ones (the *Norton Anthology of English Literature*).

Nor are all brief extracts suitable for inclusion. Some are not good enough. What is not interesting is not quoted. Others do not circulate. Quotations must be shared: as there are no private languages, there are no private quotations. Still others, for a variety of reasons, are not memorable enough. What cannot be remembered cannot be a quotation. Is there anything that these and other criteria have in common? What exactly is it that extracts that are not quotations typically lack?

Such extracts lack *quotability.* A quotation must be quotable, an extract may or may not be. One reason that quotations must be quotable is that they function as complete, if brief, literary works and so, like all literary works, must be capable of standing on their own. Though it may be drawn from some larger work, the quotation does not require the context of that larger work. As a quotation it is not part of anything. It is taken from a larger work so that it may stand on its own.

If they could not stand on their own, cited sets of words would not be freely passed around or recognized as quotations. No one would collect them. Without quotability, there is no literariness.

Literariness, as I understand it, does not necessarily entail any particular set of formal qualities. What makes a work literary is the ability to be understood and appreciated outside the context of its origin. That is why a literary work, however valuable as a document of its time, is more than documentary.

Determining the literary work's meaning is not equivalent to reconstructing the circumstances, causes, and effects of the original exchange between speaker and listener or writer and reader.[8] Rather, the work is designed or taken to be meaningful to those who neither know nor care about that context.

We might say that a work's literariness begins precisely where its documentary value ends. If one reads Gibbon as a textbook on Roman history, as one surely can, one is not reading it as literature. If one turns to Herodotus as a model of storytelling, one is. No matter what inaccuracies or documentary shortcomings may be discovered in Boswell's *Life of Johnson,* it remains a literary masterpiece.

Taken Out of Context

For a work to be literary, it must be capable of standing on its own, and to stand on its own, it must be complete in itself. If it isn't, and the larger context is required to understand it, then it is something less or other than a literary work.

All nonliterary extracts are taken out of context, or they would not be extracts at all. But when we *say* an extract is taken out of context we mean that it is taken out of context *improperly:* that is, in a way that gives a false idea of that context and so of the extract's meaning. Something important has been omitted: for example, an indication that the words in question are not intended seriously or that a term to which a precise meaning has been given now appears to mean something else. By contrast, a literary work cannot be taken out of context because it is its own context.

If one moves a painting (I mean, one not designed to be viewed from a particular place), one is changing its surroundings but not taking it out of context. By the same token, a reprint of *Paradise Lost,* no matter what else may also be published in the same volume, is still *Paradise Lost.* One can take a part of a work out of context by reprinting it on its own, but not the work itself, or it would not be a literary work in the first place.

The Frame

A literary work comes with its own "frame," defining what is and is not part of it. But nonliterary extracts have no such frame.

When critics argue whether the preface to *The Brothers Karamazov* belongs to the work, or is simply an authorial commentary no different from a letter about the work, they are arguing about the work's boundaries *as* a literary work, the point at which it is complete and can be read as such. Where is the frame? What does it include and exclude? If Dostoevsky's novel includes the preface, the whole is not there without it, but if it does not, the preface is, as we say, external. If the preface lies within the frame, then an edition that omits it—as some do—is, wittingly or not, abridged or incomplete.

Where there is a frame, internal and external evidence are qualitatively different.

Once something is a quotation, the source from which it is drawn is necessarily external. This distinction between internal and external does not apply to an extract, which we do not interpret as a complete work. If we do, we have *made* it into a quotation.

A nonliterary extract stands as something drawn from something larger. We are always implicitly invited to check whether the process of extraction has distorted meaning. That is because any line drawn between the cited words and the surrounding text is arbitrary: judgment, not a frame, defines the proper extent of the passage to be cited for a given purpose on a given occasion. No matter how long a nonliterary extract may be, it asks to be read as a part; no matter how short a literary work may be, it demands to be read as a whole.

Twinning

Dr. Johnson defined an aphorism (by which he meant something close to what we are calling a quotation) as "a maxim, a precept contracted in a short sentence; an unconnected position" (OBA, vii). By "unconnected" he meant capable of being read and remembered on its own.

In Francis Bacon's view, it is precisely because aphorisms are unconnected that they characteristically give us "the pith and heart" of things: "for discourse of illustration is cut off; recitals of examples are cut off; discourse of connexion and order is cut off; descriptions of practice are cut off."[9]

Depending on whether they are presented as connected or unconnected—as part or as whole—the very same words may be an extract on one occasion and a quotation on another.

When this happens, their meanings may diverge. If identical texts can differ, then we have another good reason to conclude that formal qualities may make a text more or less quotable, but are not themselves what makes it a quotation. It is the need to stand "unconnected" that makes quotations brief, not brevity that makes a quotation. After all, many brief sentences (like this one) are not quotations.

It is in fact easy to discover lines that have functioned as both quotations and extracts, as complete on some occasions and as a part of something else on others. Tolstoy's famous line—"All happy families resemble each other; each unhappy family is unhappy in its own way"—lives two lives, as an extract (the first sentence of *Anna Karenina*) and as a quotation used by those with no interest in the novel at all.

Such cases of *twinning,* as we may call them, characteristically invite us to read a line as an extract, a quotation, or both. We may either ask how these words function in their original context or treat them as a statement standing on its own. Countless lines of Shakespeare live a separate life, and yet in many cases we do not forget their origin.

The better known a work is, the more likely its lines will live a double life. Shakespeare and the Bible enjoy unique status in this respect, at least in English. Other sacred or quasi-sacred texts—Homer for the ancient Greeks, Virgil for the Romans—typically invite twinning of their lines.

Genres and Words That Wander

Lines may become twinned either by accident of literary history or because they were designed to be twinned from the start. Accidental twinning is more likely to lead to a significant divergence in meaning. Irony is lost when Polonius's maxims are cited as supreme wisdom. A scholar I know recently expressed her annoyance at hearing someone say: "As Robert Frost remarked, 'Good fences make good neighbors.'" In context, of course, the quoted words exemplify not a wise saying but the substitution of a saying for wisdom.

Sometimes a sort of twinning makes the same line function not as both extract and quotation but as two different *kinds* of quotation, either at the same time or in the course of literary history. A quotation of one genre begets a twin of another. That process has typically doubled famous lines of Hippocrates, who is conventionally identified as the first aphorist.

Hippocrates' aphorisms stated the precepts of a discipline, and that is one way in which the term "aphorism" has been used. But "aphorism" refers also, and now usually, to statements of moral or aesthetic norms. Hippocrates' "aphorisms" thereby came to have two distinct meanings. As usually cited, Hippocrates' first aphorism—"Art is long, life is short"— refers not to the "art" (that is, discipline) of medical practice but to one of the arts, such as poetry, painting, or music. Here is the whole aphorism in the English translation of 1735: "Life is short, the art is long, occasion sudden, to make experiments dangerous, judgment difficult. Neither is it sufficient that the physician do his office, unless the patient, and his attendants, do their duty, and that externals are likewise well ordered."[10] Conrad Sprengell, the editor of this translation, explains: "These, by way of introduction, are mentioned as necessary considerations to a practical physician . . . the circumstances of any disease are so many and various, that it is difficult to judge, whether this or that medicine may answer one's desire, or whether the disease is curable, or how it will determine" (Hippocrates, 2).

Hippocrates is not discussing aesthetics, but the quotation based on his words often does. Living two lives, it comes in two versions. The wording "art is long, life is short," rather than the reverse, reflects Seneca's rendering of the line in Latin as "Ars longa, vita brevis" (ODQ, 389). Seeming to derive from both a Greek and a Latin original, cited with its clauses in two orders, and serving as both types of aphorism, the line means different things. So does Hippocrates' aphorism "Extreme measures are most appropriate for extreme diseases," which is so often taken as general advice pertaining to any critical situation that it seems positively literalist to limit it to advice for physicians (ODQ, 389).

Quotations wander from one genre to another. Taken as a witticism, a line may be one thing; as a maxim, oracular pronouncement, or dictum, quite another. Because quotations are brief, they are easily twinned.

When twinned, the quotation may become familiar in an altered wording so that it may stand on its own more readily or work better in its new genre. Twinning is one source of variation.

Meaning and Classification

Twinning happens in many ways. Quotations twin extracts, one genre of quotation twins another, and doubling takes place deliberately, unwittingly, and every way in between. We may be well aware that, in the context of *Hamlet,* Polonius's words of advice are meant to be taken ironically, but we may nevertheless teach our children that it is prudent to be neither a borrower nor a lender and wise to be true to one's own self. We know these lines mean one thing as an extract from the play, but nonetheless we use them as freestanding quotations to mean another.

Sometimes the quotation's other life as an extract merely shadows it. Those who repeat it may be dimly aware that it means something different in its original context, but they employ it, perhaps guiltily, as a freestanding quotation nonetheless.

Such shadows of another life may be more or less detectable. Upon hearing some lines—"Fools rush in where angels fear to tread," "A little knowledge is a dangerous thing," "To err is human, to forgive divine"—we may ask ourselves: now, which works are these drawn from? Is it the Bible or Shakespeare that warns us the devil can cite Scripture to suit his purpose? To find the answer, one may consult an anthology. Indeed, one function anthologies serve is to provide substance to such shadows.

When we treat words differently, they become different. Meaning depends on classification, on the sort of thing we take the words to be.

We will see how important it is to distinguish a literary quotation from its verbally identical twin, the nonliterary extract. It is crucial to know whether to interpret something as connected or unconnected.

An extract is a biopsy, a quotation an organism.

Oral and Written

Twinning is not the only reason quotations vary. No less important, quotations also straddle the boundary between oral and written literature. They display characteristics of both and everything in between.

Witticisms may arise in conversation, be recorded, and then be quoted in subsequent conversations. The sardonic maxims of La Rochefoucauld apparently began in conversations, were edited and polished to perfection, and then were written down. Proverbs feel like a form that is at root oral even if we get many of them from the Bible or other written sources. By contrast, even if we quote an aphorism in conversation, it seems essentially written. For obvious reasons, famous last words (which I discuss in chapter 10) must be taken as originally spoken, and epitaphs (chapter 11) as written, indeed carved.

Rather than thinking of sharply distinct classes, we may rather think of a continuum. And instead of one distinguishing criterion, we may imagine several. Quotations may lie anywhere along the continuum, and they may shift from position to position, depending on use, culture, or historical period. They may alter in wording to fit a new spoken or written context. As we shall see, the problem of a quotation's accuracy is a complex one, and one reason for this complexity is the fact that quotations are dispersed along, and move along, the entire continuum.

At one end of the continuum lies the conventional model for written literature: the single, fixed original, which the textual editor seeks to restore. At the other extreme we find works of oral literature that vary constantly. For these works, it makes no sense to speak of a single original. Let me ask again: what is the correct version of a joke?

Of course, both extremes are limiting cases. As numerous commentators have pointed out, medieval written works often seem to vary by nature, and even some modern written works seem from the outset to have existed in a cloud of versions.[11] On the other hand, today's quotation anthologies often try to record, and perhaps to fix, some version of an essentially oral saying.

At one time, the ideal of a single correct original was applied to oral as well as written works. In his classic collection of ballads, Walter Scott observed: "The more popular the composition of an ancient poet, or *Maker,* became, the greater chance there was of its being corrupted; for a poem transmuted through the number of reciters, like a book reprinted in a multitude of editions, incurs the risk of impertinent interpolations from the conceit of one rehearser, unintelligible blunders from the stupidity of another, and omissions equally to be regretted from the want of memory in a third."[12] If oral poems, like the ideal of written texts, derive from a maker at a moment, then change is degeneration and what the scholar must do is restore the presumed original. But as more recent folklorists have observed, it often makes no sense to suppose an original when we are dealing with the sort of work that changes from performance to performance, passes through many hands and mouths, and alters with the occasion. The work is essentially plural.

The importance of the occasion of performance underscores that, as Ruth Finnegan's classic study *Oral Poetry* observes, "The literate model of a fixed correct version—*the* text of a given poem—does not necessarily apply. . . . Oral literature is more flexible and more dependent on its social context. For this reason, no discussion of oral poetry can afford to concentrate on the text alone. . . . There is now a growing awareness that any piece of oral poetry must, to be fully understood, be seen in its context; that it is not a separable thing but [what Dan Ben-Amos calls] 'a communicative event'" (Finnegan, 28–29).

Finnegan regards it as impossible to draw a clear line between oral and written literature. Poems may be composed in writing and then recited. Ballads may be written and published, then passed on through performance, with resulting new versions written down. In most surviving cultures, writing has played some part in oral works. It is more accurate to speak of "the continuity of 'oral' and 'written' literature. There is no deep gulf between the two: they shade into each other both in the present and over many centuries of historical development, and there are innumerable cases of poetry which has both 'oral' and 'written' elements. The idea of pure and un-contaminated 'oral culture' as the primary reference point for the discussion of oral poetry is a myth" (Finnegan, 24).

Like oral poetry, quotations pass from mouth to mouth as well as from text to text. They are frequently spoken, altered, written, and quoted aloud again. Cherished as texts, they also live in their oral use.

Quotations lie everywhere on the continua from written to oral, from fixed to variable, and from minimal to maximal role of the extraverbal occasion.

To understand them in this way is to begin to grasp their life. To do so, let us examine how an extract can become a quotation.

IV
Making a Quotation

Misextraction

A line interpreted as an independent work differs fundamentally from the same line interpreted as a part of some larger work. This apparently simple distinction between a quotation and an extract turns out to have important consequences.

Because a quotation differs from an extract, the version that appears in anthologies is in fact the accurate version of the quotation, even if it differs from its original source, as it often does. The original source defines the accuracy of the extract, the words a biographer would cite as actually said or written at a specified historical moment. But the anthology, or common usage, defines the accuracy of the quotation. The quotation as a quotation is precisely the form that is most typically quoted.

The extract and the quotation may or may not coincide. If they differ in wording, both may be accurate. One may be the accurate extract, the other the accurate quotation. By the same token, presenting the extract as the quotation would be as inaccurate as presenting the quotation as the extract.

Accuracy depends on classification. Texts are not accurate or inaccurate in the abstract. I hope it is clear that I am neither embracing relativism nor dispensing with the notion of accuracy. Quite the contrary: my point is that since there are two different ways to cite—as an extract and as a quotation— there are two accuracies.

For the sake of clarity, one should distinguish between a misquotation and a *misextraction.*

Transubstantiation

As we have seen, some quotations not only live as whole literary works, but were composed as such. The maxims of La Rochefoucauld and some quips of Mark Twain or Dorothy Parker are not extracts from anything.

Other quotations do involve a process of extraction from something larger, but mere removal from surrounding context does not suffice. For an extract to become a quotation, the isolated words must acquire quotability. They must be memorable. Above all, they must display the capacity to stand on their own and reward reading as a complete literary work. Unless and until that happens, we have an extract, but not a quotation. If it does happen, the extract becomes the mere source of the quotation.

Even when a quotation and its source are verbally identical, the quotation has become the freestanding work that La Rochefoucauld's maxims were designed to be from the start. It is now different precisely because, as a complete work, it asks to be read differently and rewards doing so.

Quotations are not born but made. Phrases are not automatically quotations; someone must author them *as* quotations, either by composing or presenting (reframing) them as such. Authors like La Rochefoucauld do the first, anthologizers the second.

Unless created as freestanding works, quotations resemble "found" art. They are analogous, say, to a piece of driftwood identified as formally interesting enough to be displayed in an art museum or to a weapon moved from an anthropological to an artistic display. Just as an art museum may contain some objects made to be exhibited and others simply found to be worth exhibiting, so a general anthology typically contains both kinds of quotations. The presenter of found art, whether material or verbal, has become a sort of artist. He has not made the object, but he has made it as art.

Reframing an extract as a quotation constitutes a kind of coauthorship. With no change in wording, the cited passage becomes different. I imagine that the thrill of making an anthology includes the opportunity to become such a coauthor. By virtue of finding, selecting, and reframing, one gets to be the collaborator of Gibbon, Lincoln, or Tolstoy. In this way, verbal creativity extends beyond verbal composition.

I sometimes wonder whether Tolstoy—who, as we shall see, composed several anthologies—enjoyed becoming the collaborator of the thinkers he most revered, Lao Tzu, Buddha, and Tolstoy himself. After all, he had already rewritten the Gospels and corrected the sayings of Jesus.

Becoming a quotation is a change in status. It is like transubstantiation, where, as theologians say, the "substance" changes even if the "accidents" do not. The bread of the Eucharist still looks the same but has become essentially different, and so have the words that become a quotation.

If a Man Takes Thy Quote

Sometimes when an extract is made into a quotation, the "accidents" do change. It may be necessary to alter wording in order to achieve quotability and enable the passage to stand on its own. Such change does not make the quotation erroneous. On the contrary, it allows it to be a quotation in the first place.

When an extract becomes a quotation, a proper name or noun may be substituted for a pronoun, allusions to the surrounding text may be omitted, and a word may be altered so that the line makes sense on its own. As I noted in the introduction: we quote Jesus saying "Turn the other cheek," and in English that is an accurate quotation. But in Matthew the line reads: "Whoever shall smite thee on one cheek, turn to him the other also" (Matthew 5:39). The reason for the change is plain and derives precisely from the fact that the passage is being made into a quotation. There could hardly be a quotation of the line otherwise.

What other wording could one use? No one says "Turn to him the other also," because it would make no sense. "Turn the other cheek" supplies the word "cheek" because the word "other" in the original text *means* "other cheek." "To him" and "also" refer to a part of the sentence not present in the quotation and so are properly omitted.

Despite these changes, I have never heard anyone reply: "You are misquoting and should say, 'Turn to him the other also.'" To object that such changes are errors is to say that one cannot make a quotation from the phrase at all. Our acceptance of such alterations testifies to our tacit understanding that a quotation and an extract do not have to match perfectly, even when we are dealing with a sacred text.

Just how different the quotation and extract can be without our sensing something wrong depends on a number of considerations. These include the ways in which the quotation is used, the degree to which an original verbal context is meant to be evoked, and the circumstances or purposes of quoting.

Genre also matters. Witticisms in drawing rooms function differently from, and allow more leeway than, citations of the law
in briefs or of Scripture in sermons.

Far from being necessary, verbal identity between an extract and a quotation is a limiting case. Even when their words
just happen to coincide, quotations and extracts are two different things, each governed by a specific set of conventions.

The Second Speaker

When a quotation differs from its source, the source may feel
like a draft of a poem or a notebook to a novel: interesting, but
not finished. That feeling may strike us as odd, because we
usually attribute a quotation to a given speaker as if he or she
had said exactly that. But in fact a quotation has its own shadowy *second speaker,* who is not identical to the speaker of the
source. Recognizing the role of the quotation's second speaker
is essential to understanding the life of the quotation.

We expect extracts to have been said or written as presented, but all quotations are "attributed"—that is, attributed
to the second speaker. That is why the quotation may or may
not double as a historically accurate extract. When a passage
lives a twinned life, as both an extract from a work and a work
in itself, each twin has a distinct speaker. One set of words may
belong to Shakespeare's Polonius; the other, verbally identical
set to the voice of proverbial wisdom.

In some cases, it is not important whether the words
were actually uttered by a first speaker at all. For all we know
and care, the first speaker may never have existed. We say:
"Supposedly, Oscar Wilde said," or "Asked an impertinent
question by a heckler, John Kennedy (or was it Abraham Lincoln?) once countered," or "I think it was Rabbi Hillel who

observed," or even "Someone once said . . ." All these ways of introducing the quotation indicate that we are not primarily concerned with whether the event actually happened or simply makes an apt story. "Supposedly," "someone," "once" (not specifying when or where)—such locutions indicate that the listener is not expected to take the tale as attested fact. They evoke not a first but a second speaker. The listener would be missing the point if he or she should demand documentation.

Anecdotes and jokes work in much the same way as "second-speaker-only" quotations. If the editors of *Bartlett's Book of Anecdotes* or the *Oxford Book of Literary Anecdotes* had demanded hard evidence that the incidents described actually happened, and happened in just that way, their collections would have been dramatically thinner.[1] The editor of the Oxford volume, James Sutherland, contents himself with "a crumb of fact" because "an anecdote may have become so much a part of literary tradition that it must be given a place in a volume like this, although any self-respecting biographer would feel compelled to reject it as untrue or only half-true" (OBLA, viii). I suppose one could imagine a Monty Python sketch about a book of meticulously authenticated and exhaustively documented jokes. Anecdotes and jokes work like a good deal of folklore, because, whether written or not, they *are* forms of folklore. In much the same way, our practices with many quotations tacitly suggest that we are citing not the historical Kennedy, Lincoln, Shaw, or Wilde, but their quotational doubles. There is Oscar Wilde and there is "Oscar Wilde."

They Will Sell Us the Quote

Sometimes we have the sense that the words we quote are "too good to be true," as I recently heard someone confess after citing Lenin's line: "When we are ready to hang the capitalists, they will sell us the rope." He did not know whether Lenin had ever made this trenchant observation, or, if he had, whether these were his exact words. Nevertheless, he explained, the comment was in character and so illustrated Lenin's way of thinking. What is more, it describes a kind of shortsightedness not limited to capitalists. So taken, it hardly matters whether the remark is attributed to Lenin, Stalin, Mao, or, with a slight change of wording, Machiavelli, Richelieu, or Talleyrand.

Whether or not the quotation is a real extract that a Lenin biographer could document, it is certainly a real saying commonly quoted and living a life of its own in political discourse. Perhaps it circulates because we have no better way to express this insight and the attitudes accompanying it.

As it happens, this quotation sharpens a longer documentable observation: "They [capitalists] will furnish credits which will serve us for the support of the Communist Party in their countries and, by supplying us materials and technical equipment which we lack, restore our military industry necessary for our future attacks against our suppliers. To put it in other words, they will work on the preparation of their own suicide" (RQ, 51). The thought behind the quotation as usually phrased is indeed Lenin's, even if the exact wording reflects a process of editing—the sort of editing that commonly occurs when a thought is made pointed enough to be "unconnected" and quotable.[2] We may be inclined to say that, as a historically documentable statement, the famous line merely paraphrases Lenin. Even so, the quotation belongs, if not to Lenin, then to "Lenin." Quotations as quotations characteristically work in this way.

Even though a quotation does not have to match what the first speaker actually said, it cannot be reworded in any way. If someone were to quote Lenin's (or "Lenin's") line as "When we are ready to shoot the capitalists, they will sell us the rifle," we might correct him or her even if we doubted whether Lenin ever said anything of the sort. Lenin mentioned neither rifle nor rope, but "Lenin" specified rope. Regardless of the extract, the speaker would have gotten the quotation wrong. Someone who quoted George Washington as having said "I cannot tell a whopper" might be faulted for misquoting even by people fully confident that "I cannot tell a lie" is entirely legendary.

How is it possible to correct lines that were never stated? The answer is that we implicitly recognize that second speakers also have rights. Though not fully embodied, they enjoy their own kind of existence and should not be quoted incorrectly. One can get a quotation right or wrong just as one can get an extract right or wrong.

Qu'ils mangent de la citation

Anthologizers typically write as if the historically accurate phrase—what I have called the extract—is their sole concern. Nevertheless, they seem reluctant to banish real quotations that are fake extracts. Why? It is all to the good that their practice rarely lives up to their theory, but shouldn't this inconsistency suggest that their theory is too simple?

Quotation dictionaries that are ostensibly committed to strict historical accuracy routinely include lines that biographers have been unable to document or have even determined to be fake. It is hard to prove a negative, but the alleged speaker occasionally has an ironclad alibi. Perhaps he could not have been where or when the words were allegedly spoken. Or the pun he supposedly uttered depends on words in a language he did not know. Sometimes the putative speaker persuasively denied having said any such thing. Yet such thoroughly debunked lines are often included all the same. They are called "attributed."

But if the anthologizer knows such attributions are false, and has aspired to cleanse the quotational record of all such errors, then why does he or she include them at all? One does not clear the name of someone proven innocent by publicizing the supposed crime as "alleged." Could the reason be that such anthologizers unwittingly recognize that the question of "accuracy" is not as straightforward as all that?

Let me return to some puzzles posed above. Historians and biographers do not believe that Louis XIV ever said "L'état c'est moi," but that *is* the accurate quotation. We tacitly mark it as such by citing it in the "original" language—the language in which the second speaker (not the first) "said" it. The quotation as a quotation circulates as an illustration of the attitude of Louis XIV, of the mindset of absolute monarchs, and of imperiousness in general.

Those who regard quotations lacking a reliable source as spurious might want to ask whether our sense of history would be more accurate if these fakes were purged. Would we understand the past better if all the famous lines that have guided people's thought and behavior, but were not said or said as quoted, were omitted and eventually forgotten?

Almost certainly, Marie Antoinette never said "Let them eat cake" or even (as the line is sometimes corrected) "Let them eat brioche" (*Qu'ils mangent de la brioche*). I am always amused at the correction of "cake" to "brioche" because, after all, one is correcting what Marie Antoinette did *not* say.[3] In French, what she did not say was "brioche." In fact, the correction does make sense once we realize that we are providing a better version *of the quotation*.[4]

Whether referring to brioche, pastry, or cake, this famous statement appears earlier. Rousseau used it, and he, in
turn, was paraphrasing a common way of indicating how the
rich understand poverty. But however historically inaccurate
the attribution to Marie Antoinette, "her" line has figured as
part of European consciousness then, since, and now. If it was
not said by the first speaker, it was said by the second; if not
by Marie Antoinette, then by "Marie Antoinette." So widely
known is this line as a quotation that to purge it would be to
make numerous parodies unintelligible: Colin Jarman's "Let
them drink Coke" and others.[5] In fact, speechmakers, authors,
headline writers, and advertisers constantly allude to, adapt,
or otherwise rely on our knowledge of many similar second-
speaker-only utterances.

Voltaire apparently never said or wrote, "I may not agree
with what you say, but I will defend to the death your right to
say it" (or any of a number of versions more or less similar in
wording). The statement belongs to a biographer of Voltaire
who was paraphrasing his thought more felicitously than Voltaire ever phrased it. Voltaire did defend free speech in other
words. So is the quotation accurate? Certainly it is, as a quotation: it has been repeatedly cited in calls for tolerance ever
since it entered our culture.[6] It functions as the opposite of
Lenin's much-quoted line about liberty being precious—so
precious it has to be rationed.[7]

The Translator's Range

Even as a historical statement, Voltaire's line is not clearly inaccurate. It is, first of all, an accurate rendition of Voltaire's
sentiment, and second, not that far from things he did say.[8]
Is that enough to be a more or less accurate extract? Where
does an extract shade into a paraphrase? Well, it depends—

principally, on the context in which we are using the line and the conventions governing that context.

In any case, we know perfectly well that whatever Voltaire said, he said it in French, so no English wording could be truly accurate. Nor is it likely there could be only one proper wording in English. We are usually aware that there are usually several ways to translate a foreign phrase.

Let us call the set of possible renditions we acknowledge as accurate "the translator's range." All foreign quotations given in English may vary within that range.

What is more unexpected is that we sometimes allow a sort of translator's range even for some quotations originally in English. We treat them *as if* they were a rendition of some foreign original and so entitled to vary in wording so long as meaning is preserved.

The range of variation we allow tends to expand when we recognize that the line has *only* a second speaker. Once we understand that we are speaking of a legend, we do not care as much whether someone quotes "Washington" saying "Father, I cannot tell a lie. I did it with my little hatchet" (MDQ, 602), or "I can't tell a lie, Pa; you know I can't tell a lie. I did cut it with my hatchet" (ODQ, 822).

A quotation that has only a second speaker resembles a translation of a nonexistent original.

The Quotation's Memory

Translations raise a multitude of problems. Sometimes a translation acquires an authority of its own. In that case, we may sense another version to be somehow wrong even if we accept it as an acceptable English rendition of the original wording. This perplexing fact shows that we distinguish between extract and quotation. We may know both wordings are accurate as extracts, but still regard only one as the accurate quotation. In fact, an extract can be an inaccurate quotation even when it is *more* faithful than the authoritative translation to the original.

For English speakers, the King James Bible has played the role of such an authoritative translation. Consider these renditions of a famous Biblical verse:

> Am I my brother's keeper?—King James version (Genesis 4:9)

> Am I my brother's guardian?—Jerusalem Bible[9]

> Am I the watcher of my brother?—Everett Fox translation[10]

I imagine that most people would be ready to acknowledge that all three may be accurate renditions of the underlying Hebrew line. One hardly needs to know Hebrew to do so, because all three lines mean the same thing, and so if one is accurate, the others are as well. All evidently lie within the translator's range.

But if we are speaking of the quotation—the words frequently quoted in English and which we can expect a literate person to recognize—only the King James version qualifies. Would anyone writing or lecturing on each person's responsibility to his or her neighbor quote any other version? Would anyone wanting to evoke the biblical story say anything but "brother's keeper"?

"Brother's keeper" evokes the Bible without mentioning it. In doing so, it calls to mind a range of associations the phrase has accumulated over the centuries and in the course of our individual lives. Precisely because it is the quotation—not the extract, but the quotation—it "remembers" the contexts in which it has appeared.

Indeed, it is one of the defining features of quotations that they have a sort of "memory."[11] (Or as people say today, they have "stickiness.")[12] Because they are familiar, because they are quoted, because we say and hear them time and again, they can be counted on to evoke a great deal more than they say. An extract has a memory only insofar as it is similar enough to the quotation to remind us of it. If there is any such evocativeness to "watcher of my brother," it is because the listener may guess that he or she has encountered a variant of "brother's keeper."

The translational equivalent of the extract is not necessarily a substitute for the quotation. Only the memorable remembers. Modernizers of liturgical as well as of biblical texts too often seem to forget that a new version, just because it is a new version, loses quotational resonance. Even if it should be poetically superior, which rarely happens, the new line forgets what the old one retains—all the more so, if the latest rendition should be just one more in a series of ever-changing editions.

"Blessed are the meek, for they shall inherit the earth" is the quotation, whereas "Happy are the gentle; they shall have the earth for their heritage" (Jerusalem Bible) is not. It would be a kind of quotational illiteracy not to know the words that follow "Blessed are the meek." In much the same way, one would be demonstrating illiteracy not to recognize "good Samaritan," "Turn the other cheek," and "Let my people go!" But who could complete "Happy are the gentle"?

I remember as a child hearing someone define "evolution" as the theory that makes a monkey in the zoo ask, "Am I my keeper's brother?" Such a joke presumes we know the quotation in the King James version—not just the sense of the passage, and not even its wording in Hebrew, but precisely its specific wording in the authoritative English translation that established the line as a quotation in English.[13] Much as one proof of your fame is that somewhere a madman thinks he is you, so one sign of a quotation is that other quotations imitate, parody, or otherwise depend upon people's knowledge of it. I am aware of no joke about the watcher of my brother.

The famous African American spiritual includes the line, "Let my people go!" It makes use of a quotation, which means that it presumes we know the version quoted *as* the quotation, regardless of how some other translation might "improve" on it. Supposedly more accurate versions—which, as we have seen, are sometimes simply other choices within the translator's range—sacrifice the quotation on which other quotations depend. Change "Let my people go!" to "Permit our community to depart" and the spiritual loses its biblical referent.

Voltaire's line has functioned as a kind of liberal sacred text of tolerance. For this purpose, it is quite good enough that the closest version to be found in his writings is: "Think for yourselves and let others enjoy the privilege to do so too." The standard line is less an extract than a paraphrase.

I may not accept it as a translation, but I will defend to the death its rights as the quotation.

The Rough Draft Rule and the Transcriber's Range

Even for an extract, standards of accuracy are anything but clear-cut. We properly, if tacitly, use different standards for different purposes.

Just as trade unions know that exactly following a company's rules will bring production to a halt (the technique of a "rule-book strike"), so journalists are aware that "the surest way to make a monkey of a man is to quote him" with perfect accuracy.[14] Anyone sounds like an idiot in a sufficiently precise transcription, including all the "ahs," "ers," and corrections in mid-sentence. So ambushed, we all resemble George W. Bush.

All-too-literal citation could make even Martin Luther King Jr., Mahatma Gandhi, or William Jennings Bryan sound inarticulate, but no one cites them this way. In these cases, we cite generously, and it is the generous version that appears accurate while the literal one, though matching the transcription, seems like a mean-spirited trick. Why?

In citing public figures, journalists usually give what the person clearly meant to say—without mid-sentence corrections, filler words, repetitions, and the sort of lapses in grammar committed by the most educated when speaking off the cuff. By convention, such alterations in accord with intended meaning are not considered inaccurate.

In his textbook for journalism students *Basic Interviewing Skills,* Raymond Gordon notes that the act of transcribing a taped interview is not purely mechanical. "The interviewer, or another person with a clear understanding of the objectives of the interview, listens to the tape and dictates onto another tape the relevant information. Whether this dictation must be in the exact words of the respondent or whether it can be paraphrased depends on the precise objectives of the interview."[15] Transcription is then made from this second tape. If the process were purely mechanical, no understanding of the interview's objectives would be needed, and the whole step of dictating a second taped version would be pointless. Why this extra step?

For one thing, the transcriber must judge the information provided by "audible but nonverbal clues such as tone of voice (of both participants), pacing, hesitations, false starts, confusions, and redundancies that are typical of unedited conversations. All of this information is particularly important" and can be reflected in the transcription eventually to follow. On the other hand, the transcriber can leave out "false starts, hesitations, confusions, and redundancies" (Gordon, 176). Obviously, judgments about which hesitations are important and which merely distracting can differ. The whole process from taped interview to edited text can lead to several versions that, by journalistic standards, might all be deemed accurate. Where there is judgment, there is variety.

Readers usually sense that some such process has gone on. I know of no case when an irate letter to an editor alleged journalistic fraud in the absence of every "er," unpronounced letter, repeated word, or throat clearing.

It is as if the journalistic convention was: Record what the person would have said had he been able to go over his own words. Treat the actual utterance as a sort of rough draft and then supply the final version. We can now see why mechanical transcription can actually falsify, because, given this convention, it presents the rough draft as if it already *were* the edited version. In so doing, the journalist implicitly claims that the way we all usually speak is the best the interviewee could do even when considering every word. In treating the transcription as if it were a formal press release, the journalist lies, not by mistranscribing words but by misrepresenting them.

The conventional treatment of actual words as somehow preliminary: let us call this the "rough draft" rule. The less prepared a remark is, the more leeway should be allowed to its intended meaning and the greater distance should be allowed between speech and cited words.

But if this, or something like it, is the convention, then it is in *not* being literally accurate that one is conventionally accurate. Clearly, there is some analogue to the translator's range: call it a "transcriber's range." As with translations, different occasions allow for different accuracies, and even the same occasion permits a range of versions. Two transcriptions of an unrehearsed question-and-answer period may differ without either being inaccurate.

Recorded, Meant, or Heard?

The rough draft rule is only one factor shaping the transcriber's range.

What listeners hear, as well as what speakers mean to say, affects our sense of accuracy. Attend a speech and read the literal transcript and you will be struck by what you have not heard. Listeners usually do not even notice the corrections made in the course of speaking.

For this reason, one might easily understand a speech yet find the transcript very hard to follow. As the organizer of a conference, I once had a transcript made of the lectures and question-and-answer periods. Reading it over, I could not even decipher portions unless the tape was playing at the same time. And yet my memory was of speakers expressing themselves clearly. Was my memory mistaken?

What does accuracy entail? Is an accurate text one that records (a) the words spoken as a tape records them and a mechanical transcript renders them; (b) what the speaker clearly meant to say; or (c) what the audience heard? If (b) and

(c) agree with each other but disagree with (a), is it so clear that (a) is the accurate version?

Citational Range

For an extract, as well as for a quotation, convention always allows a "citational range," depending on circumstances, audience, occasion, and purposes.

Even great works of literature, which we usually feel must not be tampered with, permit a range of accurate versions. Very few would call the eminent scholar William K. Wimsatt Jr. careless. Yet we find the following comment in the "bibliographical note" to his edition of *Alexander Pope: Selected Poetry and Prose:*

> The text of this edition is that of the large octavo edition of Pope's *Works* in nine volumes, 1751, by his literary executor William Warburton, except that (1) elliptical spellings (e.g., *barb'rous, int'rest, sat'rist, vent'rous, pleas'd, thro'*) have been expanded or, in the case of most second-person singular verbs, simplified by omission of the apostrophe (e.g. *deignst, knowst*); (2) archaic spellings (e.g. *chear, dipt, prest, shew, syren, Cressi, Switz*) have been changed unless in rhyming positions; (3) a good many hyphens have been eliminated (In this I have tended to follow modern American rather than British usage); (4) commas, semicolons, other marks of punctuation, and quotation marks have occasionally been changed, omitted, or added where a conflict with modern usage was disturbing to sense; (5) a few

clear mistakes have been corrected; (6) in the prose
pieces titles of books have been italicized; (7) a few
prose pieces set in italic and one set largely in
Gothic (the mock proclamation prefixed to the
Dunciad) and the italicized verse quotations in *Peri
Bathous* and *Guardian* No. 40 have been changed
to roman.[16]

In the course of the entire volume, the number of these alterations must be considerable, and yet they do not add up to inaccuracy. Why not?

Wimsatt's changes seem reasonable because an original
reader would have been familiar with spelling, punctuation,
and usage strange to a modern one, and so to reproduce them
mechanically would actually change the experience of reading. A joke we have to decipher painfully ceases to be funny;
humor delayed is humor denied. Wimsatt is evidently concerned with fidelity to the experience of reading, which is not
the same as fidelity to textual markings. If it were, he would
not have altered the text to conform to "modern American"
rather than British usage. When a conflict with modern usage
proves "disturbing to sense," Wimsatt chooses fidelity to sense.

A clear principle of editorial change implicitly operates
here: given changes in usage from Pope's time to ours, reproduce the text that is the sensible equivalent to what Pope wrote
and his audience read. If sense is the standard, then changes,
far from distorting the text, may make it more accurate.

Wimsatt also regards it as obvious why "a few clear mistakes have been corrected." Does accuracy demand the reproduction of typos? It might, if the edition was intended for students of printing and publishing. But not if it was meant for
appreciators of English literature. Given the readers Wimsatt

has in mind, and the reason the edition is being prepared in the first place, the standard of accuracy pertains not to textual markings but to their effect. Again, purpose is intrinsic to accuracy.

Nevertheless, Wimsatt's choices are not the only possible ones. Compare his principles with those adopted by Roy Flannagan in *The Riverside Milton:*

> Milton's texts should be distanced from his modern readers, because they are distanced by time and by the evolution and the fluidity of the English language. The word *grace,* for instance, meant something quite different in 1667 from what it means at present, and the word spelled *Sovran* signifies a sound quite different from that of *sovereign.* If one adds together the all-but-invisible elements of spelling, punctuation, capitalization, and italics, Milton's English as he presented it in manuscript and in print has an utterly different texture from that of acceptable modern English style. I believe that it is the modern editor's duty to preserve the texture of Milton's prose and poetry as it appeared in his own time—not for antiquarian purposes but in order to emphasize its difference and its distance from our own usage.[17]

In contrast to Wimsatt, Flannagan rejects the practice of adjusting spelling and other textual features to create a familiar experience of reading. On the contrary, he wants to preserve the difference between twentieth- and seventeenth-century English. For him, the essentials of the text include elements that could neither have been intended by the poet nor experienced by the original readers. After all, temporal distance from the original is a fact not about text, the poet, or the original readers, but about us. Flannagan's choice is as reasonable as Wimsatt's; but, whatever Flannagan may think, it is not necessarily more accurate, precisely because it imposes a temporal distance that original readers did not sense.

When I was a student at Oxford, buildings originally white had darkened over the centuries to almost black. They were later restored, more or less, to their original color. Purists objected to the change. But which appearance was "truer"? Was it the one that made the buildings look as if they were recently built, which they were not, or the one that made them look centuries old, which they were? Do we want the faded photographs of our childhood made to look as if just taken? Would that not be like colorizing a black and white film? Or, on the contrary, would erasing the signs of intervening years help photographs do what we hope they do: recreate the past as it really was, without the weight of the future that was to follow?

Flannagan and Wimsatt agree that, in some sense, the standard is sense. Nothing in Flannagan's principles, for instance, would prevent him from correcting obvious typos. Neither does he insist on seventeenth-century typefaces, which also mark our difference from Milton's time. And yet for some purposes, preservation of typefaces would be important, just as for some purposes—say, those of a sociolinguist—speech transcription should preserve not only all ers and ums, but even the precise phonetic rendition of particular words. Journalists ignore regional accents that linguists examine, and varying interests may prove relevant to particular editions.

Wimsatt and Flannagan have adopted different principles, but each edition lies within the bounds of accuracy. That is so even though Wimsatt's principles applied to Milton, or Flannagan's to Pope, would lead to editions different from the ones they have given us.

Evidently, citational range includes an "editor's range," which, like the translator's range and the transcriber's range, allows for more than one kind of accuracy.

Quotations differ from extracts, and extracts themselves may vary. In that case, what is a misquotation?

V

What Is a Misquotation?

*Quotation, n. The art of repeating erroneously the
words of another. The words erroneously repeated.*
—*Ambrose Bierce*, The Devil's Dictionary

Nice Quotes Finish Last

Recent quotation anthologies have advanced claims for unprecedented accuracy. The Internet has supposedly allowed
for previously impossible research to establish correct wording. Unfortunately, advanced technology cannot compensate
for muddled thinking.

Numerous recent books collect familiar *mis*quotations.
They offer buyers two pleasures at once, rereading favorite sayings and seeing them exposed as frauds. Choosing such titles
as *They Never Said It: A Book of Fake Quotes, Misquotes and
Misleading Attributions* (Paul F. Boller Jr. and John George),

What They Didn't Say: A Book of Misquotations (Elizabeth Knowles), and *Nice Guys Finish Seventh: False Phrases, Spurious Sayings, and Familiar Misquotations* (Ralph Keyes), authors purport to cleanse the verbal record of errors resulting from simple carelessness or malicious intent. With the ardor of a detective proving a forgery or a prosecutor exposing a backdated document, they warn us that "so many of our most popular sayings" are spurious. Having taken a "skeptical look," they provide true versions and proper attributions (NGFS, xi).

The covers of such volumes often cite the counterfeits we take for true coin. The back of the dust jacket of Knowles's book pictures a balloon with the line "Play it again, Sam," which, for all its fame, turns out to be mistaken. Keyes's title *Nice Guys Finish Seventh*—the word "Last" has been crossed out and "Seventh" written in its place—graphically dramatizes the process of catching a misquotation in the act. Keyes's later volume, *The Quote Verifier: Who Said What, Where, and When,* prints on its jacket a long list of errors now exposed: "Greed is good—Less is more—Blood, sweat, and tears—Give me liberty, or give me death—The buck stops here—The devil is in the details—Don't give up the ship!— Elementary, my dear Watson—What does a woman want?— Ain't I a woman?— Make my day—All politics is local—Go west, young man, go west—Golf is a good walk spoiled—Let them eat cake—History is bunk—Cut to the chase—Nice guys finish last—Play it again, Sam—There's no such thing as a free lunch—Show me the money!—Beam me up, Scotty—Fifteen minutes of fame—Paris is worth a mass—War is hell—Nuts!"

Apparently, we are victims of constant and colossal verbal swindles. The first blurb on *The Quote Verifier*'s first page tells us that "Ralph Keyes has made it his mission to hunt down and expose false quotations . . . *The Quote Verifier* is a much-needed corrective to the countless 'quotations' that are misquoted, falsely attributed or downright wrong. Keyes takes apart with surgical precision every dubious quotation old and new."[1] Another blurb describes Keyes as "our verifier-in-chief." Missionary, surgeon, and general, this hero reproves verbal sinners, amputates gangrenous errors, and commands the linguistic equivalent of war.

To be sure, some of these authors (especially Knowles) have a relatively sophisticated sense of what they are doing. But even the best succumb to the sheer pleasure of "gotcha!" They scold from the hip. It is one thing to find that two versions do not coincide; it is quite another to discover a misquotation. That distinction is almost always lost or obscured. In general, these volumes presume simple answers to complex questions. They seem impatient to put all subtleties aside and just ask: Is the line correctly quoted or isn't it?[2]

Misquotation books typically suffer from the two errors I have already described. First, they do not distinguish between an extract and a quotation. This error presumably derives from the double usage of the word "quotation," which can refer both to any cited passage and to several short literary forms. Second, even with extracts, standards of correctness can differ. If we examine just where these exposers of error err, we may learn a good deal about both quotations and extracts.

Becoming a Quotation

Like so many debunkers since, Paul Boller and John George list quotations (or, as they would have it, misquotations) that differ from the "real" source. Winston Churchill is usually quoted as having said, "I have nothing to offer but blood, sweat, and tears," but in his address to the House of Commons on May 13, 1940, he really said: "I have nothing to offer but blood and toil, sweat and tears." Boller and George comment: "He [Churchill] liked the words so much, in fact, that he used them again on several occasions during the war. But the public soon revised the Churchillian phrase, partly because the words 'toil' and 'sweat' seemed redundant and partly because the word order sounded a bit awkward. Before long, Churchill was being quoted as having said, 'blood, sweat, and tears,' and the words became famous throughout the world. Today, anyone quoting the original statement would be charged with garbling the quote" (TNSI, 13). Of course, blood, sweat, and tears are all bodily fluids, as toil is not, so the revision is better for more than one reason.

What Boller and George here describe is *the process of becoming a quotation.* The "public" reauthors the words while still attributing them to "Churchill," and so he comes to have said something more quotable. This process, and the sort of polishing towards quotability it involves, is quite common.

"Today, anyone quoting the original quotation would be charged with garbling the quote." And for good reason, because they *would* be garbling the quotation. The quotation, though not the extract, is precisely "blood, sweat, and tears." Once the phrase becomes a quotation, "famous throughout the world," the original wording becomes merely the source of the quotation. The repeated and anthologized version has become authoritative, but the source of that authority is the second speaker.

Usually, the process of polishing takes place beyond the author's ken or after his or her death, but sometimes the author may witness, or even participate in, the process. According to Boller and George, Churchill apparently preferred the public's version of his original words and so sometimes self-quoted them—or "self"-quoted them—in the revised form. Churchill, not just "Churchill," came to say "blood, sweat, and tears."[3] In this way, the quotation became the new extract as the former extract had become the quotation.

Churchill quoted "Churchill," the first speaker quoted the second. More precisely: Churchill saying "blood, sweat, and tears" was repeating not his own words but those made jointly by himself and "the public."

It is precisely for the sake of accuracy that we must distinguish what was said on May 13, 1940, from the quotation. If the second is inaccurate as a reproduction of the words on that date—as an extract—the first is inaccurate if given as the quotation. Or should we ask the rock group to change its name?

Moreover, even by the standard of an extract, "blood, sweat, and tears" is *not* inaccurate. Keyes, who uses the same example of a misquotation, explains that in 1939, the year before the famous speech to the House of Commons, "Churchill (who had previously used the phrases 'blood and tears' and 'their sweat, their tears, their blood' in his writing) himself used the 'blood, sweat, and tears' version in an article on the Spanish Civil War. . . . Churchill himself (or his publisher) called a 1941 collection of his speeches *Blood, Sweat, and Tears*" (QV, 15–16). If Churchill did in fact say "blood, sweat, and tears" on other occasions, and had even titled a collection of his speeches *Blood, Sweat, and Tears,* then how can it be claimed that those words are falsely attributed to him? Only if someone were to specify the speech he made on May 13, 1940, and claim that *on that day* what Churchill said was "blood, sweat, and tears," would there be an error. I imagine most people who cite Churchill's words do not name a date. If they do not, then "blood, sweat, and tears," is accurate as *both* quotation and extract.

As is so often the case, the debunkers are the ones who err. By any reasonable standard, it is mistaken to claim that Churchill did *not* say "blood, sweat, and tears."

Quote Me Sometime

Truth, Sir, is a cow which will yield such people no more milk, so they are gone to milk the bull.

—*Samuel Johnson, in Boswell's* Life[4]

Consider the following example from Keyes. Under the heading "movie misquotes," he cites Mae West supposedly saying, "Why don't you come up and see me sometime?" He comments: "What Mae West actually told Cary Grant in *She Done Him Wrong* was, 'Why don't you come up sometime and see me?' This provocative suggestion caught the public's fancy in its euphonized form. West herself used the new version in her next movie, *I'm No Angel*" (NGFS, 135).

As with Churchill's line, the change represents the process of becoming a quotation. The quotation is precisely: "Why don't you come up and see me sometime?" And here again, this version is also one of two accurate extracts, since, as Keyes allows, Mae West really said *both* versions. If in a later movie she really voiced the line as usually quoted, how can it be an error to say as much?

In short, the version that Keyes regards as accurate is correct as an extract but not as a quotation, whereas the commonly cited one is correct by either standard. What is *not* correct is classing "Why don't you come up and see me sometime?" as a misquotation.

One might offer anthologizers a guideline: if one must

choose a single version of a line, and there is one that is both the common quotation and one possible accurate extract, choose that one.

Garbo's Disavowal

As a rule, the first speaker has no veto power over the second. It would probably have been futile for Churchill to correct the public and demand his original wording. Some have tried to do just that. They have insisted on what they originally said, usually to no avail.

Greta Garbo denied having said "I want to be alone": "I only said 'I want to be left alone.' There is all the difference" (MDQ, 369). There is, indeed. But people still go on quoting Garbo as saying "I want to be alone." All she succeeded in doing is adding *another* quotation to the anthologies, usually appearing under either "Quotation" or "Misquotation," in which her words of correction are given. Disavowals are themselves a type of saying often collected.

For that matter, it is not even clear that "I want to be alone" is a mistake. Garbo did say the line in several films. It appears in *Grand Hotel* (1932), and the subtitle of *The Single Standard* (1929) is "I am walking alone because I want to be alone" (WTDS, 67). Certainly the words belong to Garbo the actress if not to Garbo the person as she existed outside her films. And in referring to film stars, we very often have in mind the character they typically play. If we credit "Make my day" to Clint Eastwood (NGFS, 106, and QV, 138), we are referring to Clint Eastwood as Dirty Harry.

Even in real life, Garbo used close variants like "Why don't you let me alone?" If so, and if the commonly cited line appears in her films, surely it is less misleading to quote these words as hers than to call them a misquotation.

Discursive Fictions

Even though they never existed physically, second speakers are real, in much the way that numerous acknowledged fictions really exist. They exist precisely as fictions. Although Hamlet, Raskolnikov, or Samuel Weller could never be found outside literary works, quotations from them are not fake.

Acknowledged fictions play an important role in social life. We may reason about rights in terms of a social contract even though we do not believe for a minute that people ever got together to draw one up. The law employs "legal fictions," rules depending on premises known to be factually false. If a husband and wife die minutes apart in an automobile accident, the law may proceed as if they had died simultaneously. Readers often interpret the *Iliad,* Aesop's fables, and books of the Bible as if they had a single author even if they do not believe such an author ever existed. If not written by Homer, the *Iliad* was written by "Homer."

In much the same way, the second speaker is real, even if not the same as, the historical person with the same name. In the case of second-speaker-only quotations, we often employ a name that is a mere placeholder: Poor Richard, Solomon, or even "a Chinese proverb." We do so even when we no more mean to make a claim about Chinese culture than when we call a game "Chinese checkers." "Yiddish saying" functions in a similar way. Such practices testify to the sense that there can be some sort of speaker other than a flesh-and-blood, historical person.

And Yet I Quote

We even have visual depictions of things never said and the speakers who never said them. Galileo almost certainly did not say "Eppur si muove!" (And yet it moves!) as he rose from his knees right after affirming, under threat of torture by the Inquisition, the fixity of the earth. He would have been an idiot to do so, and there is no evidence outside folklore or legend that he did. The editors of *History in Quotation* comment astutely: "There is no evidence for this and it is extremely unlikely. Even so, a painting by the Spanish painter Murillo, dated 1643 and depicting Galileo pointing to these words on the wall of his cell, show that it is an early tradition," not just a widely circulated one (HiQ, 370). Murillo has literally painted the quotation and painted the second speaker, and these words live as an authentic quotation even if only "Galileo," but not Galileo, said them.

At Waterloo, Baron Pierre Jacques Etienne Cambronne supposedly responded to an English demand to surrender: "La Guarde meurt mais ne se rend pas" (The Guards die but do not surrender). In fact, Cambronne did surrender and claimed that he had said something different, "*Merde.*" Nevertheless the brave words were placed on a statue to Cambronne in Nantes "and soon passed into English and other languages."[5] Here the quotation has been carved and the second speaker sculpted.

Such quotations reach out beyond their text. The very existence of statues, paintings, and legends representing quotations suggests an important feature about them. They are not just texts, but also events, and they consist of more than words alone.

VI
More Than Words Alone

In the same hour came forth fingers of a man's
hand, and wrote over against the candlestick upon
the plaster of the wall of the king's palace; and the
king saw the part of the hand that wrote.
—Daniel 5:5

A Quotation May Include Its Authorship

Anthologizers wonder: if a famous statement turns out to have
a prior source, then who is the author of the quotation? Under
whose name should the anthologizer list it?

Quotographers (to use the current term) often insist
that attribution to the more famous, but not earliest, speaker is
erroneous, and their books relentlessly expose such "misattributions." Anthologizers often demonstrate uneasiness which-

ever choice they make. Their criteria require them to credit the earliest user, but the results seem wrong.

"Ask not what your country can do for you": Should we really attribute these words not to John F. Kennedy but to Kahlil Gibran, who wrote something similar a few decades earlier in a book entitled—really—*The New Frontier* (1931)? Or should we ascribe authorship to Oliver Wendell Holmes Jr., who said in 1884: "We pause to . . . recall what our country had done for each of us and ask ourselves what we can do for our country in return" (WTDS, 7)? Should the words "iron curtain" no longer be credited to Churchill in his 1946 speech at Fulton, Missouri, because they had been used before, at times even referring to the Soviet Union (NGFS, 54–55)?

The problem here arises not only from failing to distinguish the extract from the quotation but also from not recognizing that the ascription of an author may be an intrinsic part of a quotation. So may be the identification of the specific work from which the words are drawn or the occasion during which it was uttered. In such cases, giving the author, work, or occasion is not like crediting Sheridan when quoting "Never say more than necessary" or mentioning Boswell's *Life* as the source of a Dr. Johnson witticism. Nothing in Sheridan's line demands that we know he wrote it, nor, at least in many cases, do Johnson's witticisms depend on awareness of where they can be found. But some quotations do require mentioning the author or other pertinent extratextual information. They would be incomplete otherwise.[1]

A quotation may consist of more than just its words.

Part of the point of the Beatitudes is that they were spoken by Jesus and are to be found in the New Testament. They differ from a blessing by a saint or a saying by Jesus in the gnostic *Gospel of Thomas* not only because their wording is different but also because they were spoken by the Jesus of the canonical Bible. Believers recite the Lord's prayer because it is the *Lord's* prayer. Americans repeat the words of the First Amendment not just as an eloquent endorsement of freedom of speech and religion but precisely as the first amendment to the U.S. Constitution. In many cultures or situations, a citation from Scripture (whether the Torah, the New Testament, the Koran, or the writings of Marx and Lenin) can settle a dispute as citations from anywhere else could not. In the Soviet Union, it was crucially important whether one was citing Lenin or merely Engels. The Little Red Book of *Quotations from Chairman Mao Tse-tung* is a wholly different sort of thing from *Everyman's Dictionary of Shakespeare Quotations.*[2]

Because authorship or textual location may be part of a quotation, verbally identical texts may be different quotations. For Americans, the same words, if drawn from the French Declaration of the Rights of Man rather the U.S. Constitution, would not be the same quotation, because one is not binding on the American government while the other is. Statements in the Declaration of Independence differ from statements of any specific person, including Thomas Jefferson elsewhere, even when the two coincide.

Because authorship may be intrinsic to a quotation, John F. Kennedy's famous line is his regardless of where he got it. The fact that he may have heard or read these words, or something resembling them, is an interesting fact about the line but does not make it someone else's quotation. If Holmes anticipated Kennedy, then we have *two* curiously similar quotations. "Fear itself" belongs to Franklin Roosevelt, even if he was aware that the Duke of Wellington, Montaigne, and the Book of Proverbs had expressed a similar thought in similar words.

Keyes and other experts agree that by the mid-1920s the Russian author Vasily Rozanov, a British traveler named Ethel Snowden, and an American magazine article had all referred to an "iron curtain" separating the Soviet Union from the West, but the phrase nevertheless belongs to Winston Churchill because it was his speech at Fulton, Missouri, in 1946 that shaped the Cold War.[3] Snowden may have been a predecessor of Churchill, or even a source of his *words,* but Churchill authored the *quotation.* What is more, the occasion, as well as the author, is intrinsic to the quotation. The quotation belongs to the Fulton, Missouri, speech even though Churchill himself had used the phrase in a cable to President Truman a year earlier, because that speech, that occasion, and that moment, which were constantly mentioned along with the famous words, gave the phrase its importance. Sometimes people do not bother even to mention the words and mention just the speech at Fulton, Missouri. Why else would the *Oxford Dictionary of Quotations* and the *Yale Book of Quotations* credit the quotation to that speech even though they note Churchill's earlier use?[4]

Occasion

Rembrandt's famous painting of the handwriting on the wall— the mysterious words of warning that appear to Babylonian King Balshazzar in Daniel 5:1–31—portrays the moment when the words appear, because it is the whole incident, not just the words, that make the quotation mean what it does. The quotation includes the writing hand and the wall on which it writes. The words, which the King James Bible does not translate and which even English speakers always cite in the Aramaic, are meaningless apart from that moment. They merely remind us of the occasion without which the quotation is incomplete.

The sculpture of Nathan Hale on the Yale campus also tries to give us a whole quotation. The whole quotation includes, and the sculpture depicts, the speaker and occasion, as well as the words carved into the pedestal. This is what a quotation intrinsically connected with a speaker and an event *looks like.*

Quotographers have argued that even if Nathan Hale did utter his famous words—"I only regret that I have but one life to give for my country"—he was nevertheless quoting Addison's play *Cato* (1713), in which a character says, "What pity is it / That we can die but once to serve our country!" (NGFS, 61; QV, 117, 177). Since Hale may well have known this play, they conclude, the quotation is not his but Addison's.

To argue this way is to miss the handwriting on the wall. As "iron curtain" belongs to Churchill at Fulton, Missouri, so "I only regret" belongs to Hale at the moment just before he was hanged. As the statue picturing that moment testifies, the line lived on as *his.* After all, an essential part of its import lies in the event of its uttering. It was spoken not by a fictional character, but by a flesh-and-blood young man about to die in his country's war for independence. Apart from that circumstance, these words border on the insipid, or at least they would be hardly as memorable as they are. In this case and many others, both the author and the occasion of utterance are intrinsic to the quotation.

The statue shows Hale with his hands bound, evidently about to be hanged. The line carved on the pedestal exemplifies courage in the face of death for a cause. Indeed, it is precisely because the quotation is Hale's that the quote sleuths can evoke interest by pointing out that Hale may have done some reading. Otherwise, who would care?

Quoting a Quotation

Regardless of what they may have read, Hale was not *quoting* (or citing) Addison, nor was Kennedy quoting Holmes or

Gibran. If we are to use terms with care, quoting means evoking the words of another *as* the words of another. But it would be absurd to imagine that Hale meant to say: "As one of Addison's characters puts it in his play *Cato,* 'I only regret. . . . '"

Last words require no footnote, and only a pedant, not a hero, would provide one. By the same token, Lincoln would have been a fool to mention that, in calling for "malice toward none," he was adapting words of John Quincy Adams.[5] It is possible that Kennedy was using Gibran, and Hale relying on Addison, for inspiration, but they were not directing their audience to think of their sources. Their words do not quote, they are quotations.

Of course, a speaker may be famous for quoting another speaker, and then real or implied quotation marks would be part of the quotation. When Lincoln at Gettysburg referred to the "proposition that all men are created equal," the point of his words required that listeners recognize the origin of this proposition even without intonational or graphic marks of quotation. In the Jewish *Pirke Aboth,* we find numerous famous rabbinic quotations that include, and depend on knowledge of, quotations from Scripture or earlier rabbis.[6]

Oddly enough, quotographers seem especially likely to detect misattribution when a speaker is quoting: that is, when a speaker expects the audience to recognize words *as* drawn from someone else. For quite different reasons, Adlai Stevenson and Ronald Reagan were given to using the words of others—Stevenson because he was intensely literate and Reagan because he was an actor. When Stevenson observed of Eleanor Roosevelt that she "would rather light a candle than curse the darkness," he was alluding to, if not quoting, the motto of the Christopher Society: "It is better to light one candle than to curse the darkness" (NGFS, 76; YBQ, 418). When

Reagan, after being shot by John Hinckley, said to his wife,
"Honey, I forgot to duck," he was quoting Jack Dempsey's
comment to his wife after losing the heavyweight title to Gene
Tunney (NGFS, 105–106). The appeal of Reagan's remark depends on its surprising use of Dempsey's words along with a
bit of self-deprecating humor when it was least expected. If we
miss that these are quotations that themselves quote, they lose
much or all of their point. It is hard to see why Keyes, who
describes Reagan's quip as the very same one Dempsey made,
lists it in a chapter entitled "All the President's Misquotes," or
why (in the chapter "Lyp-sync Politics") he treats the attribution to Stevenson as an error.[7] How can it be a misattribution
to quote someone quoting when that is what he was doing?

I suppose it is possible that Stevenson was, rather than
quoting, hoping no one would notice a verbal theft, but Keyes
gives no reason to think so. Reagan clearly expects us to understand not just that he is using Dempsey's words but also
to recall the situation in which Dempsey used them. Both
the earlier author of the line and the occasion of its uttering
were intrinsic to the words Reagan was using as he meant to
use them. The very point of the line requires our recognition
that it consists of more than its words.

Changing Authorship

It is quite common that a later speaker displaces an earlier one
as a quotation's acknowledged author. "Government of the
people, by the people, for the people" belongs to Lincoln even
if he did get the phrase, or something like it, from a speech by
Daniel Webster. The only question is whether Lincoln meant
his listeners to detect Webster's words behind his own. If he
did, Lincoln's line is a quotation that quotes, and if he did not,

it is simply a quotation. Of course, Lincoln could have meant his words to work both ways, depending on a given listener's knowledge.

Famous lines change authors, perhaps frequently if they survive long enough. To take the best-studied example, we credit Isaac Newton with the quotation "If I have seen further it is by standing on the shoulders of giants." Since the publication of Robert Merton's magnificent book *On the Shoulders of Giants,* it is clear that, by the time Newton wrote these words to Robert Hooke in 1676, they were quite famous. They already had centuries of history behind them, and people as educated as Hooke could be expected to know them. We are misled into thinking Newton invented the line because he did not use quotation marks.

Lack of quotation marks, however, can mean more than one thing, much as ignoring something differs from not seeing it. One can fail to mention something precisely because everyone already knows it. The absence of a sign indicating that something is present may indicate its absence, but it may also mean that its presence is obvious. To know whether someone from another age is quoting, one needs to look at more than the text.

Newton omitted quotation marks for the same reason that someone today might omit them around "to be or not to be." When a line is familiar enough, use of quotation marks might imply that one's reader needs to be told what everyone else knows. They impute illiteracy.

Like explanations of the obvious, quotation marks may be an insult. In this respect, they resemble explanatory notes. Philosophical journals do not identify Immanuel Kant, French historians rarely provide Napoleon's birth and death dates, and economists writing for each other never define marginal utility or supply and demand. Professional training includes learning what *not* to footnote. A mistake might easily betray that a young scholar has just encountered a source everyone established in the field takes for granted.

A journal in Laos might identify "four score and seven years ago," as no American source would. How about a German, Polish, or Russian publication? It depends on how well known the line is to Germans, Poles, or Russians. We might even conjecture how well known a line is in a given culture by whether it is identified or placed between quotation marks.

So is the quotation that Newton did not dream of claiming still his? Certainly it is, in our culture. Despite a long history of predecessors and variations, the "shoulders" quotation is Newton's for more than one reason. To begin with, no one today remembers earlier speakers. It is now just another one of Newton's famous lines, listed in anthologies along with many others. As he claims to "frame no hypotheses," he stands "on the shoulders of giants."[8]

Even more important, the quotation is now Newton's because the fact that the words are his has long been part of their meaning. The same words said by anyone but Newton, regarded for centuries as the greatest scientist who ever lived, would not be the same. Imagine them put in the mouth of Larry Summers or, for that matter, given as anonymous, and the difference becomes palpable. Credited to Newton, the line suggests: If even Newton stood on the shoulders of giants, then surely everyone does. As Newton's, the quotation makes the point Francis Bacon insisted on and we have come to recognize, that science is not a matter of isolated geniuses but a communal enterprise making progress over time.

In much the same way, the attribution of "L'état c'est moi" to Louis XIV is part of the quotation. It would be entirely different attributed, say, to Baudelaire or even Nicolas Sarkozy. No matter how many people may have said "I have a dream," the quotation belongs to Martin Luther King Jr. The same words said by anyone else would not be the same quotation. One cannot identify such a quotation with its text.

The phrase "pride and prejudice" now belongs to Jane Austen even though it was borrowed from Fanny Burney ("'The whole of this unfortunate business,' said Dr Lyster, 'has been the result of *pride and prejudice*'"—from *Cecilia,* 1772, as cited in ODQ, 169).[9] It is doubtful, indeed, that anyone would remember the phrase at all if not for Austen's novel. Burney almost seems to be quoting it in advance.

In such cases, authorship has changed. It has also become not just a fact about the quotation but also an intrinsic part of it.

Subsequent Significance

Sometimes a quotation may come to include not only its author and occasion, but also its subsequent significance. It incorporates later events into the story that includes its utterance. Unwelcome irony may result.

In a chapter devoted to mistaken attributions, Keyes points out that before Neville Chamberlain proclaimed he had achieved "peace with honor," that phrase had been used by Disraeli. Disraeli, in turn, was preceded by Samuel Pepys's comment about his wife that "with peace and honor I am willing to spare her anything" and Volumnia's plea to her son in *Coriolanus* to "hold companionship in peace / With honor" (NGFS, 48).

True enough, and future sleuths may detect predecessors of these predecessors. But however much he may have wished to disown it, the quotation still belongs to Chamberlain and, no less important, it belongs to that occasion. Returning from the Munich conference with Hitler in 1938, Chamberlain proclaimed: "This is the second time there has come back from Germany to Downing Street peace with honor. I believe it is peace for our time" (NGFS, 48, and YBQ, 142). We remember Chamberlain's pronouncement precisely because, as Churchill foresaw, the agreement at Munich did not achieve peace and proved anything but honorable. For many, the line also includes the photograph of Chamberlain holding up the famous "scrap of paper" with Hitler's peaceful assurances.

Chamberlain's words are shadowed by the war that followed. The quotation includes its monumental disconfirmation. For us, it is answered by Churchill's "blood, sweat, and tears" and no less famous vow to "fight them on the beaches." As Chamberlain could not have known, his words initiated a dialogue and an argument he lost.

"Peace in our time" became *proverbial*. It now *means* the frame of mind that once led to the "appeasement" of Hitler and often leads democracies to prefer peace at any price. This meaning belongs not to the words themselves, as they might be deciphered with the aid of a dictionary and grammar, but precisely to the quotation including the occasion of its uttering and that occasion's subsequent significance.

Go West, Young Man

Anthologizers also ponder yet another way in which authorship may be attributable to more than one person. Not only may a famous speaker have a predecessor or quote another famous author, he may have had his words written for him by someone else. Who gets the credit?

Statesmen employ speechwriters, and actors, if not improvising, use a script. Should we say that Churchill's, Kennedy's, and Franklin Roosevelt's famous words really belong to their assistants? In practice, the answer often depends on whether we like the politician—Kennedy keeps his best words while George H. W. Bush's go to Peggy Noonan—but that is not a standard anyone could consistently defend.

What about cases in which we attribute lines to an actor or actress even though we know perfectly well that they were probably written by some scriptwriter? Once again, Mae West frequently becomes a test case.

The editors of the *Macmillan Dictionary of Quotations* observe: "The example of Mae West typifies another difficulty. Many of her sayings are lines from films; therefore the author should, strictly speaking, be the script writer. However, remarks such as 'Come up and see me (sometime)' are so closely associated with her that it would be perverse not to include them under her name" (MDQ, viii). Not only would it be perverse, but—strictly speaking—it would be mistaken not to include them under her name. As quotations, they *are* hers.

Would her famous invitation have any point coming from a male scriptwriter or an anonymous woman? The quotation, as opposed to the extract, includes her saying it. It would even be odd to attribute the line to the fictional character she is playing, since we typically remember it as said not by the character played by Mae West but by Mae West playing a character—a character who is recognizably Mae West.

Mae West says her line in a particular tone and with characteristic gestures, which are also intrinsic to the quotation. The words composed by the scriptwriter are only part of the quotation. What we remember, and evoke when we quote, is the whole scene, which includes not only words but also body language, voice, and apparent eye contact, all of which make a line of Mae West just that. What would the line be without West's tone of sexual innuendo? The film clip, which we may have often seen and which we may remember without knowing what film it comes from, functions as a sort of visual quotation. The words are a reminder of the entire quotation, which includes much more than the words.

The Adapter's Range

In *What They Didn't Say,* Elizabeth Knowles tells us that the famous words "Frankly, my dear, I don't give a damn" should be credited to Sidney Howard, the scriptwriter of *Gone with the Wind,* but this attribution seems decidedly odd. It makes more sense to say that, as a quotation, the line belongs to Clark Gable as Rhett Butler. Here again, the words function as part of a visual quotation that is both verbal and extraverbal. Has anyone ever said, or imagined saying, "As Sidney Howard once remarked, 'Frankly, my dear, I don't give a damn'"?

Knowles explains that in Margaret Mitchell's novel, Rhett says: "I wish I could care what you do or where you go but I can't. . . . My dear, I don't give a damn" (WTDS, 40). Therefore, Knowles concludes, the changed words in the film were composed by Howard and are properly his. What a defense for plagiarists!

Does anyone think of the film as the famous Howard dramatization? Howard who? We think not of Howard but simply of *Gone with the Wind* on film. We readily accept that, in adapting Mitchell's novel for the screen, someone must have changed something, but we are concerned primarily with Clark Gable's Rhett Butler and Vivian Leigh's Scarlett O'Hara. Otherwise, we don't give a damn.

What is most surprising about Knowles's evidence is how *little* the words of the novel have been altered. One would certainly have called the film faithful even if the change had been greater. We do not equate fidelity with literal reproduction, which might take no account of the constraints and opportunities provided by the new medium. Mitchell did not have Gable's face to convey the scene. The words of a faithful film need not be identical to its novelistic source, they need only lie within the "adapter's range," which we may imagine as analogous to the translator's range, the transcriber's range, and the editor's range.

If identical wording were required, then *Gone with the Wind* would be one long misquotation. Howard is no more the author of the famous line Gable speaks than Constance Garnett is the author of Raskolnikov's sentences in her widely used translation of *Crime and Punishment.* I know of no quotation anthology that credits "If there is no God, then all is permitted" not to Dostoevsky but—"strictly speaking"—to Garnett, even though other English versions are worded differently.

It makes sense to think of the quotation as Clark Gable's, as Rhett Butler's, or as Margaret Mitchell's. It also makes sense to think of it as simultaneously belonging to Rhett Butler and to Clark Gable as Rhett Butler. But it borders on the absurd to think of it as Sidney Howard's. Even as an extract, it would be more accurate to say the line belongs jointly to Howard and Mitchell.

Not Yet the Real Thing

Sometimes the changes that quotographers call misquotations do not lessen accuracy, and sometimes they actually increase it. Consider these two examples.

1. Knowles regards Einstein's famous quotation, "God does not play dice," as a misquotation because what Einstein wrote in his letter to Max Born was: "Quantum mechanics is certainly imposing. But an inner voice tells me that this is not yet the real thing. The theory says a lot, but does not bring us any closer to the secrets of the 'old one.' I, at any rate, am convinced that *He* does not play dice" (WTDS, 43).

2. Knowles also faults those who quote Freud as saying "Dreams are the royal road to the unconscious." Citing this popular version, she glosses it: "A popular summary of the views of the Austrian psychiatrist Sigmund Freud, which has now become part of our vocabulary. (The critic John Sutherland, writing in 2001 on the vocabulary of President Bush, commented, 'As Sigmund Freud reminds us, the lapsus linguae is, like the dream, a royal road to the unconscious.') However, what Freud actually wrote in *The Interpretation of Dreams* (2nd edition, 1909) was: 'The interpretation of dreams is the royal road to a knowledge of the unconscious activities of the mind'" (WTDS, 28–29).

In both cases, the supposedly spurious version is indeed accurate as the quotation precisely because that is the version that has now become "part of our vocabulary." Otherwise, it could not be presumed the way Sutherland's allusion does. But we may still ask, are these versions erroneous as extracts?

Remember that some variation is allowed to extracts within the bounds of understood purposes and conventions. As we saw, it is not an error to say "Turn the other cheek." Imagine someone writing: "As Einstein commented, 'He does not play dice.'" This version might satisfy Knowles's standard of accuracy. But it would nevertheless misrepresent the original, which leaves no doubt about to whom "He" refers. Insofar as accuracy includes conveying sense, the same change from pronoun to noun that makes the words a quotation increases, not decreases, its accuracy as an extract. That is how pronouns by their nature work.

Extracts, too, consist of more than words alone. Sometimes a passage must change in order to stay the same. Whether spoken or written, utterances are not just texts but also events.

The Difference of a Difference

In what way is "Dreams are the royal road to the unconscious" erroneous? Knowles cites the original as follows: "The interpretation of dreams is the royal road to a knowledge of the unconscious activities of the mind." By the standards of most scholarly articles, it would be entirely correct to cite "royal road to . . . the unconscious," because ellipses are not errors and scholarly publishers encourage the brevity they allow. In speech, we rarely pronounce ellipses, any more than we give voice to brackets, unless doing so would make a difference. Even in scholarly writing, before one convicted someone of error, one would need to show that the change matters. Imagine someone using the quotation as usually given in a lecture and a questioner indignantly rising to say that what Freud in fact wrote was "The interpretation of dreams is the royal road to the unconscious activities of the mind." We would immediately ask what difference the difference makes and what misunderstanding it fosters. For with no possible misunderstanding, we might have just an alternate version of the same underlying German words. In fact, we do.

Flectere si nequeo superos

As it happens, the influential Freud scholar Jonathan Lear does argue that these changes matter. He appeals to the difference they make as support for his reinterpretation of Freud's theory. I am not convinced that the full wording Lear cites as accurate supports his interpretation any better than the condensed one, but if it does, Lear has indeed made the sort of argument needed to show that the usual quotation misrepresents the original. But what original?

Knowles insists: "However, what Freud actually wrote in *The Interpretation of Dreams* (2nd edition, 1909) was . . ." And Lear writes: "It is common knowledge that Freud thought dreams were the royal road to the unconscious. But what he actually says is . . ."[10] Both then cite the same passage, with Lear italicizing "interpretation," "knowledge," and "activities" as important differences.

The problem is, both Knowles and Lear cite the James Strachey translation as if it were itself the original. But Freud did not "actually" write those words, because Freud wrote in German. Scholars who work with foreign languages usually know that before one calls a citation a mistake, one checks the original, not a translation. Otherwise what one has detected is at best a deviation from the translator's rendition. Knowles gives no citation except this English version, and Lear's footnote directs us only to the Strachey translation in the Standard Edition.

The underlying German reads: "Die Traumdeutung aber ist die Via regia zur Kenntniss des Unbewussten im Seelenleben."[11] Lear's interpretation depends on the presence of the word "activities," but there is no corresponding word in the German. It is arguable that the earlier translation of Freud's book by A. A. Brill, to which Freud himself wrote a foreword, is closer to the original than the Strachey version. Brill translates: "At any rate, the interpretation of dreams is the *via regia* of the unconscious element in our psychic life."[12]

In the original, the famous line follows a quotation in Latin: "Flectere si nequeo superos, Acheronta movebo" ("If I cannot bend the powers, I will move the infernal regions"— from Book VII of the *Aeneid*).[13] Given this Latin context, should not the translator (as Brill but not Strachey has done) preserve "via regia" rather than translate "royal road"? Anglicizing the Latin conflates the two languages of the original sentence into one. By so doing, Strachey has omitted whatever significance the choice of Latin has in the original. And the Latin line is clearly important to Freud: It is in fact the epigraph to the whole book!

I am not arguing that the Strachey version is wrong. I am arguing that it is naïve of Lear and Knowles to cite that version as if it and it alone must be right. One may plausibly make a case for various renditions here, but one cannot properly insist on a particular English translation as the standard of "what Freud actually wrote."

For a variety of reasons, then, accuracy demands attention to more than words alone. Extraverbal elements, like authorship and occasion, often constitute intrinsic parts of quotations. And the process of making an extract demands attention to more than words if sense itself is to be preserved.

How many supposed misquotations are neither misquotations nor misextractions at all?

VII
Mis-misquotations

The Canon of Misquotations

A growing canon of misquotations reappears in numerous volumes. Often enough, however, it is the accusation of error that is itself erroneous. These supposed mis-quotations are better called *mis-misquotations.*

As we have seen, "blood, sweat, and tears" is a mis-misquotation. By now, this phrase, like many others, lives a double life, as both a quotation and a mistaken example of a misquotation.

The same mis-misquotations are flagged not only in Keyes's *Nice Guys Finish Seventh,* Boller and George's *They Never Said It,* and Knowles's *What They Didn't Say,* but also in special entries of recent general quotation anthologies. They have become a category of their own. It is as if popular interest in commercial malfeasance or Chicago politics had led to a bubble in exposés of verbal fraud.

Both the *Macmillan Dictionary of Quotations* and the *Oxford Dictionary of Quotations* include such entries. The Oxford's table of contents lists "Special Categories" including not only expected topics like advertising slogans, epitaphs, last words, mottoes, sayings, slogans, and toasts, but also misquotations.

As we have seen, quotations are often assigned to this dubious genre on dubious grounds. We therefore need to distinguish between genuine and fake misquotations. When counterfeits become valuable, people forge them.

Old English

If one treats the accuracy of an extract as an all-or-nothing proposition, rather than a matter of conventions, audiences, and purposes, one easily falls into a sort of verbal fundamentalism. Like all fundamentalisms, the quotational kind makes complex issues misleadingly simple.

For all his insistence on absolute literalness, Keyes does allow himself some alterations. His author's note explains: "Although I have always reported the most accurate wording available of material in question, old English generally has been converted to modern, and British spelling to American" (NGFS, xii). Here "old English" does *not* mean the language of *Beowulf* but anything Keyes feels to be rendered in something other than the current way. He does not tell us how old "old" is. As we have seen from an editor of Milton, such differences as Keyes elides can matter. "Sovran" is not "sovereign."[1]

My point is not that such changes should never be made; it is that even a literalist almost inevitably makes some changes. It requires judgment to determine which changes, and how broad a range of variants, to allow. Not only do quotographers permit themselves some changes when faulting others for the slightest deviations, but they also differ from each other as to what variation to allow.

Boller and George give Churchill's words as "I have nothing to offer but blood and toil, sweat and tears." Keyes has him say: "I have nothing to offer but blood, toil, sweat and tears" (NGFS 53). Shapiro (in the *Yale Book of Quotations*) corrects to: "I would say to the House, as I said to those who have joined this government: 'I have nothing to offer but blood, toil, tears and sweat'" (YBQ, 152). In the *Oxford Dictionary of Quotations,* Knowles insists on: "I have nothing to offer but blood, toil, tears, and sweat" (ODQ, 221). So:

> blood and toil, sweat and tears
> blood, toil, sweat, and tears [no "and" after blood]
> blood, toil, tears and sweat [again no "and" after blood, but with tears before sweat]
> blood, toil, tears, and sweat [almost like the third version but with a comma after tears]

These experts apparently agree only on the incorrectness of the quotation as usually given and the availability of the correct alternative. But if correctness is such a simple matter, why do they differ from each other?

(In a kind of inverse fundamentalism, Hesketh Pearson has famously contended that misquotations are bound to improve—in fact, to perfect—a quotation. The "people" make it better until it can be improved no more: "They are the final and usually unimprovable. Misquotations are the only quotations that are never misquoted."[2] But if that were so, why do so many of them still exist in multiple versions?)

A String of "Misquotations"

Louis Menand begins his *New Yorker* review of the *Yale Book of Quotations* by restating a series of its surprising revelations:

Sherlock Holmes never said, "Elementary, my dear Watson." Neither Ingrid Bergman nor anyone else in "Casablanca" says "Play it again, Sam": Leo Durocher did not say "Nice guys finish last"; Vince Lombardi did say "Winning isn't everything, it's the only thing" quite often, but he got the line from someone else. Patrick Henry almost certainly did not say "Give me liberty, or give me death!"; William Tecumsah Sherman never wrote the words "War is hell"; and there is no evidence that Horace Greeley said "Go west, young man." Marie Antoinette did not say "Let them eat cake"; Herman Göring did not say "When I hear the word 'culture,' I reach for my gun"; and Muhammad Ali did not say "No Vietcong ever called me nigger." Gordon Gekko, the character played by Michael Douglas in "Wall Street," does not say "Greed is good"; James Cagney never says "You dirty rat" in any of his films; and no movie actor, including Charles Boyer, ever said "Come with me to the Casbah." Many of the phrases for which Winston Churchill is famous he adapted from the phrases of other people, and when Yogi Berra said, "I didn't say everything I said," he was correct.[3]

Most of these examples are, and long have been, commonplaces of the misattribution industry. Using the evangelical irony endemic to this genre, Menand introduces his readers to its core examples.

There now appears to be a special kind of quotation authorship, the person who did *not* say something. Who did not say "Let them eat cake" or "Give me liberty or give me death!"? Marie Antoinette and Patrick Henry. You and I simply never said these things (except as a "misquotation") but these famous people are—or are now—*the ones who never said it.*

Menand has ascertained that what Ingrid Bergman really said was "Play it, Sam," not "Play it again, Sam." He comments: "When you watch the movie and get to that line, you don't think your memory is wrong. You think the movie is wrong." Well, we don't literally "think" that the movie is wrong, of course, but we may experience surprise. This reaction does not tell Menand what it should: that a quotation and its source are two different things and that the quotation, though not the same as its source, really is "Play it again, Sam."

Who would ever quote, "Play it, Sam"? Adding "again" preserves the tone and whole point of the line, and that is why one would quote it in the first place. One would be getting the quotation wrong to say "Play it, Sam," just as one would be getting the Churchill quotation wrong to say "blood and toil, sweat and tears."

He Did Too Say It

Menand's ascriptions of error err. Take the example from Leo Durocher, a discovery that the Yale volume credits to Keyes. Keyes has ascertained that the frequently used phrase "Nice guys finish last" must be corrected to "Nice guys finish seventh." As I mentioned above, that change supplies the title of Keyes's book: "*Nice Guys Finish Seventh": False Phrases, Spurious Sayings, and Familiar Misquotations.* On the book's cover, the word "Seventh" is written over a crossed-out "Last," a change that evidently exemplifies verbal correction itself.

Nevertheless, by Keyes's own account, although Dodgers manager Leo Durocher originally said of the losing New York Giants that, as nice guys, they finish seventh (not last), he did later publish an autobiography entitled *Nice Guys Finish Last*

(1975). He recalled having said, "Nice guys. Finish last." Since he was speaking then, he evidently supplied punctuation later. So either he did say "Nice guys finish last" or wrote it as the title of his autobiography later. He also repeated the line as his own on several occasions. It is clear that on *some* occasions he did indeed say "Nice guys finish last" (NGFS, 142–144).

As the phrase is used, "Nice guys finish last" does not refer exclusively to baseball. Still less does it demand a knowledge of how many teams were in the National League at a given time. The quotation as a quotation applies to any competition. By contrast, "Nice guys finish seventh" makes no sense unless one knows the specific context of baseball at the time, when the two major leagues each had no divisions but eight teams. After all, seventh out of eight is different from seventh out of a dozen or a hundred.

Durocher's first version of the statement, the one with "finish seventh," depends on a specific, ephemeral context. To remove the statement from that context is to change, if not entirely obscure, its meaning, even if—or rather, precisely because—its wording remains the same. Is preservation of that wording more faithful to the original event of utterance even when it entails losing both the original meaning and the clarity that made the line memorable? And why insist on that now senseless wording, if Durocher did in fact use "finish last" on another occasion? Keyes's flagship change destroys the quotation without increasing the accuracy of the extract.

Correction is a royal road for the unthinking.

Not So Elementary

Back where I come from, we have universities, seats
of great learning, where men go to become great

thinkers. And when they come out, they think deep
thoughts and with no more brains than you have.
But they have one thing you haven't got: a diploma.

—The Wizard of Oz *(film)*

The example from Sherlock Holmes has become part of
the industry's folklore. Knowles, Keyes, Shapiro, and Boller
and George all cite the incorrigible error. It is routinely pointed
out that nowhere in the works of Conan Doyle do we find
Sherlock Holmes saying precisely, "Elementary, my dear Watson." But we do come fairly close. In *The Crooked Man,* Doctor
Watson narrates:

> "Excellent!" I cried.
> "Elementary," said he.

The usual explanation of the "misquotation" is that in the 1929
film *The Return of Sherlock Holmes,* the actor playing Holmes
(Clive Brook) does say "Elementary, my dear Watson, elementary" and that "it was Basil Rathbone, British actor playing the
ratiocinative sleuth in a series of Hollywood movies appearing
in the 1930s and 1940s, who made the words famous" (TNSI,
47). Alas, the explanation continues, ever since, people have
carelessly mistaken these words for those of Holmes.

But how else would one quote Holmes's memorable response? One could not very well say, "'Elementary,' said he." If
one wants to quote a single line from a dialogue, one often
must supply the verbally missing but contextually present information. As we have seen, such changes are a common part
of the process by which quotations come to stand on their own
as quotations. If one is to quote this particular memorable response at all, what else could one come up with except "Elementary, my dear Watson"? That is how the phrase became

the quotation—it appeared as such, before the 1929 film, in P. G. Wodehouse's novel *Psmith, Journalist* (1915)—and why it became commonplace in so many dramatizations.

As with "Turn the other cheek" and "God does not play dice," we typically recognize that, by convention, the process of extracting words often entails changes. In most cases, unless the difference makes a difference, we do not sense an error, any more than we do when a typo in an original source is not reproduced in the extract or when a transcript of a speech adds a comma where the speaker did not pause. Ban all such changes, and take most quotation with it.

One reason for our awareness that the original may have been changed to make it quotable is that we ourselves make such changes when citing others. We substitute nouns for pronouns and make a missing question clear. After all, we quote for a reason, not mechanically to repeat certain words, however senseless. Magic spells require verbal exactitude, because the words themselves are supposed to be efficacious. But quoting is not casting a spell. The words themselves do not change anything directly; rather, they convey meaning.

The *quotation* is clearly "Elementary, my dear Watson," for, as the quotographers note, that is what is said in countless dramatizations and paraphrases. But even as an extract, the words *are* Holmes's. Strictly speaking, it is not true that—I again quote the opening phrase of Menand's review—"Sherlock Holmes never said 'Elementary, my dear Watson.'" The film character Sherlock Holmes says precisely these words. Menand does not specify Conan Doyle's Sherlock Holmes. Even if he did, how do he and the quotographers know that the people who quote these words have in mind Conan Doyle's text rather than one of the films? More than likely, quoters think of neither. They probably have in mind some generalized folkloric image of Holmes, a composite of many renditions that have become part of our culture. That is how folklore works.

Holmes is not the only literary character to outgrow the work in which he initially appeared. Many characters break free from their original source, or even their original author, and acquire new adventures and voice new sayings over time. Dracula, Frankenstein, Superman, Tarzan, and Dorothy of Oz have all lived a life after text, in sequels by other authors, in various dramatizations, or both. They function in our culture the way mythological heroes have in other cultures. There is no way to squeeze Frankenstein back into Mary Shelley's novel, any more than one can confine Dorothy to Frank Baum's original Oz novel. She lives far beyond that book, which differs from the even more famous film. There are thirteen other books by Baum, nineteen by Ruth Plumly Thompson, three by John J. Neill, and four by Jack Snow, not to mention stage renditions of some of these works and sequels by other "non-canonical" authors.

Biographical accretion of this sort does not constitute a series of errors. For the Greeks, there was no single biography of Heracles, and Diogenes the Cynic accumulated many new witticisms over time. The King Arthur story kept growing. In much the same way, Tarzan lives far beyond the covers of the novel in which he originally appeared and is known to countless people who have not read or even heard of the original. Some characters of this sort have experienced more than one death, depending on which version we are following. One need not regret that they have but one life to give to their legend.

Sherlock Holmes is just such a folkloric hero living a biography of accretion. Tourists are routinely shown the location of his lodgings on Baker Street—the lodgings of a fictional character at an address which, in fact, does not exist. Is it not possible that people who quote "Sherlock Holmes" are citing not a specific source but a whole tradition? Such citations may be accurate extracts, as well as quotations, from that tradition. Unless quoters name Conan Doyle as the source of the famous line, they do not err in citing the line as commonly given.

One Small Quote

Like other anthologies, the *Macmillan Dictionary of Quotations* insists that the accurate version of Neil Armstrong's statement, when he became the first person to set foot on the moon, is: "That's one small step for man, one giant leap for mankind," which makes no sense at all. After all, "man" without an article *means* "mankind." As the editors note, "probably what he intended" to say was "small step for a man."[4]

If Armstrong had the word "a" in mind; if the audience heard it as he intended it; if it is clear to everyone that that is what he meant; if it is even possible that the recording did not pick up a softly spoken or obscured sound; and if what the recording has preserved makes no sense—then what difference does it make that the "a" is absent from, or inaudible in, the recording? It is hardly obvious that the nonsensical version immediately recognized as either a slip of the tongue or a failure of transmission is the correct one.

Armstrong, if he indeed left out the article, evidently made a sort of verbal typo. Whether a slip is spoken or written, preserving it at the expense of intended meaning is itself misleading and therefore mistaken.[5] If anything, the "correct" version without the article is the misquotation.

Is one quoting sounds or an utterance? Verbal fundamentalists treat utterances as if they are nothing but strings of words. But an utterance is not a string of words. It is a communicative act that uses words as material. It is constituted *as* an utterance by a place in an exchange, which means it includes not just words but overall meaning and purpose.

Titles

We implicitly recognize that different kinds of citations are governed by different conventions. When titles of novels, stories, critical studies, or articles are citations, they enjoy some liberty. In practice, they function as quotations held to the standard of allusions and lie somewhere between the two. We do not sense Faulkner's title *The Sound and the Fury* as inaccurate, even as an extract, simply because it adds articles. Nor do we sense Hardy's title *Far From the Madding Crowd* as erroneous because it changes "crowd's" to "crowd." Cleanth Brooks entitled his famous study of poetry *The Well-Wrought Urn* even though the phrase from the Donne poem he analyzes is "a well-wrought urn."

Sometimes, as we saw with *Pride and Prejudice,* a title that began as a quotation loses its source. A familiar line it once cited or recalled ceases to be familiar. At other times, it is unclear whether a title is quotational at all. By entitling his book *War and Peace,* Tolstoy may have meant to quote either Proudon's treatise *War and Peace* or a fragment of Heraclitus: "God is day and night, winter and summer, war and peace, surfeit and hunger" (BFQ15, 69). Or the title may have been meant to be self-sufficient, and it now surely is. Because we realize that titles commonly are quotations or allusions to quotations, we may suspect such allusion even when it is not present.

Sometimes, allusions in titles make the title a dialogue: Marx's *The Poverty of Philosophy* replies to Proudhon's *The Philosophy of Poverty.* Or, rather, it once did.

From Reproduction to Paraphrase

Conventions change with genre, over time, from culture to culture, and from profession to profession. They typically allow some changes in moving from speech to writing, from writing to speech, or from one context to another. To know what is and is not permitted in extracting words one needs to know governing conventions.

After the Revolution, the Russian alphabet was modernized, but few, if any, insist that present versions of *War and Peace* should use pre-revolutionary spelling, complete with the letters no longer preserved. Not even the meticulous editors of the ninety-volume complete works of Tolstoy (published from 1929 to 1958), or the editors of the even longer complete works now in progress, return to the nineteenth-century orthography, although one can imagine that, for some purposes, one might want to do so. Occasionally, it would disambiguate a homonym by restoring different spellings.[6]

When these matters are of concern, we may consult an autograph or facsimile. But not everything short of a facsimile is a misextraction. If it were, every other edition would be erroneous.

In short: there is a continuum between mere paraphrase and absolute reproduction of an extract. The border between accuracy and inaccuracy shifts with context, convention, and purpose.

Allusion

What is an allusion? We sense that it lies somewhere between an extract and a paraphrase. An allusion *reminds us* of a quotation. It does so neither by offering a presumably exact reproduction of it, nor by merely describing it, but by evoking a verbal impression of it. It must sound like the original without being close enough to the original to be mistaken for it.

The title of Henryk Sienkiewicz's novel *Quo Vadis* quotes, rather than alludes to, the Vulgate Bible, and *The Well-Wrought Urn* is close enough to the original to be mistaken for it or to constitute a variation necessary to make a title. By contrast, the 1996 TV movie about football *The Halfback of Notre Dame* alludes to, but does not cite, the usual English title of Victor Hugo's novel.

To evoke a verbal impression, the allusion may include a few well-known words of the original. Or it may sharpen the original. Or "refute" it, as Marx's title refutes Proudhon's. As a result, allusion easily slides into caricature or parody, and indeed, the same words may function as either allusion or caricature depending on context. What distinguishes the two is purpose. Once again, we are dealing with more than words alone.

As an allusion may be verbally identical to a caricature, so it may also, as a limiting case, be verbally identical to an exact reproduction. It is possible, though rare, to allude to a line by repeating it, so long as it is clear that one means to allude rather than quote. The allusion is offered and understood as offering a verbal image of the passage. An extract is understood as offering an exact reproduction. A builder could publish a book entitled *Uncle Tom's Cabin* or a typographer one entitled *The Scarlet Letter* and genre itself would indicate that allusion, not quotation, is intended. The very same words may be offered either way. Sometimes we are surprised to discover that, in alluding, we have in fact reproduced the original verbatim.

Quotographers often write as if an allusion differing from the original were a misquotation, but that is to misunderstand what allusions are. When Dorothy Parker commented that "Just before they made S. J. Perelman, they broke the mould," she was neither quoting nor misquoting Ariosto's line (in *Orlando Furioso*) that "Nature made him, and then broke the mould": she was alluding to it. This example appears in *I Said It My Way: The Guinness Dictionary of Humorous Misquotations,* but it neither is nor could be a misquotation at all.[7] Only what is offered as a reproduction can be an error if it is not a reproduction.

Quotations (in the sense of short literary works) resemble allusions in this: they may or may not be verbally identical to an extract. A process of verbal sharpening can make either an allusion or a quotation, and so it is easy for one to give rise to the other.

Parody may be regarded as a special type of allusion that creates a verbal image of an original in order to discredit it. Parodies usually exaggerate characteristic verbal features of the original, but as a limiting case, they may, like other allusions, repeat the original verbatim. Such "identical parodies" can be especially effective because they suggest that the original is absurd on its own. In his classic anthology of parodies, Dwight MacDonald includes a section of "unconscious self-parodies" that reproduces targets word for word. He includes without alteration a speech by Eisenhower, only adding an introduction and footnote mimicking the president's garbled logic and syntax: "As a bipartisan," the footnote reads, "I must point out that, although the syntax seems to put the Republican Party on record against freedom and liberty, the speaker almost certainly intended to say the opposite."[8]

Quotations and extracts do not have to coincide word for word with the original, and parodies may. Purpose is not in the text itself. The failure to understand that utterances consist of more than their texts gives rise to numerous mis-misquotations.

Quotations live complex lives. How and where do they live?

VIII
How and Where Quotations Live

Hermit Quotations

It is bad enough to see one's own good things fathered on other people, but it is worse to have other
people's rubbish fathered upon oneself.

—*Samuel Butler (CHQ, 623)*

We have already seen that quotations belong to the second speaker, who may or may not coincide with the historical
first speaker of the extract. Still more strangely, the second
speaker can change. As hermit crabs find new homes, so what
we might call "hermit quotations" find new authors.

Once we understand that the ascription of an author
may be an intrinsic part of a quotation, the behavior of hermit
quotations makes sense. Certain genres of quotation demand
a specific *kind* of author, who is recognizable as such. When
one such author ceases to be known, another readily takes his
or her place.

Keyes correctly mentions the existence of "flypaper people" to whom quotations stick (NGFS, 24), but there are also flypaper quotations to whom authors of a given kind stick. As if they would do anything to remain current, such quotations capture a presently appropriate speaker. If the quotation lives long enough, it may accumulate a long list of "originators."

Genre is key. Witty insults are much more likely to be ascribed to George Bernard Shaw or Winston Churchill than to St. Francis, Confucius, or George Washington, all four of whom are also flypaper people, but not for witticisms. As soon as an anecdote begins "Once Dorothy Parker . . ." one can rule out certain gnomic statements of timeless wisdom. One knows and expects the sort of remark she is famous for. Heroic pronouncements seek the soldier more readily than the artist or fop. To my knowledge, no one has attributed a saying like "We have not yet begun to fight!" to Oscar Wilde.

The converse is also true: our image of certain people is partly composed of the genre of quotation they attract. Their image includes their legend, and their legend includes sayings as well as doings. That is one reason that cultures come to ascribe both to the figures that define it. Schoolchildren learn famous words and heroic deeds, while skeptical grown-ups are often surprised when some of them turn out to be real. The anecdotes and quotations that Lenin, Lincoln, and Napoleon acquired shaped the sense of who they are. In Russia, the image of General Kutuzov, who defeated Napoleon, has long been liberated from the historical figure as he was understood in his time, and replaced with the contrary picture of him offered in Tolstoy's *War and Peace*. This Kutuzov might as well be a Taoist sage on horseback. Blind in one eye, he came to be all-seeing, and his corpulence symbolized contempt for futile chivalric "heroism." Even recent historians seem unable to think of him without the profound insights and wise sayings Tolstoy authored for him.

When a hermit quotation migrates, it typically finds the speaker who, at that moment, best exemplifies its genre. If two speakers specializing in the same genre appeal to different audiences, the quotation may be attributed by some to one, and some to the other. "Churchill" and "Shaw" thus respond to the same insults with the same or similar words. Disputes over authorship in such cases really concern the best second speaker, the one who makes the comment most effective.

Often enough, when a historical person actually said the quoted words, they turn out to be taken from someone else, either another historical person or a fictitious second speaker. If this modern sage should eventually become the best exemplar of such a saying, the sense that he was quoting someone else is especially likely to be lost. As we have seen, that is apparently what happened with Newton's famous comment about the shoulders of giants. Ironically enough, he was credited with the very words he used to acknowledge his debts. Standing on the shoulders of giants, he was mistaken for the giant itself.

As they change authors, great lines lose their past. As if by a discursive law, quotations evolve in wording, occasion, and ascribed author as they struggle for continued existence. Only the most quotable, and most adaptable, survive.

Promiscuous Quotations

Sometimes a quotation acquires multiple speakers not only because people dispute who said it but also because its very nature demands many possible speakers at the same time.

Such promiscuous quotations are never satisfied with a single author.

Promiscuity differs from disputability. Doubting who the author is does not mean doubting that there *is* a single author. Promiscuous quotations live precisely as ones that could have been said by several people. A given person who quotes the line may even ascribe it variously on different occasions, as one or another possible author or appropriate set of circumstances is mentioned. Most of us, I imagine, have told an identical story about different famous figures and attributed the same sage or stupid words to different heroes or idiots. In quoting promiscuous lines, people imagine not one speaker but a cloud of possible speakers.

An anonymous witticism thus finds itself in the mouths of Shaw, Wilde, and Churchill, not only because no one knows who said it, but also because it is the sort of thing any of these wits could have said. Cohabiting with multiple speakers at the same time, such "could have" quotations enjoy special rhetorical power.

A promiscuous witticism seems as if it was somehow seeking the *perfect* wit, and so no single, necessarily flawed individual would do. Often enough, it may have already acquired attribution to multiple wits of earlier eras. Ripostes once credited to several twentieth-century figures may once have been credited simultaneously to John Wilkes, Samuel Johnson, and Voltaire.

Both Wilde and Disraeli are said to have issued a challenge that they could speak well on any subject. When someone suggested "the Queen," each is said to have replied, "Her Majesty is not a subject."

There is no evidence that Churchill, who apparently

made some nasty comments about Clement Atlee, actually said: "An empty taxi arrived at 10 Downing Street, and when the door was opened Atlee got out."[1] But it is easy to see how such a line is bound to be attributed to someone else in describing another empty politician. I imagine that Lyndon Johnson was neither the first nor the last politician to insult a rival—according to these stories, Gerald Ford—by saying he was too dumb to fart and chew gum at the same time, or that he too often played football without a helmet.[2]

Hermit quotations, in short, may switch not only from one author to another, but also from one set of possible authors to another. Some change speakers, while others inhabit clouds of possibility.

Barnum and Lincoln

Things are seldom what they seem,
Skim milk masquerades as cream.
—*W. S. Gilbert,* HMS Pinafore

P. T. Barnum supposedly said, "There's a sucker born every minute." But only a sucker of sorts would fail to suspect that "Barnum" is nothing more than a genre-appropriate speaker for a quotation about hoaxing. And that is apparently the case. The *Yale Book of Quotations* reports research purporting to show that the line originated with a notorious con man and was later falsely attributed to Barnum. It reports another researcher who claims: "Barnum doubted ever having uttered these words, though he conceded he may have said 'The people love to be humbugged.'" Doubted? Could the line have been so appropriate to Barnum that he wondered whether he might have said it? Or was he wondering whether he could get away with claiming it?[3]

Hermit quotations sometimes, if rarely, change not only authors but also kinds of author. Then they become especially different even without any change in wording. Lincoln supposedly said: "You may fool all the people some of the time; you can even fool some of the people all of the time; but you can't fool all of the people all the time" (ODQ, 485). But the identical words are also attributed to Barnum! As author shifts, so does meaning. As Lincoln's, they seem to promise that ultimately deception is unmasked and truth wins out. As Barnum's, they work as advice to hucksters: you can always find a sucker, and some suckers never learn, just don't try to sucker everyone at once too often.

The fact that the same line becomes quite different demonstrates that authorship, not just words, is an essential part of the quotation. Or should we, at some point, speak of two quotations that just happen to coincide verbally?

Place

Quotations also seek out genre-appropriate places. If a comment would be more effective if said in a given physical or social location, that location, like the most effective author, often becomes intrinsic to it. Conversely, certain locations attract appropriate quotations.

Much as adventure stories love the open road, so heroic pronouncements favor a podium, battlefield, scene of disaster, or other locale where people gather at dangerous moments. Where war is, there defiant challenges will be; battlefields where corpses still lie attract words of reverence; graveyards want eulogies. By the same token, there are also genre-inappropriate settings. Hazy revelations of deep mysteries are heard on mountaintops, not in public squares, while sermons avoid the solitary sanctuary. No one has ever placed a witticism of Wilde, Wilkes, or Shaw at Gettysburg or Normandy.

Since the words themselves may not mention the location, titles added by others often do it for them. Jesus did not call his exhortations the Sermon on the Mount, nor did Lincoln name his words the Gettysburg Address. Precisely because of its identification with the place it was delivered, Lincoln's speech came to disprove its own assertion: "The world will little note nor long remember what we say here, but it can never forget what they did here."[4] Quite the contrary, we remember what they did there primarily because of what he said there. The place is hallowed by the words, and the words demand to be placed at the spot they hallow. In cases like this, the title naming the speech or quotation is part of it, regardless of whether the author or someone else provided it.

Genre Speakers

Because genres often demand a speaker of a given sort, we may identify what might be called "genre speakers": Shaw for insults, Mayor Daley and George W. Bush for humorously mangled English, Dan Quayle for ignorant nonsense. Each of these people has developed, or has had ascribed to him, a persona that makes him appropriate to voice a given set of words.

Some genre speakers are aware of this status. When Yogi Berra explained that "I never said all the things I said," his apparent contradiction pointed to his double identity, as the baseball player Yogi Berra and as a particular genre speaker who came to be known as "Yogi Berra." Dorothy Parker commented on the tendency of quotations to migrate to the best-known, genre-appropriate voice:

> If, with the literate, I am
> Impelled to try an epigram,
> I never seek to take the credit:
> We all assume that Oscar said it.

(YBQ, 579)

George S. Kaufman complained in turn: "Everything I've ever said will be credited to Dorothy Parker" CHQ, 623). Dr. Johnson recognized the process: "Pointed axioms and acute replies fly loose around the world, and are assigned successively to those whom it may be the fashion to celebrate" (BBA, xxi), including Johnson himself. Fashion, of course, is notoriously fickle.

Scrupulous anthologizers typically list such statements as "attributed," which is true enough, but fail to distinguish between two kinds of "attribution." Some attributions are part of the quotation while others are just guesses about who the author might be. Questionable ascription of words may reflect mere loss of evidence, but it may also occur at the behest of the quotation itself.

Some figures appear in anthologies solely as genre speakers. It is as if they lived entirely as symbols of a quality or set of qualities. Bartlett's fifteenth edition, for instance, includes three entries for Louis XIV, all attributed (BFQ15, 312). In addition to "L'état c'est moi," we find:

> Has God forgotten all I have done for him? (Dieu
>   a donc oublié tout ce que j'ai fait pour lui?)
> —*Attributed remark upon hearing the news of the
> French defeat at Malplaquet (1709)*

> I almost had to wait. (J'ai faille attendre.)
> —*Attributed remark when a coach he had ordered*
> *arrived just in time*

Imperiousness, thy name is Louis. Other anthologies have the Sun King comment on this very image of himself as super-human. On his deathbed, he responds to the tears of his at-tendants: "Why are you weeping? Did you suppose I was im-mortal?" The question recalls the Roman practice of deifying emperors at death. We may think of the emperor Vespasian's supposed remark when dying: "Dear me, I believe I am be-coming a god" (MDQ, 317).

Just Possibly

We do not read Vespasian's comment and then, weighing evi-dence, decide whether he really said it. Just as some quotations exist with authors who just might have said them, others exist as words that just might have been said.

Vespasian's comment belongs to the set of quotations that are neither real nor fictional but just possibly real. It is a genuine quotation, of course, but as an extract, we experience it as the sort of thing that *could* have been said, as lying some-where between fact and fiction. When the line is quoted, this experience accompanies it.

"Just possibly" is its own way of being. Some quotations are surely real as extracts, others certainly are fake, but in be-tween we find everything from the barely possible to the highly plausible. This is the middle realm of the hypothetical. Even when an extract is "almost certainly" real, the force of that "al-most" may cast upon it a shadow of the hypothetical; and even when it is highly unlikely, it can still feel like it just might be true.

Some genres thrive precisely in the middle realm. There we

find telling put-downs, profound last words, and the very best witticisms. Is something "too good to be true" necessarily false? Not at all: it is too good to be above suspicion, but suspicious things do happen. Given enough time, as Aristotle observes, "it is probable that a thing may happen contrary to probability."[5]

We also find in the middle realm of possibility unverified comments that have so long been treated as important that, by mere dint of their influence, they cannot be sacrificed. We look for reasons to believe they could be true. In Russian literature, Dostoevsky's supposed observation that Russian writers "have all come out from under Gogol's overcoat" fits this category. So does the comment that soothed nineteenth-century Russian radicals when their cause seemed almost hopeless. They would compare socialism in their day to Christianity when it was still a small, persecuted sect. Looking forward to Christianity's triumph, they would then cite the barely plausible dying words of the last pagan Roman emperor, Julian the Apostate: "You have won, Galilean!" (ODQ, 474).

Sometimes just possible utterances are used to express hope for just possible outcomes.

Anonymizing

As some kinds of quotation seek to acquire an author, others try to lose one. It is the absence of an author that is intrinsic to these quotations. Their very nature entails the destiny of *dis*-attribution.

When quotations express timeless wisdom, applicable to all, they readily become anonymous. To be proverbial is to belong to no one in particular.

We can sometimes catch the process of "anonymizing" in the act. Somewhere on the way to authorlessness, the quotation's author is still known to some people even though most use it as if it did not have one. They are surprised when informed that an identifiable writer, not the voice of the people, stands behind a saying. They may even be disappointed, for one person's opinion, however felicitously worded, does not carry the force of a people's combined wisdom. Often enough, the most authoritative author is precisely nobody.

The section on proverbs in the *Oxford Dictionary of Quotations* lists most selections as anonymous. In these cases, it provides not the author, but the earliest known use. But a few examples still have authors clinging uncertainly to their words:

Hope springs eternal. (Pope)

Style is the man. (Buffon)

None but the brave deserves the fair. (Dryden)

Man is the measure of all things. (Protagoras)

Many say "Hope springs eternal" with no awareness that the saying belongs to Pope, any more than they know that "broke the mould" belongs to Ariosto.[6] Even if they should learn of Pope's and Ariosto's authorship, they may still sense these lines as different from fully authored quotations. They have *proverbiality*. It is almost as if Pope discovered and polished, not created, this way of saying what oft was thought but ne'er so well expressed. Indeed, with another of his proverbial lines—"To err is human"—he did.[7] And that line, too, has all but forgotten Pope's authorship.

The *Oxford Dictionary* also lists some half-proverbial sayings under their authors' names. These quotations resemble those that are anonymous to almost all people except that their authorship is somewhat more widely known.

A little learning is a dangerous thing. (Pope)

Tell me what you eat and I will tell you what you
    are. (Brillat-Savarin)

When in Rome, do as the Romans do. (a para-
    phrase of St. Ambrose)

We may guess that over time this second category will move
into the first, if it has not already done so according to other
anthologies. From "known to many but far from all users" to
"known to very few users" is an easy transition. One sign that
very few know the authorship of "When in Rome" is that
St. Ambrose's words have been altered considerably.[8] We may
surmise that these sayings will eventually achieve full detach-
ment from their creators.

    Does anyone citing "The more things change, the more
they remain the same" (or simply "*plus ça change*") think of its
author, Alphonse Karr (ODQ, 441; MBSSQ, xvii)? Or is it one
thing as a line from Karr, another as an anonymous proverb?

Climate of Quotation

I don't want to be quoted, and don't quote me that I
don't want to be quoted.
—*Winston Burdett*[9]

We have seen that when a phrase loses an author, it may
become an idiom. Conversely, use as an idiom gradually strips
away an author.

    No one but a person who studies quotations, I expect,
recognizes the common phrase "climate of opinion" as a quo-

tation from Joseph Glanvill (YBQ, 312) or "steal my thunder" as coined by John Dennis. As the story goes, Dennis had invented thunder sound effects for an unsuccessful play. Hearing the same effects used in the same theatre for a performance of *Macbeth,* he remarked: "They will not have my play, yet steal my thunder" (YBQ, 194). The idea of stealing thunder proved amusing enough for the phrase to be repeated. Used often to describe a particular sort of situation, it both lost its author and became metaphoric. By now, the word "thunder" in this phrase does not indicate an event of the weather (or the stage) or, for that matter, a sound at all. Learning the story of the phrase's origin, we may be surprised it really is about literal (if imitated) thunder.

No one thinks of saying something like: "What someone once called 'the climate of opinion' has changed." "Climate of opinion" no longer functions as a quotation from anyone, just a fixed phrase. We no more think of climate in speaking of climate of opinion than we think of thunder when someone steals our thunder. True, we *could* discern the underlying meteorological metaphor if instructed to do so, but, by the same token, we might just as readily accept the spurious explanation that "steal my thunder" is a corruption of "steal my flounder" much as "Welsh rabbit" is mistakenly assumed to be a corruption of "Welsh rare-bit."[10] So far have these uses of climate and thunder strayed from the status of someone's quotation, that a correct explanation seems no more convincing than a wholly fictitious one. No one using either phrase would be charged with plagiarism for not giving a source, even though there is a source, because each is simply an idiom of the language.

The idiom "to call a spade a spade" has an identifiable, because strange, coinage. The author of the phrase was Erasmus, but he did not mean to author it: he mistranslated a

Greek original saying meaning something closer to "to call a skiff a skiff." In the same way, he unwittingly turned Pandora's jar into Pandora's box (AE, xxxix). Even though experts know of Erasmus's authorship, the phrase "to call a spade a spade" is nevertheless now authorless. Like Dennis's unwitting coinage, Erasmus's has lost its author by becoming an idiom. An author who did not know he was an author has lost his authorship.

As we have seen, truly successful neologisms also lose their author. "Différance" may still have Derrida clinging to it, as "double bind" has Bateson, but very few remember Merton as the coiner of "self-fulfilling prophecy." Neologizing and anonymizing go hand in hand.

Genre Occasions

Historical occasion, as well as author and place, may become part of a quotation, intrinsic to its meaning. The editors of *History in Quotations* turn this fact to their advantage. Taken together, each chapter's quotations, along with accompanying descriptions of how and when they were uttered, add up to a historical narrative. Supplying circumstances and ordering entries chronologically, the editors transform a mere anthology into a highly readable story.

Some quotations require an occasion to make sense at all. Others must have it or lose their significance. "How could they tell?" is utterly baffling until one is informed it was Dorothy Parker's response to the news that Calvin Coolidge had died. Most witty replies fall into this category:

Neither am I.

—Peter Cook . . . on being told that the person sitting next to him at a dinner party was "writing a book" (attributed—MDQ, 478)

> I have known many an instance of a man writing a letter and forgetting to sign his name, but this is the only instance I have ever known of a man signing his name and forgetting to write the letter.
>
> *—Henry Ward Beecher . . . said upon receiving a note containing the single word: "Fool" (MDQ, 479)*

As we have seen, Bartlett's needed to provide not just the author but also the occasions of Louis XIV's famous comments. The meaning of the phrase "Four score and seven years ago," which can appear allusively by itself, depends on our locating it both textually and contextually. When we speak of "Lincoln's Gettysburg Address," we are naming author, location, and occasion, all of which are intrinsic to these famous words.

Some situations have given rise to quotations so often that they have become conventional for quotations of a specific kind. As we have genre authors, we have genre occasions. As a remark may acquire an author, so it may attract the appropriate occasion. Solemn words look for a gathering after a tragedy.

One could assemble an anthology in which quotations are classified by genre occasion. The possibility of doing so testifies again to the fact that quotations consist of more than words alone.

In such a collection, perhaps the most fascinating selections would include "famous last words" and "epitaphs," genres of occasion to which we now turn.

III
Quotations of Occasion

IX
Famous Last Words

Life itself is a quotation.
—Jorge Luis Borges (ODLQ, 238)

The Last Occasion

"Famous Last Words" evoke strong interest. After all, no one has experienced the end and everyone must do so. When the final moments arrive, how will we feel and what will we say?

Many other reasons insure interest in last words. They provide closure to biographies. Many locations of dying—the gallows, the stake, the guillotine, the battlefield, the deathbed with disciples or relatives as witnesses—fascinate for their own reasons. Great farewells often belong to great people, whose deaths interest us because their lives interest us. Countless volumes collect last words from antiquity to the present. No matter how many are spoken, "last words" themselves never end.

Famous last words are grouped together because they share an occasion. That occasion shapes their significance. The same words spoken in some other situation mean something else entirely. When famous last words are quoted, the genre occasion is invariably provided.

Examples of the form often share little else. They vary considerably in theme, tone, and diction, and would not be classed together on other grounds. Ranging from trivial matters to ultimate questions, and from lighthearted whimsy to "dead" seriousness, they neither say similar things nor use a similar style. Rather, they share something extraverbal, a specific moment in life.

When last words appear in an anthology of last words, the occasion for each example need not be specified. More general anthologies of quotations may (and often do) include a section devoted to last words so that a single heading may supply the occasion. The Oxford and Macmillan volumes both devote sections to "last words." In other collections, last words conclude the quotations listed for a specific person. In that case, a note supplies the quotation's status as last words.

However comic it may seem, people seek to die on a podium. Some, perhaps, love public display at all moments and so take advantage of one that convention offers. What a pity to waste such an opportunity! Other people may ward off loneliness with conversation. Besides, the possibility that last words will be remembered offers the chance for an afterlife of sorts.

The desire to make a memorable final pronouncement has itself served as a conventional topic, last words about last words. When Karl Marx's housekeeper offered to write down his last words for posterity, he allegedly replied: "Last words are for fools who haven't said enough" (FLW, 27). The fact that the line is quoted belies it.

Tolstoy made the most of any possible tribune. Near death several times, he used such occasions for profundity or even comedy. One anecdote has the supposedly expiring old man summoning Chekhov to place his ear to his mouth, only to hear Tolstoy say: "You know, Shakespeare's plays are bad enough, but yours are even worse!"[1]

Possibly the Last Words

In these days Rumor took an evil joy
In filling countrysides with whispers, whispers,
Gossip of what was done, and never done.
—*Virgil,* The Aeneid

If we were to demand only verifiable, historically accurate last words, anthologies would be impossible. We would have almost no examples.

Are we to ask the speaker if he or she really said those words when dying? We are told in Laura Ward's collection *Famous Last Words: The Ultimate Collection of Finales and Farewells* that Henry James died making a Jamesian remark: "So here it is at last, the distinguished thing." Ward notes: "Generally regarded as the dying words of Henry James (d. 1916), American born novelist. They gained credence through being recorded by Edith Wharton in *A Backward Glance* (1934) as reported to her by Lady Prothero, a confidante of James. James actually claimed to have heard the words when he had suffered his first stroke, on December 2, 1915" (FLW, 27). It is thus rather unlikely that James said these words when dying, but his comment nevertheless lives on as a classic example of the genre.

So do General Custer's supposed last words, "We've

caught them napping!" But how could we possibly know that Custer actually said them? Ward comments: "Possibly the last words of General Custer at the Battle of the Little Big Horn, 1876, although no one knows for sure, as not one of his men survived" (FLW, 106). Possibly? Did the words somehow report themselves without human mediation? Were they carried by Virgil's goddess Rumor?

If "possibly" means there is some plausible but insufficient evidence, Ward's statement is nonsense. But it may indicate something else entirely. It apparently exemplifies a convention governing how famous last words are understood. Listeners are expected to regard them as things that *could have been* said. The genre occupies the space between certainty and impossibility. Last words need only be possible in the sense of not absolutely impossible.

The same considerations apply to other last words attributed to Custer: "Where did all those damned Indians come from?" (DLW, xxiv). Questions about historical accuracy hardly matter, for this genre depends not on historical accuracy, but on literary appropriateness of various sorts.

The genre almost creates the words. It is as if our awareness of the form prompted us to ask: What *would* Custer, More, Thoreau, Rabelais, Napoleon have said last? What would anyone interesting, either because of who he was or how he died, have said? If the hypothetical answer is a good one, it finds whatever evidence it can to support its captivating, if factually dubious, existence. It lives as literature.

More Quotes

The only thing that really saddens me over my demise is that I shall not be here to read the nonsense

that will be written about me. . . . There will be lists
of apocryphal jokes I never made and gleeful misquotations of words I never said. What a pity I
shan't be here to enjoy them!

—*Noël Coward (ODLQ, 64)*

Almost all examples of the form could easily find their way
into a misquotation anthology. What would count as reliable
evidence? Most examples rely on alleged witnesses, who do
not hear the same thing, who readily omit whatever was said
right after something quotable, who usually know what the
form demands, whose memories are faulty or all too active,
and who have an understandable interest in reporting something interesting. To be sure, there are rare instances of words
mechanically recorded: We appear to have the last words on
September 11, 2001, of a passenger on Flight 93 ("Let's roll!").
Kalakaua, a king of the Hawaiian Islands, died recording a
message on a New Edison recording machine. A police ste-
nographer took down the last ravings of a feverish "Dutch"
Schultz, the gangster (DLW, ix). But such instances are vanish-
ingly rare. Most examples are as dubious as James's, or even
Custer's.

We are told that Beethoven died saying, "Too bad! Too
bad! It's too late!" (He had ordered wine.) A second version
"has the deaf composer saying, 'I shall hear in Heaven.' In yet
another story, he sat up in bed, shook his fist (at what, who
knows?) and fell back dead" (FLW, 38). Each version testifies
against the historical reliability of the others—and against the
last words of other people "known" in a similar way.

One would have to be credulous indeed to overlook the
conventionality of many deathbed scenes, in which the dying
person, who enjoys full possession of his faculties, has at-

tracted an audience eager to record his words accurately. Such accounts come from many cultures and historical periods. All the problems of oral testimony are multiplied when the audience knows it is supposed to hear something worth repeating.

Could anyone actually hear the last words of a soldier in battle? Or fail to be influenced by earlier heroic utterances when reporting what he or she heard?

With the exception of suicide notes, which of course may have been followed by statements spoken out loud without record, we must rely on reports of words spoken. Spoken, because, so far as I know, reality offers no example of the Monty Python scene in which anthropologists find last words carved into the wall of a cave, including the cry of surprise when the carver was attacked from behind.

Musical Quotes

Any audience at a famous person's death would be inclined to hear what *should* have been said. The *Macmillan Dictionary* prefaces its selection of last words: "Not always the actual last words said, but including remarks made when dying. Many are apocryphal, hence the fact that some people have more than one set of attributed 'last words.'" "Not always the actual last words said": this qualification distinguishes the real circumstance from the conventional genre occasion. By convention, "last words" are not necessarily last words. Rather, they are understood *as if* they were.

The phrase "made when dying" proves elastic enough to encompass utterances made weeks or more before death (if they were made then). It is as if the occasion reached out and gathered to it as much as could plausibly be linked to it. In including remarks made weeks before death, the Macmillan volume acts in the spirit of the genre. Misquotation hunters notwithstanding, editors who list such examples need have no qualms.[2]

As the literary nature of quotations would lead us to expect, the attribution of more than one last utterance to a given speaker is common. Beethoven's case is almost the rule for people who suit the genre occasion especially well. Rabelais, Thoreau, and More each have three well-known examples. Such multiplicity shows we are dealing not with history but with folklore. The situation of last words is too good, too inviting, to be surrendered just because it has already been occupied.

When a new good possibility arises, we play a game analogous to musical chairs—call it musical quotes—to assure a temporarily empty space.

Historical Novels

By convention, historical novels narrate events that *could have* taken place. Readers are supposed to wonder: did occurrences, more or less like these, happen to real people with different names? After all, to understand what it was like to be alive at a different time is to sense its field of possible events. What were people anticipating, fearing, hoping for? Their lives, like ours, include such shadowy possibilities, events that genuinely could have happened even if they did not. We are, in part, what we might have been. The might-haves of one culture and period differ from that of another. The historical novel, because of its inclusion of fictional as well as real events, has served as a good way to describe the genuinely possible.

Historical novels have a special standard of truth. They cannot make up just anything: they must honor the genuine possibilities of the time, or they will seem false. Real events are of course included because, as Aristotle observed, "What has happened is manifestly possible; otherwise it would not have happened."[3] But they are included precisely because they must have been possible.

In describing possible events, historical novels must not contradict real historical outcomes. Napoleon cannot win at Waterloo. More precisely, they cannot contradict historical outcomes that the reader is likely to know.[4] But they can contradict ones known only to specialists. The less readers know of history, the more leeway the author has with historical fact. Historical novels are then free to imagine anything else that enables them to achieve plausibility. So long as readers can indulge a sense of possibility, they are safely in the realm of "might have been."

"Famous last words" resemble a moment from an unwritten historical novel: they require and evoke a sense of "what might have been said." As the historical novel invites us into a vanished era, famous last words invite us into a vanished moment that just might be more or less true. Many last sayings can be attributed to the same person because he or she might have said any of them. Only one historical utterance can have been uttered last, and so only one can be actual last words. But many could have been said last, and so many can belong to the genre of quotations we call "last words."

Last as Essential

One type of last words indicates a person's essential qualities. Ward confesses to "a foolish—possibly romantic—notion that a person's departing sentence, however brief, can tell us something about the life that preceded it, and perhaps even throw fresh light on that individual" (FLW, 8–9). Of course, the expectation that a "departing sentence" somehow sums up a life depends on an analogy between a life and a well-written story. It is essentially literary.

The convention governing such examples directs us to presume that the person's full life, consciously or unconsciously, shapes his or her last words. For Whitman, such last words "are not samples of the best, which involve vitality at its full, and balance, and perfect control, and scope. But they are valuable beyond measure to confirm and endorse the varied train, facts, theories, and faith of the whole preceding life" (DLW, viii).

We imagine: a person's final words tell us who he or she really was. In this type of famous last words, the point is how characteristic the words are of a given set of qualities or activities. Consider the following examples:

Leave the shower curtain on the inside of the tub.
—*Conrad Hilton (FLW, 116)*

What's the news?
—*Clarence Walker Barron, publisher of the* Wall Street Journal *(FLW, 17)*

Tomorrow I shall no longer be here.
—*Nostradamus (FLW, 117)*

Stand away, fellow, from my diagram.
—*Archimedes (FLW, 118)*

Hilton and Barron die attending to business, Nostradamus predicting the future, and Archimedes, who is all too absorbed in a mathematical problem, ignoring a command given by a conquering Roman soldier.

In most such cases, such perfectly appropriate last words work because the speaker goes about his business as if life would never end and so says something unconsciously fitting. He does not say his last words because they are fitting, but they fit because he is who he is.

The irony that gives such utterances their interest belongs to the destiny that shapes human lives. That destiny seems to know us better than we know ourselves. It shows what we either hide or fail to recognize. A man's character is his fate, and his death reveals his character.

The Essential, Intended

If some last words work because they are not intended as such, others succeed precisely because they are. A person may take advantage of his or her dying moment to say something appropriate to his or her life. The last words of martyrs are sometimes of this sort:

> Hold the cross high so I may see it through the flames.
> —*Joan of Arc (FLW, 51)*

> This side is roasted enough.
> —*Saint Lawrence (martyred by being roasted on a griddle; FLW, 50)*

It as if the last moment of these saints does not just express but actually contains the significance of the entire life. The martyrdom either serves as the culmination of everything else or itself constitutes the most important thing the speaker has ever done. The martyr has lived to die in just this way. The final moment and the last words contain everything that matters.

Posthumous Speech

There is no such thing as sudden death to a Christian.
—*Samuel Wilberforce (FLW, 54)*

Wilberforce's dying comment illustrates another way in which last words can express essential qualities. They may sound as if the speaker has been granted a moment just after his or her life so as to survey it as completed. He or she speaks posthumously about a story now over.

"Posthumous" words are spoken in the strange sort of temporality we might call "epilogue time." Novelistic epilogues narrate events, but these events cannot alter the significance of what has gone before. If they could, they would not belong in an epilogue. Though part of a biography, such moments are sensed as extrabiographical.

In such an extrabiographical moment, a true believer like Wilberforce expresses absolute certainty, while a doubter betrays ultimate uncertainty:

I don't know, I don't know!
—*Abelard (FLW, 16)*

Despite all his theological arguments, then, Abelard has not convinced even himself!

If we discover or hear about a comment that would work well extrabiographically, we place it by convention at the speaker's deathbed. No matter when Abelard or Wilberforce said these words, if they said them at all, they would be quoted as final.

Some last words sound posthumous in a different way. It is as if the moment of crossing over to the afterlife provides a glimpse of mysterious truths that the last words, however dimly, express to those left behind. These words, made in and for our world, struggle to describe another. Writing as both physician and theologian, Thomas Browne (died 1682) hopes for just such a transitory moment so that, when soul and body are separating, he might still offer the living an audible revelation: "Men sometimes, upon the hour of their departure, do speak and reason above themselves; for then the soul, beginning to be freed from the ligaments of the body, begins to reason like herself, and to discourse in a strain above mortality" (DLW, viii). In our time, reports of people declared dead but returned to life, or of other apparently impossible "out-of-body" experiences, offer similar revelations of what we might know if our body did not blind us.

The aging Tolstoy once wrote a letter of advice to Tsar Nicholas II, whom he addressed presumptuously as his "brother." The novelist explained that, being so near death, he could offer advice as if from the other world, where rank does not matter and insight unavailable to mere tsars is available. Tolstoy never ceased exploring the implications of speech acts that aspire beyond ordinary human life.

The Last Words of Jesus

Whether they sum up a life or reveal truths otherwise unavailable, such words are "last" not just because they are latest in time but also because they are conclusive. What is conclusive can appropriately be placed in a concluding spot.

Multiple final utterances for the same person can therefore reflect something more interesting than divergent testimonies. They may express the multiplicity of meanings his or her life contains. Each meaning requires consummate expression, and so we may accept accounts of last moments that, if taken literally as occurring at the very same time, would be incompatible with each other.

In Matthew and Mark, Jesus's last words are "My God, my God, why hast thou forsaken me?" (Matthew 27:36 and Mark 15:34); in Luke, he says, "Father, into thy hands I commend my spirit" (Luke 23:46); and John testifies: "When Jesus therefore had received the vinegar, he said, It is finished: and he bowed his head, and gave up the ghost" (John 19:30). Each of these testimonies comments on the meaning of Jesus's death and his own understanding of it. Since this death signifies many things, one need not find these reports contradictory.

In the ancient world, last words served as a recognized form in which the essence of a life, and not necessarily a historical event, was reported. Jesus's words may rely on the conventions of a well-known genre. One would have to be a literalist, and insensitive to literary conventions, to find mere contradiction here. In any case, the compilers of the Gospels could not have missed the presence of different last words, and so we may presume that *they* saw no necessary incompatibility.

Each of Jesus's final utterances is both biographical and extrabiographical, much as, for the believer, Jesus is both human and divine.

Jesus Quotes

The last words of Jesus rely on our understanding of quotation. In Mark we read:

> And at the ninth hour Jesus cried with a loud voice, saying, Eloi, Eloi, lama sabachthani? which is being

interpreted, My God, my God why hast thou forsaken me?

And some of them that stood by, when they
heard it, said, Behold, he called Elias.

And one ran and filled a sponge full of vinegar,
and put it on a reed, and gave him to drink, saying,
Let alone; let us see whether Elias will come to take
him down.

And Jesus cried with a loud voice, and gave up
the ghost. (Mark 15:34–37)

The evangelist must quote Jesus's words in the original because
no translation will do: for without "Eloi, Eloi" one could not
grasp why the witnesses heard him summon Elias. The story
narrates how people mishear and why reports differ. Symboli-
cally, perhaps, we humans may not be ready to take in divine
words. Ears do not suffice for true hearing.

Jesus is not calling on Elias or on anyone else. He is
quoting, for he repeats the opening of the twenty-second
psalm, "My God, my God, why hast thou forsaken me? Why
art thou so far from helping me, and from the words of my
roaring?" For Mark and Matthew, this citation is apparently
too obvious to be noted as such.

Presumably, we are to think not only of the psalm's opening words of despair but also of the consolation and glorifica-
tion of God at its conclusion. If we do not know the quotation
well enough to supply its textual context, we will miss this
point. For that textual context belongs to the words not as
words but as quotation.

If one turns to this psalm, one sees that quotationality
extends further than one might at first suspect. Read in light
of Jesus's life, as its quotation at his death might prompt, the

psalm's metaphors acquire an unexpected and literal accuracy. The evangelist reports that passersby "railed on him, wagging their heads, and saying, . . . Save thyself, and come down from the cross" (Mark 15:29–30). The chief priests also mock and dare Jesus: "He saved others; himself he cannot save. Let Christ the King of Israel descend now from the cross, that we might see and believe. And they that were crucified with him reviled him" (Mark 15:31–32). The psalmist seems to foresee this mockery: "All that see me laugh me to scorn: . . . they shake the head, saying, He trusted on the Lord that he would deliver him: let him deliver him, seeing he delighted in him" (Psalms 22:7–8).

The psalmist complains that "they pierced my hands and feet," a line that he apparently offers as metaphoric, but that turns out to describe literally the demise of the One who quotes this psalm. John also seems to develop the psalmist's statement "I am poured out like water" when he reports that, when the soldiers pierced Jesus's side, "forthwith there came out blood and water" (John 19:34).

Reverse Quotation

John then explicitly cites two earlier scriptural verses:

> For these things were done, that the scripture should be fulfilled, A bone of him shall not be broken.
> And again another scripture saith, they shall look on him whom they pierced. (John 19:36–37)

John is of course citing Scripture to show fulfilled prophecy, but he does so in a less than obvious way. Usually, the fulfilling of a prophecy proves the insight of the prophet, but that is not what is happening in this case. Instead of events confirming the prophecy, here prophecy confirms the event. The point is not to show that the Scripture is divine because it predicted what happened to Jesus, but to show that Jesus is divine because the Scriptures referred to events that happened to him. The sanctity of Scripture is not verified but presumed.

Consider the logic of omen and prophecy. When people invoke omens to foretell an event, they are relying on backward causation: the event that is to come—that in a sense has already happened in the future—sends a sign backwards that can be read by the prophet or oracle. The flight of fowls or the disposition of an animal's entrails take their shape not because they will cause the event-to-come but because they are caused by it. An omen is to history what foreshadowing is to a novel. Both indicate that events are not just pushed but also pulled, that they result not only from prior causes but also from future ones. Omens and foreshadowing show that events complete a design in which past, present, and future events all have a meaningful place, visible at a glance when the design is at last seen in its entirety.

The soldiers do not pierce Jesus instead of breaking his bones with the intent of fulfilling Scripture. Rather, their doing so shows that scriptural verses predicted what was to happen. When Jesus quotes biblical verses, he does so not to confirm signs or omens but to show that these verses *were* signs or omens. It is only after the fact that the words of the twenty-second psalm turn out to have been prophetic. They are perfectly meaningful by themselves, and no one would suspect them of prophecy if subsequent events had not revealed them as such. The event makes the prophecy, not the prophecy the event.

In much the same way, the evangelists not only quote the Scriptures; they also reveal that the Scriptures were quoting the words and actions of Jesus in advance. The psalmist writes "My God, my God, why has thou forsaken me?" *because* Jesus was to say the same thing: that is the logic of the Gospels. The other passages cited also turn out to have been quotations from the future. The New Testament gives us case after case of *reverse quotation,* quotation of an utterance in advance of its uttering. Nowhere is reverse quotation so important as in these accounts of Jesus's last actions and last words.

Burden of the Future

In the fourth century, Aelius Donatus wrote a line that frequently appears in today's quotation anthologies: "Confound those who have said our remarks before us" (ODLQ, 237). But with reverse quotation, our predecessors are quoting us! Instead of a "burden of the past," in which the achievements of earlier generations rob us of opportunities for creativity, there could be a burden of the future, in which what we say merely echoes words to come. Imagine objecting: That man was quoting what I am going to say. He plagiarized what I am destined to write.

However odd, it is a feeling we sometimes have. We know we created a certain thought or set of words, and so, when we discover them already expressed long ago, it feels as if they had been stolen from us in advance. Sometimes, a person may ascertain from his notes that he himself is the one who did the advance stealing: reverse déjà vu.[5] Confound those who say our remarks after us.

Two Kinds of Possibility

Of course, Jesus is a special case, and last words are usually not examples of reverse quotation. Neither are cases of multiple last words typically offered as Gospel. But even with ordinary mortals, we are rarely disturbed to hear more than one final statement attributed to a famous person. We grasp, if only by tone and experience, the form's convention that this is something the person *might* have said. It would be in character and only too appropriate for him or her. All three versions of Rabelais's last words are Rabelaisian; Thomas More was capable of saying any of the last words attributed to him. Each ending of these lives represents a possible ending.

We are all sufficiently complex for life to have more than one suitable ending. None could be fully suitable.

A few "last words" are demonstrably impossible, but even these may be reshaped so that they are neither verifiably true nor verifiably false but rather possible—or, at least, barely possible. Such reshaping testifies to the fact that last words typically belong to the "middle realm" of "might have been said." This intrinsic quality of possibility characterizes last words as a literary form rather than a historical report.

Let me stress: the category of "possible" in this special sense differs from "possible" in the usual sense of "still unverified but in principle verifiable." When an event is possible in the sense of still unverified, we look for evidence that will decide one way or another. Possibility-as-still-unverified describes not the utterance but our knowledge about it. But when an utterance is possible the special way last words are possible—when they are taken as a literary form inhabiting the middle realm—possibility pertains to the utterance itself. It is a state of its own. If anything, the utterance discourages attempts to determine whether it is true or false.

Instead of verifiably true or false, last words are verifiably *possible.*

Anecdote and Possibility

In this respect, last words resemble anecdotes. Walter Gratzer, the editor of *Eurekas and Euphorias: The Oxford Book of Scientific Anecdotes,* wisely advises: "It remains only to concede that authenticity is an ever-present bugbear in a collection of this nature. Some stories have attached themselves to more than one protagonist; where this is the case, I have noted as much. Nor can I, with hand on heart, swear that none is apocryphal, but I have taken the view that if they deserve to be true then they are worth including. I may, therefore, have erred in leaning sometimes on the editor's friend, *ben trovato.*"[6] The same anecdote attaches itself to more than one person, much as certain quotations have sought and found different speakers. Gratzer cannot swear that the anecdotes in his collection are true, only that they are not demonstrably false, and that is enough so long as they are good (ben trovato) by the standards of anecdotes. We read them with the sense that we would like them to be true, that they "deserve to be true," and that they just might be true. Gratzer is describing stories that, like certain quotations, belong to the middle realm.

Anecdotes of scientific discovery divide into different genres, each of which requires and finds a certain kind of protagonist, the way witticisms demand and seek out a suitable wit. We have scientists appropriate for illustrating absent-mindedness (Mott) or problem-solving by dreams (Kekulé). So long as the stories are possible, genre determines their shape.

Unless we lack a sense of story or humor, we do not object to Gratzer's practice. We would nevertheless hope a biographer would not take these stories at face value. After all, in reading a biography we are usually seeking fact. Our standard is "true or highly probable," not "possible and deserving to be true."

We apply different standards on different occasions, and we turn to different genres for different purposes.

Either This Quotation Goes or . . .

In practice, we often recognize genres of the middle realm. We appreciate them in literary rather than biographical terms. Someone who does not understand them as intrinsically possible, rather than insufficiently verified, comes off as a bothersome literalist—or a "quotation expert."

Does it really matter whether Oscar Wilde's remark "Either that wallpaper goes, or I do" (FLW, 27; MDQ, 317) was actually his last utterance or, as is apparently the case, one spoken (not exactly in those words) some days before? The witticism only makes sense as an example of last words and so is correctly presented as such: by "correctly," I mean in terms of the utterance as oral literature.

The Great Perhaps

In any literary form, constraints offer opportunities. The need to express oneself in fourteen lines with a certain rhyme and meter scheme does not imprison imagination, but creates the very possibility of a sonnet. In much the same way, capable hands can make the most of the convention that last words were uttered an instant before death.

Wilde's remark depends on the idea that having said it, he promptly dies, while the wallpaper remains. Several other famous last words depend on their being *very* last words:

Die, my dear Doctor, that's the last thing I shall do!
—*Lord Palmerston (MDQ, 316)*

Nonsense, they couldn't hit an elephant at that distance. [sometimes given as: ". . . at that dist—"]
—*General John Sedgwick (MDQ, 317)*

Death seems to answer Sedgwick. It offers a disproof he cannot hear. Palmerston's words depend on a sort of grammati-
cal pun. It treats death as an action even though dying is
not something we "do" but something that happens to us. Perhaps our language should have us say something like, "It died
to me."

Some humorous last words depend on other aspects of a
conventional occasion—for example, the crowd gathered in
expectation of a benediction, the friends urging extreme unc-
tion, or the priest waiting for a sign of repentance:

I owe much; I have nothing; the rest I give to the
poor.
—*Rabelais (MDQ, 116)*

I did not know that we had ever quarreled.
—*Thoreau, urged to make his peace with God (FLW,
26)*

I do not have to forgive my enemies. I have had
them all shot.
—*Ramón Marvia Narváez, Spanish general and
politician, asked by a priest to forgive his enemies
(MDQ, 316)*

God will pardon me. It's his trade.
—*Heine (MDQ, 316)*

Is this a time to be making enemies?
—*Voltaire, asked to renounce Satan (FLW, 15)*

In other cases, the dying person exploits the ability to at last speak freely with no fear of consequences:

No, it is better not. She will only ask me to take a message to Albert.
—*Disraeli, offered a visit on his deathbed from Queen Victoria (FLW, 100)*

All right, then, I'll say it: Dante makes me sick.
—*Lope Félix de Vega Carpio (MDQ, 315)*

Some of the most memorable examples take advantage of the pathos of the situation for a display of feeling or courage:

See in what peace a Christian can die.
—*Addison (MDQ, 315)*

Let not poor Nelly starve.
—*Charles II, about Nell Gwynne (FLW, 80)*

My dear hands. Farewell, my dear hands.
—*Rachmaninov (MDQ, 316)*

Others give added weight to a favored truth:

> Even in the valley of the shadow of death, two and
> two do not make six.
> —*Tolstoy, asked to reconcile himself with the Russian Orthodox Church (MDQ, 317)*

Perhaps most movingly, last words can evoke the sense of mystery and an imminent encounter with the unknown:

> I am going to take my last voyage, a great leap in the
> dark.
> —*Hobbes (MDQ, 316)*

> I am going in search of the great perhaps [*le grand
> peut-être*].
> —*Rabelais (MDQ, 316)*

> More light!
> —*Goethe (FLW, 15)*

> I see the black light!
> —*Hugo (FLW, 23)*

Subgenres of Occasion

One may die in many circumstances, but some are conventional. Conventions of occasion define not only last words as a genre but also specific subgenres. Some last words, for exam-

ple, are uttered on the scaffold, before the guillotine, or facing
a firing squad:

> O Liberty! O Liberty! What crimes are committed
> in thy name!
> —*Madame Roland, before being guillotined (FLW,*
> *111; HiQ, 523)*

> Just one more moment, executioner, just one more
> moment! (Encore un moment, monsieur le bour-
> reau, encore un moment!)[7]
> —*Madame du Barry*

The same occasion allows for a witty last request:

> Why, yes. A bullet-proof vest.
> —*murderer James Rodgers (FLW, 70)*

> Ah, you might make that a double.
> —*murderer Neville Heath, asking for a last whiskey*
> *(FLW, 65)*

The suicide note defines a different subgenre:

> And so I leave this world, where the heart must
> either break or turn to lead.
> —*Chamfort (FLW, 128)*

> Everything disgusts me. (Je suis dégouté de tout.)
> —*Crevel (FLW, 130)*

Other subgenres include wills, comments to one's doctors, or (in the following example) answers to questions about manner of burial:

> Above ground I shall be food for kites; below I shall be food for mole-crickets and ants. Why rob one to feed the other?
> —*Chuang-tzu (MDQ, 316)*

> Surprise me!
> —*Bob Hope (FLW, 46)*

In Advance

Many authors have composed "last words" long before the occasion, another sure sign that we are dealing with a literary genre. Well in advance, Dreiser wrote, as his "intended last words," the appallingly tasteless comment: "Shakespeare, I come!" (MDQ, 315). The novelist Henry de Montherlant devoted his last words to last words: "A lot of people, on the verge of death, utter famous last words or stiffen into attitudes, as if the final stiffening in three days' time were not enough; they will have ceased to exist three days hence, yet they still want to arouse admiration and adopt a pose and tell a lie with their last gasp" (MDQ, 314–315). My favorite last words responding to the very form of last words belong to Pancho Villa. Desperate but unable to say anything worthy of the occasion, he (supposedly) died pleading: "Tell them I said something!" (FLW, 92). He did.

X
Epitaphs

Epitaph, *n. An inscription in a tomb, showing that
virtues acquired by death have a retroactive effect.*
—*Ambrose Bierce,* The Devil's Dictionary

Literary and Lapidary

Like final utterances, epitaphs constitute a genre of occasion.
No less than their words, their physical location on a tombstone and the moment of their carving for a memorial are intrinsic to their meaning.

No one either expects epitaphs to report unbiased facts
or demands verification of their praise. Dr. Johnson's well-
known observation that in lapidary inscriptions a man is not
under oath points to the genre's literariness. Its conventions
allow considerable latitude.

Precisely because familiar conventions govern the form, epitaphs have invited parodies using a similar diction to confer abuse. These parodic epitaphs—or anti-epitaphs, as we might call them—borrow conventions from the epigram and other short satirical forms.

Much as people have composed "last words" as an exercise in cleverness, so both epitaphs and anti-epitaphs have been written with no expectations that they will actually be used. As a literary form, epitaphs require not carving but the possibility that they could be carved. Like any other form of writing, epitaphs become literary when they are of interest outside the circumstances of their origin, in this case, when our interest is not confined to the information they convey about the particular person or mourner. Anthologies of epitaphs testify that they may be interesting even to those who care nothing for the deceased.

We look to epitaphs for certain kinds of wisdom and wit. A special pleasure accompanies appreciation of the skill employed to take advantage of the occasion and make the most of the form's constraints. The very brevity of epitaphs presents a challenge. It is difficult to make a statement, short enough to carve in stone, that is both appropriate to the particular person commemorated and interesting to those who never knew him or her. Some epitaphs demand, along with a summation of a person's essential qualities, an important statement about death itself. Anti-epitaphs typically require a witty insult both specific enough for a particular person and yet broad enough to comment on human vice in general. Both epitaphs and anti-epitaphs take the occasion as a way of demonstrating the power of mind.

Solemnity

Epitaphs often use the solemnity of death to great effect. As they convey the essence of the life ended, they may recommend it as a model. Or the model may be the way in which the person died. In either case, a brief phrase must suffice: complexity is expressed simply, and contrary to what one might have supposed, almost effortlessly. We sense the author's intelligence in the solution to these problems.[1]

Solemn epitaphs typically work by concealing their art so as not to detract from their subject. Such concealment, we know, is an art of its own. The author's intelligence must be felt and yet not advertise itself, which would be bad taste and defeat the purpose. The composer of the epitaph is there to commemorate not his own skill but "these honored dead." Indeed, the Gettysburg Address, too long to be an epitaph but surprisingly short for a speech, borrows a good deal of its power from the modest insightfulness of solemn epitaphs.

Posthumous Solemnity: Simonides and Herodotus

Consider these four epitaphs:

> Go, stranger, and tell the Lacedemonians that here we lie, obedient to their commands.
>
> —*to Leonidas and his men who died at Thermopylae (MDQ, 190)*

> Where savage indignation can lacerate his heart no more. Go, traveler, and imitate him if you can, a man who to his utmost championed liberty.
>
> —*to Swift (YBQ, 742)*

This is the true philosopher's stone.
—*to Hobbes*[2]

If you seek a monument, gaze around.
—*to Sir Christopher Wren (YBQ, 841)*

The first of these epitaphs belongs to the poet Simonides, who was alive to carve it shortly after Thermopylae; it is quoted in Herodotus.[3] The poet has allowed the dead to speak posthumously. Their lives completed, Leonidas's soldiers receive the chance to express what is most important to them, and they choose, yet again, to do their martial duty by conveying the news of the battle.

For these heroes, facing death with courage and calmness is just another job. They obey this command selflessly, as they obey all others. Their own lives as particular people go without mention, for that is what it is to be a Spartan.

Thermopylae, of course, was the greatest battle of Greek history. For Herodotus, and even more as time went on, it seemed pivotal because Greek liberty and the culture that was to shape the West turned out to depend on victory in that war. In subsequent centuries, readers of Herodotus and students of ancient history knew, even more than Simonides and Herodotus, the significance of that battle. All the more could they appreciate these brave men, who would have made the same sacrifice had nothing depended on it.

One cannot be sure how important an occasion for courage will turn out to be. One does one's duty *as if* the occasion could not be more important. When these men did so, the result turned out to be of greater significance than they could have imagined. Their bravery is all the more impressive because they did not know what we do about their choice. They die, we praise.

Epitaph and Story

Like many quotations, this epitaph achieves power as a summarizing moment in the narrative it concludes. We sense Herodotus's complete story in its ending. Today that story is known to relatively few and remembered clearly by still fewer. By presuming a knowledge of Thermopylae, this epitaph once gained much power now lost. But not entirely lost: if we take the trouble to learn the story, or come across it in Herodotus, this quotation seems, in its simplicity, to express as much by its silences as by its speech.

For Herodotus, Simonides' words represent the climax not only of this episode but also of his entire history. As he states in his opening, Herodotus proposes to tell the story of Europe's conflict with Asia going back to the Trojan War and culminating in the Persian invasion of Greece. The narrative represents this conflict as a drama of opposing values. Greeks and Persians fight about what is truly important in life. As we would say today, Herodotus reports a clash of civilizations.

Thus we see the imperial Xerxes, drunk with power, and angry that a storm has destroyed his Hellespont bridge, ordering the sea to be tortured with branding instruments and flogged by men saying "these barbarous and impious words: 'Thou bitter water! Thy master inflicts this punishment upon thee, because thou hast injured him, although thou hadst not suffered any harm from him; and King Xerxes will cross over thee, whether thou wilt or not . . . thou art both a deceitful and briny river!'" (Herodotus, 424). Nothing could be further from Leonidas than such boastfulness.

Asked by Xerxes how the Greeks will react to his gigantic army, Demaratus, a Greek exile at the Persian court, tells him they will fight. Xerxes refuses to believe that anyone would resist when outnumbered thousands to one, but Demaratus explains that, however hopeless the cause, Greeks will resist because they are not slaves to a monarch but free men governed by their own law. As it links hubris to slavery, this story identifies devotion to duty with freedom.

Herodotus's account describes a few thousand, and in the end a few hundred, Spartans and their allies resisting millions of Persians. We may find Greek resistance all the more striking when we are told, in the sober *Oxford History of the Classical World,* that Herodotus's numbers are ludicrous because there couldn't have been more than a few hundred thousand Persians![4]

After holding off the Persians for days, the Spartans are at last betrayed by a Greek who reveals the pass that will enable Xerxes' soldiers to attack from behind. Knowing the ambush is imminent, Leonidas's men change nothing. The augur Megistias tells them they will die that morning. The allies leave and only the few hundred Spartans remain. By contrast, the Persians at the battle use scourges from behind to force their men forward. Told that when the Persians let loose their arrows, their sheer number obscures the sun, the Spartan Dieneces replies: all the better, for in that case the Greeks will "fight in the shade" (Herodotus, 488).

Leonidas falls early in the fight and then the Greeks actually contend for and secure his body. Of course, they will all soon be dead bodies themselves. But securing the body of the heroic leader is simply what one does.

A monument to those who died before only the Spartans were left reads: "Four thousand from Peloponnesus once fought on this spot with three hundred myriads" (Herodotus, 488–489). Leonidas's Spartans, speaking in Simonides' epitaph, do not call attention to such unimportant facts. Their epitaph is all the stronger for the contrast.

Herodotus confides that he has discovered the names of every man in the three hundred who remained. Those names could easily be listed, but Herodotus does not bother. For the Spartans, bravery at Thermopylae was nothing more than what was expected of them, worthy only of minimal notice. These are not unknown soldiers, but soldiers who see no reason to be known.

It is only now that Herodotus gives us Simonides' epitaph. As the culmination of this story, and of the entire history, it conveys meaning not only by what it states but also by what it does not trouble to state. In addition to calm determination, aversion to boastfulness, and devotion to duty, it demonstrates the power of freedom that neither tyrants nor tyrannized can understand. Simonides' epitaph says nothing about these men, as they would say nothing about themselves. Even after death, they speak only to fulfill their last duty—to "tell the Lacedemonians" what might be pressing military news—which means, since such information could be news only once, that they scorn the immortality they have earned. Courage disdains fame and wins it.

When epitaphs offer words that might be spoken by the deceased—a conventional practice—those words are typically spoken in "epilogue time," as if the speaker had been granted a moment after the end of life in order to sum it up for others. In epilogue time, as we saw when discussing last words, old accomplishments are reviewed but new ones are not attempted. But the words Simonides composes for the Spartans are *not* spoken in epilogue time. They decline the offer to summarize, which would constitute a form of self-glorification, and instead use the extra moment to fulfill yet another duty of life.

As if to honor this refusal of boastfulness, Herodotus does not end his account of the memorials here. He removes Simonides' epitaph from the climactic position by adding another one: "This is the monument of the illustrious Megistias, whom once the Medes [Persians], having passed the river Sperchus, slew; a prophet who, at the time well knowing the impending fate, would not abandon the leaders of Sparta" (Herodotus, 489). Of course, that is true of the three hundred as well, but they do not say so.

Simonides' classic epitaph sets the standard of nobility.

Epitaphs: Swift

> Why is it that we rejoice at a birth and grieve at a funeral? It is because we are not the person involved.
>
> —*Mark Twain,* Pudd'nhead Wilson[5]

A misanthrope's death invites an especially interesting epitaph. If humanity is essentially evil and life an intolerable burden, then death, even if still dreaded, offers a different sort of vantage point.

In such cases, death may be represented not only as a release but even as a reward. Human moral depravity makes *this* world hell. For the misanthrope, heroism lies not in facing death but in continuing to live. He endures a misanthrope's martyrdom: not flinching before the truth everyone else conceals. In *The Devil's Dictionary,* Ambrose Bierce defines a cynic as "a blackguard whose faulty vision sees things as they are, not as they ought to be. Hence the custom among the Scythians of plucking out a cynic's eyes to improve his vision" (DD, 39).

For such reasons, it seems, Yeats described Swift's epitaph as "the greatest epitaph in history." Yeats rewrote it:

> Savage indignation there
> Cannot lacerate his breast.
> Imitate him if you dare,
> World-besotted traveler; he
> Served human liberty. (YBQ, 847)

The original epitaph and Yeats's revision memorialize Swift's celebrated hatred of humanity as uncanny insight combined with fortitude. The "liberty" championed is neither political nor economic. It is above all liberty of vision, and it was championed not by any particular stance Swift took but by his very nature. His life was savage indignation, a constant laceration of the heart so intense we wonder how he could have endured it. Death not by his own hand therefore becomes the hero's triumph and crown.

Like Simonides' celebrated epitaph, to which it probably alludes, the epitaph to Swift addresses the spectator, who necessarily still belongs to the world of the living. "Go, stranger" and "Go, traveler" exploit the physical situation of a monument, visible to any passerby, in order to speak to whoever might be present.

Unlike Simonides' epitaph, this address speaks to the passerby in words belonging not to the posthumous dead man but to the poet who appreciates him. "Go, traveler, and imitate him if you can"—Yeats strengthens it to "if you dare"—makes the life, like that of all martyrs, a challenge. The power of this misanthrope's epitaph belongs not to its words alone but also to its occasion, which is an intrinsic part of the quotation.

Epitaphs: Hobbes

The epitaph to Hobbes cited above was one he himself considered and rejected. Allegedly, he remarked not long before death that "he was ninety-one years finding a hole out of this world and at last found it" (Tuck, 39). The sentiment suits a thinker almost as misanthropic as Swift. "A hole" is a properly physical exit for a materialist.

"This is the true philosopher's stone" presumes not only its situation on a tombstone but also the material of stone itself. "This"—the tombstone—is the only philosopher's stone there can ever be. The philosopher's stone sought by the alchemists was supposed to transmute base metals into gold. By implication, it would at the same time convert mere facticity into pure significance and make mortality give way to eternal life. Death therefore marks the failure of any quest to find the precious stone.

Meaningfulness disappears along with immortality. In this epitaph, therefore, the absence of any meaning is itself the meaning. The quest for understanding succeeds in a way neither desired nor anticipated. Wisdom is achieved, but it is the wisdom of recognizing the futility of human striving.

As the epitaph's irony depends on the word "stone," it relies as well on the word "philosopher." In the fixed phrase "philosopher's stone," "philosopher" means someone who sees into arcane truths beyond the power of mere reason. But since we use the same term to refer to rational thinkers like Hobbes himself, the word becomes a kind of pun or homonym. The rational "philosopher" may mock the mystical one, but in the end they are very much alike. After all, how different is the belief in Truth from the belief in Immortality? The message of the stone applies no less to this kind of philosopher: mortality spells the limitation of reason, and wisdom lies in recognizing its own paltriness.

Moreover, this epitaph commemorates not any philosopher but specifically Hobbes, a celebrated materialist. Stones are a conventional symbol of the material, and so the tombstone becomes, in yet another way, a part of the message to be carved on it. Materialism, it appears, does not escape the futility of all philosophy in the face of death. However much it may pretend otherwise, it, too, constitutes a misguided attempt to triumph over the physical world by the sheer power of comprehending it. The materialist implicitly believes that even if there is no providence, there is at least gnosis: but that faith turns out to be as much a comforting self-delusion as any other. Death and the stone mock materialist dreams, while nature's irony turns out to be all the greater for ambushing one who thought to escape the consoling deceptions of others.

Supposedly, a cleric commented to Hobbes that this epigraph would itself have had "religion in it"; and that seems correct. For if materialism itself is no match for death, then, perhaps, the futility of materialism leads us back to faith. It is precisely the grave that leads to the cross. Perhaps that implication explains why Hobbes chose not to use this epitaph. If so, the fact that it was *not* used—that the stone on which it was carved was only mental—is the most significant thing about it. The materialist's epitaph remains in thought alone. This epitaph includes not only its setting, its material, and author, but also its virtuality, its existence as a merely considered possibility.

Epitaphs: Wren

Would be equally applicable to a physician buried
in a churchyard.
—*Horace Smith (1779–1849) (EAD, 268)*

Christopher Wren's epitaph, probably written by his son, makes the most of its location in St. Paul's Cathedral, which Wren built: "If you seek a monument, look around." The real tombstone is not, as we might initially expect, the tablet on which these words are written, but the building in which we stand.

This epitaph confounds our expectations of what a monument is. What we first took to be the monument turns out to be no more than a sign pointing to it. The true monument does not just celebrate Wren's achievement, it is his achievement.

The epitaph's posthumous speech commands viewers to look around, and if they do, they see not only the building but also other viewers. The monument includes the people in it, who have come to use it and look at it. If so, it includes us. By the mere fact of reading these words, we ourselves become part of the monument.

To be sure, Wren's epitaph may seem altogether too boastful, too sure that the work of human hands will endure. Perhaps it sounds more like Xerxes than Leonidas. Mortality should have taught humility. Reflecting on these words, we may readily think of Shelley's "Ozymandias," which describes another epitaph gesturing to ostensibly eternal works, but these have long since crumbled away. The sign pointing beyond itself points to nothing:

> And on the pedestal these words appear:
> "My name is Ozymandias, king of kings:
> Look on my works, ye Mighty, and despair!"
> Nothing beside remains. Round the decay
> Of that colossal wreck, boundless and bare,
> The lone and level sands stretch far away.[6]

We recognize time itself as the real creator of this monument. The emblem of eternity is neither sculpture nor building nor any human achievement, but mere ruins. Whatever we build for all time, for "eternal memory" as they say in Russian, courts the response shown here. And even ruins are not the end, but a visible moment in the process of ending, since, they, too, will disappear.

Round the decay, "nothing beside remains," and "*Nothing* beside remains," as the line can also be read. This Nothing now means something, perhaps everything. Ozymandias created for eternity, but Time has made his absent monument its own.

A monument—in fact and by convention—lasts when the one memorialized is gone, but even a monument has its end. The artifice of eternity persists only so long. Stone disintegrates and continents erode. Perhaps when St. Paul's has gone the way of all stone, the epitaph, like the words on Ozymandias's pedestal, will still survive. Wren's son and all other fabricators of eternal monuments overlook time's irony, which uses pride to teach humility.

To be significant, an absence must be in the right place. Like the Nothing around Ozymandias's inscription or the potential disappearance of Wren's cathedral, an absence has meaning because a presence is expected. Should only the tablet with the verbal portion of Wren's epitaph survive, what would be significant would be not mere empty space but the vanished cathedral, and the cathedral can be vanished only right there. Let stones crumble to dust and time discredit pride, the genre's conventions still rule supreme. Whether we think of what the monument means to suggest or the thoughts it unwittingly evokes, the nonverbal part of the epitaph still governs our understanding.

Epitaphs as Pure Form

Once we recognize the epitaph as a literary genre, we may readily anticipate that many more have been composed than carved. The ostensible location on a tombstone becomes purely notional. Such epitaphs offer a rough analogue to closet drama—a work in the form of a play meant not for performance but for silent reading. The very existence of "closet epitaphs" shows the literariness of the form. If great writers ever start composing closet e-mail signatures or closet insurance letters denying benefits, we may be sure that those forms, too, will have achieved the status of literature.

Many significant writers have written epitaphs or closet epitaphs. Death, actual or merely anticipated, offers an opportunity for ingenuity. Auden, Dryden, Franklin, Gay, La Bruyère, and others composed epitaphs for themselves and others, or used them as embedded genres in a larger work. As we have seen, Yeats rewrote Swift's epitaph. Johnson displays his mastery of tone in his epitaph for Goldsmith: "To Oliver Goldsmith, A Poet, Naturalist, and Historian, who left scarcely any style of writing untouched, and touched none that he did not adorn" (MDQ, 190). Pope's epitaph to Newton testifies to the sage's genius while exemplifying the poet's:

> Nature, and nature's laws lay hid in night;
> God said, *Let Newton be!* and all was light. (YBQ, 599)

So clearly an exercise in wit, this epitaph almost defeats itself by calling attention to its own cleverness. For if Newton's discovery is analogous to God's creation of the universe, then Pope's words proclaim themselves a new Book of Genesis.

Another Significant Absence

Most anthologies of epitaphs quote generously from Gray's "Elegy Written in a Country Churchyard," which derives its power from eulogizing not the famous but the nameless. The "Elegy" depends on this reversal of conventions and therefore testifies to them. Its language constantly alludes to what it is *not* about ("Some mute inglorious Milton here may rest, / Some Cromwell guiltless of his country's blood").[7]

Belonging to one genre, the elegy, Gray's poem embeds another, the epitaph. Both mourn loss. In this case, it is the loss of those the poet never knew in the first place. In the churchyard, nameless people are remembered by nameless authors, who, instead of composing their own words, quote those of "many a holy text." Their mute reliance on citation carries its own tongue-tied eloquence, the eloquence of "th' unlettered Muse."

The poem ends with an epitaph that could not be further from Pope's in tone. It marks the grave of a "youth to Fortune and to Fame unknown" upon whom "Science [knowledge] frowned not":

> No further seek his merits to disclose,
> Or draw his frailties from their dead abode,
> (There they alike in trembling hope repose)
> The bosom of his Father and his God.

Human hopes tremble before fame and before heaven, goals that they may never reach. The goals are unsure, which is why they *are* hopes. Gray's poem memorializes things that might have happened. Looking forward, it also memorializes future things that might not happen. It applies to all graveyards to come.

This elegy evokes the hypotheticals of past, present, and future. It remembers, and anticipates, unwritten poems and tyrannies only dreamed of. Most epitaphs, eulogies, and elegies recall deeds, but Gray's poem recalls mere possibilities. It senses that life includes the might-have-beens, the opportunities we missed and the choices we failed to make. To understand a person is to grasp not only what he did, but also what he could have done, his subjunctive self.

Just as we all die, we all leave potentials unrealized. That is what human mortality entails. Gray's poem is about all of us. We are all people who could have been quite different and accomplished things now not even imagined. Appropriately enough, the "Elegy" concludes with an epitaph that is purely fictional, one that exists only in the poem itself. Part of a poem, an imagined thing, it remembers what never was, and only hoped for.

This is the true philosopher's epitaph.

Anti-Epitaphs

For obvious reasons, anti-epitaphs are almost always closet epitaphs. The author uses the convention of commemorating a person's essential qualities as a platform to "celebrate" flaws and vices. Anthologies now typically include the following parodic epitaphs:

> At last God caught his eye.
>
> —*Harry Secombe, Welsh comedian, for a head waiter (MDQ, 190)*

> She sleeps alone at last.
>
> —*Robert Benchley, for an actress (MDQ, 189)*

> Here lies my wife; here let her lie!
> Now she's at rest, and so am I.
>
> —*Dryden (MDQ, 189)*

Commemoration achieves retribution, and the dead become exemplary for their failings. Instead of shedding the conventional tears, the survivor rejoices. Of course, since parodies belong to a tradition, this rejoicing is also conventional.

The problem with anti-epitaphs is that they easily turn into unwitting satires on their composer. He must have the last word, even when his opponent is dead, and he thinks himself so clever:

> Poor G. K. C., his day is past—
> Now God will know the truth at last.
>
> —*E. V. Lucas on G. K. Chesterton (ODLQ, 92)*

GKC's day is past in two senses: his life is over and his beliefs are outmoded. But is there a cheaper argument against a set of beliefs than that they are no longer in fashion? One may not accept Chesterton's religious views, but surely they were based on deeper, and more rational, considerations than this objection!

The second line of the couplet attributes a smug certainty to Chesterton on no other grounds than that he had faith; but who is really being smug here? And what could be easier than suggesting that the religious person equates himself with, or even places himself above, God? This mock epitaph accomplishes the reverse of what it intends because it exemplifies the puerile criticism that Chesterton had to endure. GKC had the courage to go against the prevailing opinion of his circle, whereas Lucas relies on everyone agreeing with him.

There is inevitably something cowardly about such epitaphs. If the target is dead, they preclude an answer. Even if the target is alive, they make any answer seem humorless. Self-defense would have to be self-praise, and so unappealing. Either way, these anti-epitaphs exploit an unfair rhetorical advantage.

And yet, a successful reply is not impossible. The satirist John Wilmot, Earl of Rochester (author of the brilliant "Satire Against Mankind") insulted the reigning Charles II with the following premature epitaph:

> Here lies a great and mighty king
> Whose promise none relies on;
> He never said a foolish thing,
> Or ever did a wise one. (ODQ, 319)

The king replied: "This is very true; for my words are my own, and my actions are my ministers'" (ODQ, 209). The king bests the earl by answering not imperiously but modestly, so that he, rather than the satirist, becomes the one devoted to truth. In so doing, he takes away the satirist's power of exposure.

Rather unexpectedly, it is Rochester who seems petty. Charles acknowledges justice in the accusation, though in an unexpected way that puts it in a new light. He shifts the force of Rochester's epitaph from the insulting last line to the praising penultimate one. That praise, originally offered as a set-up for scorn, now seems justified for a man wise enough to extract, from a personal attack, a subtle point about power. Rochester revels in his cleverness. Charles shows himself intelligent enough to turn an insult to his advantage.

Self-Parodic Epitaphs

Some parodic epitaphs are written on one's own tombstone, at least notionally:

> Over my dead body.
> —*George S. Kaufman (EAD, 141)*

> Pardon me for not getting up.
> —*Hemingway (EAD, 118)*

The problem with these and similar epitaphs is that the author seems willing to trivialize death for the sake of a witticism. They keep saying: look how brave and clever I am!

More successful are these self-composed epitaphs:

> Here lies Joseph, who failed in everything he undertook.
> —*Joseph II (1741–1790), Holy Roman Emperor, reflecting on the failure of his attempts at reform (attributed—MDQ, 190)*

Here lies one whose name was writ in water.

—*Keats (MDQ, 190)*

For all their self-pity, these lines take death seriously. For that matter, self-pity, like regret, belongs to the essence of facing death. Joseph II and Keats capture an aspect of human experience we all recognize in ourselves.

Dorothy Parker's Genius

So long as they avoid trivializing death, parodic epitaphs tend to be more successful when they mock their author. To hit oneself when down demands a kind of courage, if only the courage of misanthropic despair. Of course, one must really be hitting oneself, not, like Hemingway, just showing off how clever one is.

The modern master was Dorothy Parker, who entitled her collection of short works *Enough Rope*. Parker knew not only how to insult herself with genius, but also to put herself down for the very act of doing so. She includes in her self-deprecation the desire to seem clever. Her laughter therefore pertains not only to her own weaknesses, but also to human nature, whose weaknesses she exemplifies with brilliance.

Parker evinced a contempt for life so profound that even suicide seemed not worth the effort:

> Guns aren't lawful;
> Nooses give;
> Gas smells awful;
> You might as well live. (YBQ, 579)

Verses like these work because they are not simply displays of pride at one's own clever cynicism. The tone dismisses these very verses as the verses dismiss the author. That is one reason Parker surpasses Oscar Wilde, who so often seems to revel in his own cleverness. His cynicism begs approval, hers does not.

Told she would die in a few months, Parker replied: "Promises, promises!" She could never have wanted an epitaph like that of her fellow misanthrope, Swift, because, as Yeats appreciated, it made the misanthrope noble. The true misanthrope neither exempts herself from contempt nor values her life enough to take its ending seriously. Parker suggested for her tombstone:

> This is on me. (MDQ, 411)

> Excuse my dust. (MDQ, 411)

These lines may at first sound like Hemingway's, but they are quite different. Parker displays not her wit but her futile attachment to wit. What is parodied here is the impulse to parody, which takes itself as more significant than anything in life could be. As so often with Parker, laughter makes the dark even darker.

IV
Literary Composition and Decomposition

XI
The Anthology as Literature

When is an anthology of quotations more than an anthology of quotations? Can a treasury become a jewel in its own right?

Collections of quotations have fascinated great writers. Several have hit upon the idea of transforming an anthology into a literary work. After all, literature contains many kinds of composite creations that make a whole from a collection of discrete parts.

Works like the *Decameron* and the *Canterbury Tales* consist of numerous complete stories. The *Arabian Nights* is a kind of narrative encyclopedia, a story about stories about stories. Sonneteers have written "sequences" and lyric poets "cycles," in which each poem, complete in itself, also belongs to a larger poem.

These examples combine works belonging to the same genre, but it is also possible to form a whole from different genres. Dostoevsky intended his longest creation, *A Writer's Diary*, as a new kind of literature, which would incorporate an amazing variety of literary works, all of which he would write himself.[1] Published monthly, this genre of genres made its pe-

riodical form an essential part of its aesthetic. Each issue responded to events of the preceding month, usually with a
whimsical variety of pieces united by a common concern—
say, the experience of children. Some of Dostoevsky's best
short stories first appeared in the *Diary*, alongside their own
first drafts, crime reports, autobiographical reminiscences, letters from real and imaginary readers, and a dizzying variety of
parodies, long and short. Numerous pieces can be read either
as plans for future stories or stories that take the form of plans,
in much the way that sketches for paintings can be works of
their own. Dostoevsky's experiment did not prove entirely
successful, and the *Diary* has usually been read as a mere
collection rather than as the integral work Dostoevsky intended. But it is nevertheless clear that its stories make a different impression and convey a different meaning when read
in context. They seem to invite reading both as freestanding
works and as responses in a dialogue with other parts of the
Diary.

Despite Dostoevsky's claim to novelty, his "new genre"
followed a number of precedents.[2] He probably had in mind
Dickens's experimental weekly, *Master Humphrey's Clock,* a
miscellany presented as the proceedings of a small club that
met at "Master Humphrey's" to "beguile time from the heart
of time itself." Members would read papers they placed in the
pendulum closet of Master Humphrey's clock (BoG, 26). As
Dickens explained, he planned to "write amusing essays on
the various foibles of the day as they arise; to take advantage
of passing events; and to vary the form of the papers by throwing in sketches, essays, tales, adventures, letters from imaginary correspondents, and so forth, and to diversify the contents
as much as possible."[3] He also decided to include installments
of a novel, *The Old Curiosity Shop,* which first appeared as the

Personal Adventures of Master Humphrey in the fourth number of the *Clock,* but before long it took over the entire publication.

The ancients called works consisting of diverse genres
"menippean satires," from Latin *satura* (medley) and Menippus,
the legendary curmudgeon who created the form and often
appeared as a character in works by later practitioners. Petro-
nius's *Satyricon* and Lucian's *Dialogues of the Dead* are perhaps
the best known ancient examples of this fascinating farrago. In
the Renaissance, Erasmus's *Praise of Folly* and More's *Utopia*
reflect the genre's influence, while inspiring in turn the books
of Rabelais. The form has continued to thrive, in high and
popular culture, up to the present. John Barth's novel *The Sot-
Weed Factor* and Mikhail Bulgakov's ever-popular fantasy *The
Master and Margarita* make constant and self-conscious use of
its resources. Whenever the devil is made comic, as in the 1967
film *Bedazzled,* we see the decisive influence of Dostoevsky's
greatest contribution to the genre: the chapter in which a pal-
try Satan haunts Ivan Karamazov while mocking his idea of
evil as something grand instead of merely banal. Each half-
hour segment of *Monty Python's Flying Circus* perfectly em-
bodies the menippean legacy.

Composite works need not be playful. They may reflect
the aspiration to gather all wisdom into one place. The Bible
itself may be read as such a composite containing separate
works of diverse genres. So can particular biblical books.

If it is possible to combine stories and poems, then surely
one could make literature by bringing together the shortest
literary works, quotations. For example, one might compose a
story in which a character cites wise sayings or a narrator composes sardonic maxims. Ecclesiastes and the Book of Job can
be read this way. Alternatively, a treatise or essay readable as a

whole might also be interesting for the countless quotations it contains. Or one might make literature directly out of an anthology.

All these ideas have inspired literature from the Renaissance on. They raise fascinating questions about quotations, anthologies, and literature itself. Can such works be said to have a structure or an ending? What is the relation of part to whole? In what order should each be read? In numerous ways, composite works challenge our usual assumptions of what literature is.

Let us look first at some important examples of anthologies as literature and see how they are made.

Erasmus, Seneca, Burton

Burton, that unsystematic predecessor of Bartlett.
—*Robert Merton (OTSOG, 12)*

In chapter 1, I mentioned that Erasmus's *Adages* enjoyed enormous influence in the Renaissance. Each entry provided a classical saying along with an explanatory essay. The collection was reprinted, amended, and pillaged countless times, and some of the essays—most notably, the one on "war is sweet to those who have not tried it"—became classics. Over the decades, Erasmus kept bringing out larger and larger editions, until a work that began with fewer than a thousand adages expanded to more than four thousand. In *The Praise of Folly,* the goddess Folly makes fun of its author's never-ceasing hunt for new proverbs and sayings.

Erasmus's work adumbrates an aesthetic of infinity. It seemed capable of growing indefinitely, at least in principle. In this way, the collection resembles several other Renaissance classics that dispensed with the need for an ending, from Montaigne's *Essays* to Burton's *Anatomy of Melancholy.* Montaigne and Burton were both fascinated with the same impulse to collect quotations that had inspired Erasmus. They also developed Erasmus's insight that one could make a literary work out of quotations, a kind of patchwork interesting both as a reference work and as a special kind of creation all its own.

But how can a collection of other people's words be creative? "I hate quotations. Tell me what you know," Ralph Waldo Emerson observed (WoW, 297). Ironically enough, this much-quoted line itself quotes (unwittingly?) from Seneca, who famously attacked quotations and assemblages of quotations in much the same terms. In his essay on maxims, Seneca refuses a request to put together a collection of wise stoic counsels. He explains that learning simplistic sayings is suitable for children capable of no more, "but for a man advanced in study to hunt such gems is disgraceful; he is using a handful of clichés for a prop."[4] Still more important for Seneca, one ought to learn to think for oneself rather than quote others, and create new thoughts rather than act as a "clerk" for earlier thinkers:

> "Zeno said this." What do *you* say? "This Cleanthes said." What do *you* say? . . . Produce something of your own. All those men who never create but lurk as interpreters under the shadow of another are lacking, I believe, in independence of spirit. . . . They exercise their memories on what is not their own. But to remember is one thing, to know another . . . knowing is making the thing your own, not depending on the model, not always looking over your shoulder at the teacher. "Zeno said this, Cleanthes that"—is there any difference between you and a book? . . . if we rest content with solu-

tions offered, the real solution will never be found.
(Seneca, 186–187)

Evidently, collections of quotations were common enough even in the first century to occasion such comment.

Burton and Montaigne, mindful of Seneca's contrast of creativity with mere compilation, indulged their sense of irony with a list of suitably chosen tropes, clichés, and learned quotations that justified the act of quoting—before proceeding to turn their own work into exemplars of how something genuinely new could be made from the old. In his *Anatomy,* Burton addressed the Senecan objection squarely, demonstrating complex creative possibilities within this seemingly simple form.

The Muse of Quotation

Burton's *Anatomy* announces itself as a peculiar kind of anthology of quotations, linked together by a theme and an authorial personality. The very possibility of making literature out of a compendium suggests that compendia were common in Burton's time, as in fact they were. Assuming the name "Democritus Junior"—a name that is itself a quotation—Burton explains his method: "As a good housewife out of divers fleeces weaves one piece of cloth, a bee gathers wax and honey out of many flowers, and makes a new bundle of all, *Floriferis ut apes in saltibus omnia libant* (as bees in flowery glades sip from each cup), I have laboriously collected this cento out of diverse writers."[5] As a result, "I have only this of Macrobius to say for myself, *Omne meum, nihil meum,* 'tis all mine and none mine" (Burton, 24).

> The matter is theirs [other authors'] most part, and yet mine, *apparet unde sumptum sit* (it is plain whence it was taken) (which Seneca approves),

aliud tanem quam unde sumptum sit apparet (yet it becomes something different in its new setting); which nature does with the aliment of our bodies incorporate, digest, assimilate, I do *concoquere quod hausi* (assimilate what I have swallowed), dispose of what I take. I make them pay tribute to set out this my *Macaronicon*, the method is mine own; I must usurp that of Wecker *e Ter., nihil dictum quod non dictum prius, methodus sola artificem ostendit*, we can say nothing but what has been said, the composition and method is ours only. (Burton, 25)

I cite rather than paraphrase this passage to convey how it does what it describes, that is, makes something of its own out of the words of others. Creation creates nothing; it incorporates, digests, assimilates. But assimilation is itself creative, or we would be nothing but the food we eat.

Burton here outlines a special sort of aesthetic, which may be called the *aesthetic of incorporation*. It evokes the pleasure of assembling a work that burgeons in several directions at once. Burton often says the same thing as others (and says he says it) and at times says it twice, in the original language and in English. He calls his work a "macaronicon": macaronic, a term from the late fifteenth or early sixteenth century, referred specifically to common words made by giving Latin endings to vernacular words and more broadly to works made from more than one language. The macaronic word or work flaunts its status as something new that is forged from something recognizably old, a creation showing its origin the better to mark its departure from it. It quotes and changes the quoted words so they are different but recognizable: transformation captured while the work of creativity remains incomplete, metamorphosis frozen.

A peculiar combination of modesty and hubris characterizes "anatomical" works made from the words of others. On the one hand, they appear self-effacing by relying so heavily on others' words, and yet, in their discovery of a new muse of quotation, they also display boastfulness. "Assimilation" calls attention to others and oneself simultaneously. Burton catches this paradoxical attitude well: "Though there were many giants of old in physic and philosophy, yet I say with Didacus Stella, 'A dwarf standing on the shoulders of a giant may see farther than a giant himself'; I may likely add, alter and see farther than my predecessors" (Burton, 25). We know this saying from its use later in the century in Isaac Newton's letter to Hooke, also poised between modesty and condescension.

Burton was not alone. We may speak of a class of assimilating or "encyclopedic" works (one sense of "anatomy" is "an encyclopedic work") made from extracts and quotations from the books of others. Quotation is heaped upon quotation, as readers are invited to recognize this process as potentially infinite. There is never nothing more to quote, as someone once said.

Burton's sixth edition, the last he prepared and which appeared posthumously, reflects on the changes made in the previous ones. So long as possible, the work had kept lengthening, much as Erasmus's had. Like Erasmus, Burton did not confine himself to adding material at the end of his book but, as is common with encyclopedic works, expanded existing sections as well. Paragraphs grew and then split, digressions begat digressions, and one quotation suggested another and yet another. Indeed, perhaps a good definition of encyclopedic literature—including "anatomies," parodic dictionaries, stories serving primarily as points of departure for digressions, and similar fructiferous oddities—would be "works that may lengthen from multiple points." They encourage us to wonder whether departures, additions, or digressions, when invited by the work's design and listed in its table of contents, are really departures at all. The plan is to deviate from any plan, and in an unplanned way.

Nothing is ever finished; all is a trial (an "essay") setting the stage for more trials. Montaigne used this encyclopedic method with his collection of essays, which he expanded not only by adding ever more essays but also by interpolating more quotations and observations into earlier ones.[6] Montaigne made annotations of his last, 1588, edition (the "B" text) in which he added over a thousand more passages for a "C" text.

Text begets ever more text, quotations suggest other quotations, in what amounts to a display of sheer fecundity and potential infinity. The novelist (if that is what we are to call him) Laurence Sterne took Burton as a model—and quoted Burton's quotations—when he made his wandering masterpiece of imaginative gestation and encyclopedic aspiration, *The Life and Opinions of Tristram Shandy, Gentleman*. Model, of course, is as an odd word for something that copies a repeated departure from earlier models and comments on commentaries on the models departed from, ad infinitum. Tristram's story, his "life," seems to exist, but not quite entirely, for the "opinions" to which it gives rise. And those opinions are, often enough, opinions about other people's opinions of opinions. Thus the epigraph Tristram chooses from Epictetus—"It is not actions, but opinions concerning actions, which disturb men"—changes from a serious Stoic maxim into a parodic rule for the breaking of rules. Tristram transforms Epictetus's words from a recommendation of calmness into its opposite, a promise of frenetic randomness.

Although many of Tristram's quotations alter the original, others, as with the epigraph, manage to preserve the original's wording and yet somehow "misquote" it. As Burton has warned, "The matter is theirs . . . and yet mine . . . it is plain whence it was taken . . . yet it becomes something different in its new setting" (Burton, 25).

In the famous opening to Book V of *Tristram Shandy*, Tristram chooses two epigraphs, which he credits to Horace and Erasmus, but which he actually draws from Burton's—or Democritus Junior's—amended quotation of those authors in *The Anatomy of Melancholy*. Tristram not only quotes but quotes an act of quoting and misquoting. Tristram cites Democritus Junior citing Erasmus: "Si quis calumnietur levius esse quam decet theologum, aut mordacius quam deceat Christianum—non Ego, sed Democritus dixit" (Should anyone judge my writings harshly as being in a lighter vein than suits a theologian, or more biting than is appropriate to a Christian—not I, but Democritus said it.)[7] This chain of borrowed borrowings leads to Tristram's vow in Book V, chapter 1: "By the grace of God, said I . . . 'I will lock up my study door at the moment I get home and throw the key of it ninety feet below the surface of the earth, into the draw-well at the back of my house.'" James Work annotates this line:

> A characteristic example of Sterne's roguishness. Having declared that he has locked his study door— *i.e.*, that he has separated himself from the authors whom he was wont to plunder—he breaks into a castigation of plagiaries in an impassioned passage which is itself cribbed from Burton! "Cribbed," however, is too strong a word. That Sterne has here, as in practically every other case of "borrowing," deftly altered and heightened (and, inciden-

tally, miscopied) his original, and has made the
passage incontestably his own, will be evident to
anyone who compares the following paragraphs
with their sources in the *Anatomy of Melancholy*,
"Democritus Junior to the Reader" . . . Burton himself had borrowed heavily in these particular passages, and in any case Sterne expected his learned
readers to recognize his source and to laugh with
him at the absurdity of inveighing against plagiarism in a plagiarism. (Sterne, 342n1)

Yes, but: Burton's work was a rarity at the time, much more so
than it was to become. Only a very learned reader—not the
many who made *Tristram Shandy* a bestseller—could be expected to recognize the source. I am arguing not that Sterne
is really committing plagiarism, but that even readers who
cannot tell exactly what has been quoted can still recognize
that *something* has been. They sense Sterne quoting the act of
quoting.

Professor Work appears to have missed a point subtler
than the one he has made: we live in a linguistic world consisting of more than original statement and quotations. It contains as well something in between: partial, possible quotations, whose authors (or authors citing other authors) are
sensed but unknown. A great deal of what we know as famous
words has been said precisely by "someone somewhere," and
that is how we use them. Reference books like Bartlett's or
Erasmus's *Adages*, which seek to identify that someone, testify
to the ubiquity of partial, possible quotations.

Whatever we may say can be taken by another, but it is
no less the case that another may turn up to claim our words
as his or hers, unconsciously borrowed. It is given in the na-

ture of language, and still more of literature, that, with our consent or not, words are made from others' words. That is, in fact, what Tristram goes on to say:

> Tell me, ye learned, shall we for ever be adding so much to the *bulk*—so little to the *stock?*
>
> Shall we for ever make new books, as apothecaries make new mixtures, by pouring only out of one vessel into another?
>
> Are we for ever to be twisting, and untwisting the same rope? for ever in the same track—for ever at the same pace?
>
> Shall we be destined to the days of eternity, on holy-days, as well as working-days, to be shewing the *relicks of learning,* as monks do the relicks of their saints—without working one—one single miracle with them?
>
> Who made MAN, with powers which dart from earth to heaven in a moment . . . to go sneaking on at this pitiful—pimping—pettifogging rate?
>
> I scorn to be as abusive as Horace upon the occasion—but if there is no catachresis in the wish, and no sin in it, I wish from my soul, that every imitator in Great Britain, France, and Ireland, had the farcy for his pains. . . . (Sterne, 342–343)

Horace attacks "the servile heard of imitators" who commit catechreses (misuse of words) as they imitate.[8] Tristram is of course imitating the castigation of imitators, but making something inimitable in the process. For that matter, his many similes seem to imitate themselves and yet to be something new, making miracles from relics.

It is not quotations, but quotations quoting quotations, that disturb men.

An Aesthetic of Spontaneity

When such a dynamic of digression and expansion is ongoing, we sense that the work has no final form. Any given edition can be no more than a moment arbitrarily fixed from a process that in principle never concludes. You cannot step into the same edition twice. Every quotation is a sort of bud that may generate more leaves and branches with their own new buds.

Such encyclopedic works advertise their sheer processuality. We are always catching them in the act of remaking themselves. Each achievement imitates and intimates another already under way. In effect, there is nothing but a middle of ever-expanding girth: literature as Falstaff.

Such writing not only displays that it *has* been made by assimilating, it also shows off that it is *still* being made that way. We see material just being absorbed. In many places, the assimilation is incomplete, a lump only partially digested. Burton explains: since I am always pressed for time, and incapable of accomplishing a task that only grows the more is done, I "was therefore enforced, as a bear doth her whelps, to bring forth this confused lump; I had not time to lick it into form, as she doth her young ones, but even so to publish it as it was first written, *quicquid in buccam venit* (whatever came uppermost) in an extemporean style, as I do comply all other exercises, *effudi quicquid dictavit genius meus* (I poured out whatever came into my mind) out of a confused company of notes, and writ with as small deliberation as I do ordinarily speak. . . . *idem calamo quod in mente* (what my mind thinks my pen writes)" (Burton, 31). I had no time, whatever came into my mind, what my mind thinks my pen writes: The *Anatomy* is like life, unrehearsed, and life is like the *Anatomy*, a first draft.

Works of assimilation insist—partly truthfully, partly by convention—that they are published before they can be shaped with the whole in mind. In fact, there is no whole, because a work that by design grows indefinitely and unpredictably can never be whole. A "principle of expandability" governs.[9] To waste time in polishing means to lose that many new inspirations.

As a result, the creative process is caught as it is ongoing. We see lumps half digested, quotes half assimilated, words still resisting their incorporation into the work of another. Half-assimilation easily leads to images that disgust, as in Rabelais, since disgust by its nature reflects a weakening of the shaping power of form. Disgust is evoked above all by the process of decomposition; and works of assimilation seem to compose and decompose at once. The *Anatomy of Melancholy, Tristram Shandy*, and Erasmus's *Adages* are all compositions of decomposition.

We usually see art that has been carefully shaped, but here we see the ongoing act of shaping. These works seem not to have happened, like a story already over, but to be happening now, like a game still being played or an improvisation still in process.

In such works, quotations, like some recently conquered province, seem to protest inclusion in another empire. They have not yet acquiesced to their new status and struggle to regain their former one, like Tibet in China, Estonia in the Soviet Union, or East Timor in Indonesia. Sometimes they seem to be newly liberated but not yet fully separate, like Finland after World War I. They either cling to a precarious independence or seem not quite to belong, but to be on the way to belonging.

The works that contain such half-assimilated quotations depend on and teach an aesthetic of spontaneity. The reader gazes with fascination not at an artifact but at an impatient and imperfect activity.

Stringing

> It could be said of me that in this book I have only made up a bunch of other men's flowers, providing of my own only the string that ties them together.
>
> —*Montaigne (ODQ, 545)*

Because assimilation is unfinished, a composition like Burton's can be appreciated equally well two ways. It works simultaneously as an anthology of other people's utterances complete with editor's encrustations—Bartlett's with commentary—and as a creation in its own right.[10] It is both at once, and Burton has rewarded both kinds of reading.

Like Burton, Montaigne refers frequently to his work as still in the making, as incompletely assimilating the words of others. He writes of his "attempt to match the level of my pilferings" with an art that makes of them something new without ceasing to display them as something old.[11] There are those who "turn up their nose at our borrowed incrustations," but, Montaigne explains, he exhibits them for two opposing reasons: so that readers can use his book as a sort of list of quotations and so that they can see what such a list can be made into (Montaigne, 108).

Whenever the reader wants to read the book as a complete work, some digression, or a mere list of odd words and things, reminds him or her that it is still materials not quite formed, an anthology. A list, it would seem, is not a work, nor even a recipe for a work, but just raw material. On the other hand, should the reader grow content with the separate pieces and delight in randomly heaped gems, the author reminds him or her that sheer listing of quotations is not an end in itself: "I do not speak the minds of others except to speak my own mind better" (Montaigne, 108).

With Montaigne, as with Burton, assimilation and potential infinity lead to an aesthetics of spontaneity. We enjoy not a product but a process. Montaigne insists not only that he writes spontaneously without polishing his "essays"—his "trying-outs"—but also that their own theme of constant mutability indicates why no more structured form is possible. "I aim here only at revealing myself, who will perhaps be different tomorrow, if I learn something new which changes me," as he always does (Montaigne, 109). A self in motion can fix nothing, because before it can do so it has itself changed. Montaigne resembles his work precisely in being always in process, in having older habits not yet reintegrated into a changing self, and in experiencing a mind still populated with language and sentiments felt to be outgrown.

Lists and Crumbs

Anthologies and other encyclopedic reference works are one step from mere lists. They would be unusable without some ordering principle, and so they typically pick an arbitrary method of organization, like the calendar, the alphabet, chronology, or a scale that, like the number line, is infinitely divisible. Tolstoy's anthologies provided quotations for each day of the year. Today, Bartlett's is still arranged by the birth date of the author, with Shakespeare coming before Byron. The *Oxford Dictionary of Quotations* proceeds alphabetically by author. So does the *Yale Book of Quotations,* which also takes its cue from the Oxford by interspersing special sections devoted to specific quotational genres, like "advertising slogans" and (rather vaguely) "sayings." In the *Macmillan Dictionary of Quotations,* author and topic are alphabetized together, so that Margaret Thatcher immediately follows Terrorism. Some anthologies alphabetize topics, while others group topics by association of ideas, so that Sex leads to Marriage and Sin to Death. *The 2,548 Best Things Anybody Ever Said* numbers its entries.[12]

When an author makes a reference work into literature, the arbitrary principle of organization often remains. That is why it is still possible to use such compositions as mere collections. It is also why reading them as literature can prove challenging and interesting.

These authors create by cataloguing, and a catalogue always has room. Burton's *Anatomy* has no maximum size. Whether a library arranges books by topics, author, date of acquisition, or size, it will always be possible to fit in another volume. A literary work so organized could never be a seamless whole or complete structure. It would evidently have been created *so as* to grow. Incompleteness is not just a fact about it, but also an intrinsic part of its aesthetic design. That may also be true of parodic reference works, like Ambrose Bierce's ever-expanding *Devil's Dictionary.*

In effect, all such works make literature from a list, or something close to it. By its very nature, a list is something unformed, a mere heap, an omnium-gatherum, a pile, hodge-podge, medley, mosaic. The shaping impulse either has not been applied to the matter or has not completed its work. Or perhaps whatever principle began to shape the matter has changed many times and become a sort of list itself.

List, lump, and heap are one thing and art another; the encyclopedic literary work somehow lies halfway between the two categories. Its essential paradox lies in making that *half-wayness,* that activity of seeking form, into a special kind of form—a form in formation. One of the most interesting recent anthologies of quotations, *The Chatto Book of Cabbages and Kings,* collects lists in literature, which means it is itself a sort of list of lists. The editor, Francis Spufford, shrewdly observes:

> There is a stage in composition when the elements of the subject that is waiting to be articulated seem to lie higgledy-piggledy . . . it is the stage just before language changes its status by becoming imaginative, ceasing to be a simple denotation for objects and becoming a body in itself with its own self-sufficient rules. It is also a point of divergence. What most often happens next is a struggle for the lacking verbs, with the tools of list-reading applied to a collection of perceptions to discover affinities and contrasts that can then become syntax. Sometimes, however, it can seem appropriate for the original collection of stuffs to remain a collection, as a form of anticipation in itself, equally reshaped by imagination yet with the artistry concealed in a deliberate choice to use the elementary tools of list-reading as the only ones. Crumbs should not be scorned; from time to time they have been made into a very satisfactory banquet in themselves.[13]

A form of anticipation of form, a meal of residues: a banquet of crumbs is a fine simile for an anthology as literature.

Either the author—who is also editor—applies an encyclopedic aesthetic or the reader can become maitre d'hors d'oeuvres.

Readers often extract lines from existing quotation anthologies in order to make their own personal collection. Sometimes they juxtapose quotations so as to create unexpected conversations.[14] In many anthologies, cross-references serve as prompts for doing so.

Dead Quotes

Sometimes anthologies may be seen not as parts of wholes in the making but as remains of wholes fallen to pieces. They may testify not only to composition but also to decomposition.

Quotations may seem, and indeed often are, the mere remnant of magnificent lost originals. After all, the only lines from Heraclitus we have are quotations in other writings. Medieval collections of quotations, like the widely copied Stobaeus, seem to be fragments stored against the ruin.

For that matter, older anthologies can seem like vain attempts to keep no longer familiar quotations in use. Not only the original Bartlett's, or the once popular Putnam's, but even *Magill's Quotations in Context* (originally, 1965) can create this impression. Bartlett's and the Oxford can sell new editions every few years not only because people have said memorable things since the last edition, but also because what is judged familiar or recommended as worthy of familiarity has changed. Like all literary works, quotations are subject to the shifting tastes that make a canon. Where are the quotes of yesteryear?

Quotation anthologies often keep alive bits and pieces of works that would otherwise be forgotten. They sometimes seem to reflect the effort to salvage remnants of masterpieces that live only because of the quotations they have left behind. The halfwayness of works assimilating quotations can therefore produce opposite impressions. It may suggest either creative activity or disintegration.

For Burton and the *Chatto Book,* lists and heaps of words offer opportunities for new dialogues and fresh constructions. And in the more recent *History in Quotations,* we can hardly help setting great lines against each other and allowing historical developments to cast irony on past judgments. Reading it, we find ourselves creating conversations, as if the authors of great lines could meet in the afterworld—which is exactly the premise of such works as Lucian's menippean satire, *The Dialogues of the Dead.* We begin to sense human achievement as a great symposium that overcomes time.

Nikolai Gogol's menippean satire, *Dead Souls,* returns again and again to the ways in which lists and heaps can either invite creativity or testify to ruin. Literally, a "dead soul" was an adult male serf who had actually died but was still legally alive for purposes of taxation. Serf-owners had to pay taxes on them until the next census, which made them negative assets. The hero of the novel, Chichikov, gets the brilliant idea of buying up these legal entities for a song and using them as collateral for a government mortgage. But of course the term "dead soul" also suggested human beings reduced to the level of zombies.

For Chichikov, the list of souls he has bought fires his imagination, as each epithet for a dead serf suggests possible life stories. Yet he cannot help seeing in lists and heaps troubling signs of decay. When he visits the miser Pliushkin, Chichikov discovers stinginess has actually made Pliushkin poorer. That is because he never produces anything but only accumulates what others have discarded and what he should discard. His possessions pile up, and the disordered heap, much like his populous hoard of dead souls, symbolizes the once magnificent property now falling apart. When Chichikov enters the proprietor's house, he sees nothing but piles of long untouched objects.

> The top of a bureau, with a marquetry of mother-of-pearl mosaic, which had already fallen out in pieces and left behind it only yellowish little grooves and depressions filled with crusted glue, was a great and bewildering omnium-gatherum: a mound of scraps of paper, closely covered with writing, pressed down with a paperweight of marble turned green and having an egg-shaped little knob; some sort of ancient tome in a leather binding and with red edges; a lemon, so mummified that it was no bigger than a walnut; a wine glass with some kind of liquid and three dead flies, covered over with a letter; a bit of sealing wax; a bit of rag picked up somewhere; two quills, stained with ink, and as emaciated as if they had consumption; a quill toothpick, perfectly yellowed, which its owner had probably been picking his teeth with before Moscow's invasion by the French. . . . One could by no means have told that a living creature inhabited this room had not an old, worn nightcap, lying on one of the tables, proclaimed the fact.[15]

A mosaic, a composition of parts, is returning to its constituent pieces. The omnium-gatherum of scraps offers no possibilities for future creation. All distinctions are being erased, and Chichikov at first takes Pliushkin for the housekeeper because the master has evidently lost all signs of his sex and social class. He is no longer a man, as he no longer has a living soul.

That mummified lemon on the bureau symbolizes what may happen to culture. One can thoughtfully assemble a miscellany or collection, but it can also accumulate from chance residues of bygone achievements. All museums of historical relics and all anthologies of quotations may come to seem like the mummified acts and words of a past long lost to rot. It is perhaps just such an impression that modern anthologies seek to avoid by including tag lines from *The Simpsons*, advertisements touting soft drinks, or slogans of current political movements.

A collection of verbal or nonverbal fragments may be either a composition or a decomposition because halfway goes either way. Reading composite literature like Burton, Rabelais, or Sterne, one may lose oneself or feel lost, and readers of these works have reacted in both ways.

Auden and Kronenberger

If we survey literary history, we will see a dynamic in which "compilations that are published as compilations," as Montaigne calls them, beget new works. Their progeny include both new compilations made from the old and encyclopedic literature flaunting its origin in mere compilations.

Encyclopedic literature returns the favor by supplying material for new compilations. It becomes a source for the quotations it has collected and for the memorable observations on them it has added. Burton supplies many of both. Anthologies rely on him for lines and for what Burton says about them, in much the way that they take both from Diogenes Laertius's ancient biographies of philosophers. Sterne, as we have seen, quotes Burton and Burton's quotations, while providing Shandyisms for collections to come.

Even works that profess to be no more than compilations may lie somewhere between impersonal reference books and literary self-display. A book can lie closer to one end of the continuum or the other. A compilation if there ever was one, Erasmus's *Adages* nevertheless rewards reading not only as a reference work but also as a display of Erasmus's wit, especially in the lengthy essays later extracted for separate publication. W. H. Auden and Louis Kronenberger edited the *Viking Book of Aphorisms: A Personal Selection* as just that: it is so "personal" (or rather, doubly personal) that it constitutes a statement of its own. It is simultaneously a *co-edited* reference work and a *coauthored* work of literature.

The title page of this volume uses neither "editor" nor "author." It simply reads: "A Personal Selection by W. H. Auden and Louis Kronenberger." To be sure, the word "by" standing alone more likely suggests authorship, since one usually needs to say "edited by" to indicate editorship but not "authored by" to indicate authorship. Nevertheless, a work called by the formula "Publisher's Book of X"—in this case, *Viking Book of Aphorisms*—tends to indicate a reference work rather than an individual literary creation. Then again, reference works typically claim objectivity and so do not describe themselves as personal.

In short, signs point in different directions. This book seems to enjoy its ambiguous classification, dual citizenship, and congenital in-betweenness. It is not quite a canonical work of Auden's. But it is too idiosyncratic a reference book to have survived as long as it has without that "not quite." "Not quite," like "just possibly," is itself a special status.

In their introduction, Auden and Kronenberger instruct: "Aphorisms are essentially an aristocratic genre of writing. The aphorist does not argue or explain, he asserts; and implicit in his assertion is a conviction that he is wiser or more intelligent than his readers. For this reason the aphorist who adopts a folksy style with 'democratic' diction and grammar is a cowardly and insufferable hypocrite" (VBA, vii–viii). There is nothing democratic about this passage, which neither argues nor explains but simply asserts. The authors treat their taste as a moral, as well as aesthetic, standard. One either accepts their judgment or condemns oneself.

To read this anthology as offered is to credit the editors' superior wisdom. Should one fail to see the profundity of a given aphorism or to understand why a sequence of selections is ordered as it is, one must try again. If that does not help, one can only regret a deficient sensibility. If Auden and Kronenberger have correctly characterized the aphorism, then their book as a whole is aphoristic. The aristocratic tone of the particular entries informs the entirety.

The *Viking Book of Aphorisms* displays another characteristic of collections that disdain to be mere collections. As idiosyncratic and personal, they offer minimal documentation. It is as if providing verifiable sources, naming the works from which quotations are drawn, or even giving authors' birth and death dates were beneath the notice of aristocrats and artists educated enough to work from memory. "Les references? Nos valets les feront pour nous." With such a sensibility guiding work, even lapses in accuracy, should there be any, are bound to be improvements. When Auden quotes Howell, Halifax, or Hoffer, surely any emendation redounds to their glory.

As Hesketh Pearson observed, "Misquotation is, in fact, the pride and privilege of the learned. A widely-read man never quotes accurately, for the rather obvious reason that he has read too widely."[16] I have seen highly literate Russians, who recite lengthy poems from memory, deliberately insert a mistake, just to indicate that they have not bothered to check a source, as the less literate would. Some errors indicate ignorance, others superior knowledge.

Pride in tasteful lapses, or in errors superior to mere correctness, does not characterize the editors of Bartlett's or the Oxford. The name "Yale University Press" is supposed to suggest reliability. Anthologies sold as authoritative erase signs of editorial idiosyncrasy. They boast of meticulous research and feature careful documentation. One reason Justin Kaplan was so criticized for his edition of Bartlett's is that, as he admitted, he let his personal prejudices (especially political ones) affect his choice of "familiar quotations": he deliberately left out those that were well known but by his lights should not have been. Mr. Gorbachev, tear down this quote. Reviewers pointed out that such an exercise of prejudice marks a personal selection, not an authoritative reference work. After all, this is not *Kaplan's Familiar Quotations* but *Bartlett's Familiar Quotations,* and Bartlett, like Webster and Roget, has become a trade name indicating authoritative, impersonal reliability.

If the name on the title page is Auden, we look for something it takes Auden to do. But if we buy a Bartlett's that acts as if it were Auden's when it is only Kaplan's, we are victims of quote and switch.

A reference volume typically lists credentialed experts so as to emphasize its impersonality and unimpeachable scholarly reliability. The less subjective it appears, the greater authority it can claim. Its editor can be expected to inform readers how many scholars have examined how many primary sources and earlier anthologies. Even the acknowledgments not only thank others for help but also implicitly boast of yet more verifiers. The most recent anthologies also advise that the Internet has allowed for unprecedented accuracy, but claims of unprecedented accuracy, we soon recognize, are themselves a formula. Benham boasted of his "twenty years of continuous research"—did he never take a break?—for his 1926 edition of Putnam's (PCBQ, v).

In Benham, we may discover not only the author and work, but also the chapter or part of the work, from which a quotation is drawn. By contrast, Auden and Kronenberger attribute an aphorism simply to "Halifax" or "Connolly." (Surely those names are as familiar as Milton or Lincoln?) A first name is rarely provided; when it is, we are not told why this case is different. Why does one quote belong to "Chazal" but another to "Simone Weil"? You ought to know why, and if you don't, the editors cannot be bothered to explain. If anything, the omission of names and dates seems part of a strategy to make checking difficult, as if the truly educated are their own reference works and the entries are meant to serve as mere reminders. Or is it that in an anthology of aphorisms even the references should be aphoristically brief?

Reference works usually include an index, or several indices of different sorts, to help the reader locate quotations, but Auden and Kronenberger provide instead "An Informal Key-Word Index" by Edwin Kennebeck. "Informal," of course: a personal selection demands a personal index. This one contains an introductory note explaining—in a tone we now expect—that "it is not a complete concordance. It is intended not so much to help the reader track down a particular aphorism he has seen or heard before as to help him find an appropriate thought for a given occasion, mood, or purpose" (VBA, 410). Even this help follows no editorial rules: "Those who find the listings too imprecise are respectfully referred to Dr. Johnson's remark about dictionaries (page 288)," which, when consulted, reads: "Dictionaries are like watches; the worst is better than none, and the best cannot be expected to go quite right." That criterion—better than none—allows a lot of leeway. Yet one might expect a good deal more effort before someone invokes Samuel Johnson.

Taken together, all these personal, aristocratic, unscholarly assertions and practices make it hard not to hear each aphorism as doubly authored, first by the speaker whose last name follows the quotation and then by the editors, more generously identified as "W. H." Auden and "Louis" Kronenberger.

This work deliberately situates itself somewhere between dictionary and "anatomy," between mere reference and independent creation.

Commonplace and Composition

Auden and Kronenberger found another way to personalize quotations: under Viking Press's William Cole imprint, each author published a commonplace book. A commonplace book, as those in the know know, is a sort of informal, personal anthology. It collects "commonplaces" (in the original sense of "passages"): quotations, aphorisms, poems or parts of poems, newspaper stories, overheard conversation, and anecdotes. Recorded over a long period of time, these entries appear in the haphazard order in which they came to the author's attention. The OED offers a quotation from 1578: "A studious young man . . . may gather to himselfe good furniture both of words and approved phrases . . . and to make to his use as it were a

common place book." Cole describes his version of the form as
"an annotated personal anthology." The annotations guide
readers through the author's associations of ideas provoked by
what he hears or reads, what "the passages have led *him* to
think about" (jacket back of Kronenberger's volume). In principle, the citations can be about anything. Thus Kronenberger
titles his commonplace book *Animal, Vegetable, Mineral.*

Like diaries, commonplace books are a private form, but,
also like diaries, they can be made public. In that case, they
resemble other literary genres that imitate communication
with oneself, such as some types of lyric poetry and that pecu-
liarly Russian form called "notes."[17] A published commonplace
book commands, or is expected to command, interest apart
from any possible use as a reference work, much as a published
diary may serve not only as a biographical document but also
as an exemplary record of self-exploration.

As literariness may be either imposed or designed, so
private forms may be made public by a later editor as well as
by the author. When literariness is conferred by another,
the reader becomes a sort of voyeur, as we necessarily are
when reading Anne Frank's diary. Just as eavesdroppers believe more readily what they think they were not meant to
hear, so voyeurism may transform what one sees. *The Diary of
Samuel Pepys* (1660–1669, not published until 1825) is all the
more interesting as literature precisely because it was not intended to be literature. On the contrary, Pepys did everything
he could think of to keep his record of indiscretions secret,
even writing in a cipher it took more than a century to decode.
Special poignancy therefore attaches to the diary's end, in
which Pepys confides to himself that his near blindness makes
continuation impossible. To continue, he would have to dic-
tate his secrets to an amanuensis, and then they would no longer be secret.

The book as we have it concludes: "And so I betake myself to that course [of life I must follow], which is almost as much to see myself go into the grave; for which, and all the discomforts that will accompany my being blind, the good God prepare me!"[18] In writing this conclusion, Pepys did not know if it was the very last entry or if he might just continue by adding the occasional note while he was still able; but we can see, by the blankness that follows, that he did not. We are left to wonder whether the self-knowledge he accumulated did indeed prepare this active man for dependence. And so this book, which was intended to continue as long as the author had energy to continue his adventures, displays strong closure in spite of itself. The ending moves readers all the more because the author never intended it as an ending and never meant to have readers at all. The nineteenth-century editor transformed an intensely private record into one of the classics of English literature.

With commonplace books, as with diaries, publication may be part of the design, or it can turn the reader into a receiver of stolen goods. Dostoevsky's *Diary* was designed to be published and Pepys's to be absolutely private. Sometimes, however, diaries and commonplace books begin halfway between private and public. For example, an author may compose with the thought that the work just *might* someday be published. Or one can intend that a work be published "against one's will" and enjoy in advance the posthumous regard it may receive.

E. M. Forster's commonplace book continued one begun by someone else in a large leather-bound tome Foster inherited along with a house. He intended his continuation to remain as private as the beginning he had stumbled upon. And how private is that? Forster kept this set of quotations and observations for four decades, but, as he doubtless knew was possible, the book was discovered, just as he had himself discovered the book of another. A scholar adapted it for publication after Forster's death. It is not easy to determine whether this book welcomes its readers.[19]

When an editor publishes a private diary or commonplace book, readers witness, or imagine they witness, genuine spontaneity insofar as they assume that literariness has been imposed. By contrast, when an author designs a work that strategically takes the form of a diary or commonplace book, spontaneity is merely imitated. The original features of the form have now become conventions to be exploited. A diary (or commonplace book or any other originally private form) written so as to be published is as much a literary effort as an epistolary novel. Such "diaries" follow the logic of a stage whisper.

Literary works in the form of anthologies may imitate various private forms of collected material just as they may imitate impersonal reference works. Some authors exploit both possibilities at once.

For the editors/authors of the *Viking Book of Aphorisms,* the opportunity to compose and publish a commonplace book offered yet another way to make literature out of quotations. In such cases, they knew, one speaks by presenting what one hears. There is style, but at one remove. In a published commonplace book with very few words of his own, Auden allows us to sense how he perceives experience in his own distinct way. Appropriately enough, he called the book *A Certain World.*

Auden explains that the biography of a writer, whether written by others or by himself, "is usually in bad taste"; and so a writer can properly be revealed, or reveal himself, only indirectly. Paradoxically, he can speak most personally through the words of others. "This compilation is a sort of autobiography," he explains, all the more so because he has kept even annotations to a minimum and let others speak for him. Or rather, he speaks through them. The result is a "map of my planet." A map, unlike a drawing or photograph, does not look like a landscape, but indirectly conveys a sense of it. Maps require a key, as photographs do not, and though they conceal some features, they may reveal others all the better for the indirection.[20]

Reading as Roaming

Kronenberger's *Animal, Vegetable, Mineral* opens: "Let me begin by saying that this book lacks one of the essentials of a commonplace book, since it has for the most part been compiled, not accumulated [over many years]; and envisioned in print, not copied out with a pen" (AVM, xi). Rather than a conventional commonplace book, then, Kronenberger explicitly offers a literary work in the form of a commonplace book. The author experiments with making literature by "assembling" (AVM, xii). The book's privacy is staged, and its passages have been selected not as personal discoveries but as guides to a specific kind of reading—the reading we do when confronting well-thought anthologies. "There are people, to be sure, who dislike anthologies. . . . But as against high priggishness in one reader, there are dozens of readers who like to spend half an hour roaming through, or revisiting books like these; it is people at the opposite pole, people who having started a book feel compelled, however bored, to finish it, that I have never quite understood" (AVM, xv).

Reading as roaming: that is the distinctive characteristic of anthologies, whether as reference books or as literature. They allow, invite, or even demand haphazard, rather than sequential or guided, consumption. No one reads Bartlett's from beginning to end, nor is there any incentive to do so. In a good anthology, as the editor of *The 2,548 Best Things Anybody Ever Said* explains on the first page of the introduction, "you should be able to open the book to any page, and be glad that you did." One can easily read Erasmus and Burton in just this way, and Montaigne tends in the same direction. Haphazard reading is just what Kronenberger means his anthology-made-literature to preserve: "A commonplace book, unlike a novel or play, permits—indeed, all but requires—your opening it anywhere" (AVM, xiv). The result of opening a book "anywhere" and continuing at random, or perhaps by mere association, is a special kind of "exploratory zest" (AVM, xii).

In works of this sort, the author creates not a specific experience but the possibility of an indefinitely large number of experiences that could not be imagined in advance. This combination of authorial guidance and readerly freedom constitutes the special appeal of any kind of anthology made into literature. The experience of consulting a nonliterary anthology, which is a necessary consequence of the kind of reference work it is, here becomes the very point of the composition.

The artful anthology, the formless heap that displays the potential for many forms, the list made so that its very listiness is intriguing: writers, if not critics, have proven well aware of what we might call *listerature*.

Tolstoy Quoting Tolstoy

In the later years of his long life, Tolstoy, long an obsessive note-taker and notebook keeper, hit upon his own way to make literature from an anthology of quotations. By this point, he had already turned his diary, once genuinely private, into a work to be published some day "against his will."

Tolstoy once boasted that Russian literature, more than any other, seeks out or invents unusual literary forms: "From Gogol's *Dead Souls* to Dostoevsky's *Dead House,* in the recent period of Russian literature there is not a single work of artistic prose, at all rising above mediocrity, that quite fits the form of a novel, a poem, or a story."[21] That is why Tolstoy stressed all the ways in which *War and Peace,* which has come to be thought of the world's greatest "novel," does *not* resemble a novel. He insisted on calling it instead a "book." He was always on the lookout to create unusual "books."

Tolstoy loved to copy out quotations and to invent quotable lines for his fiction, so it is hardly surprising that he, too, hit upon the idea of making an anthology of quotations into literature. If not unprecedented, the form was at least odd. Since he was also concerned after his religious conversion to present himself as a great moral teacher, he readily recognized that a collection of sayings—by others and by himself—might serve that purpose, too. He certainly had in mind as models the biblical books of Proverbs and Ecclesiastes, as well as the *Tao Te-Ching* and other highly quotable non-European books of wisdom.

As early as 1884, his diaries record the idea of creating "a circle of reading for myself: Epictetus, Marcus Aurelius, Lao-Tzu, Buddha, Pascal, The New Testament. This is necessary for all people" (PSS, 39:xxii). Within a sentence something ostensibly created "for myself" has become a work that could be read, indeed that must be read, by all. This envisioned collection first appeared in 1904, was expanded considerably in more editions until 1910 (when Tolstoy died), and changed its name several times in the process: from *A Wise Thought for Every Day* to *A Calendar of Wisdom* to *Wise Thoughts by Many Writers on Truth, Life, and Behavior Collected and Arranged for Every Day of the Year by Leo Tolstoy* to *The Way of Life*. There were also three different subtitles. Editions expanded and reorganized earlier editions. At one point, Tolstoy added not only eight hundred of his own thoughts but also a short story for every week of the year. Two hefty volumes of his collected works are devoted to his largest collection, *A Circle of Reading*.[22]

It would be hard to imagine an anthology more overshadowed by its "editor" than Tolstoy's. To begin with, each day's quotations (occupying about a page) feature one by Tolstoy himself in italics stating the day's main theme; they usually contain other sayings by Tolstoy; and at times they offer none by anyone else! Imagine *Bartlett's Quotations from Bartlett and Others, Required Reading for All Persons*. Even the quotations not by Tolstoy are usually coauthored, as Tolstoy explains in his preface:

> When I translated thoughts by German, French, or Italian thinkers, I did not strictly follow the original, usually making it shorter and easier to understand, and omitting some words. Readers might tell me that a quote is not then Pascal or Rousseau, but my own work; but I think there is nothing wrong in conveying their thoughts in a modified form. Therefore, if someone desires to translate this book into other languages, I would like to advise them not to look for the original quotes from the English poet Coleridge, say, or the German philosopher Kant, or the French writer Rousseau, but to trans-

late directly from my writing. Another reason some
of these thoughts may not correspond to the originals is at times I took a thought from a lengthy and
convoluted argument, and I had to change some
words and phrases for clarity and unity of expression. In some cases I even express the thought entirely in my own words.[23]

Assimilation and the imprint of the editor's personality could
hardly go further. We may regret that Auden and Kronenberger do not identify sources, but at least we may *hope* to find
them. But if an author entirely rewrites a selection, what good
would it even do to know its "source"?

Tolstoy has here foregrounded and taken to an extreme a
fact about all quotations: they reflect the quoter as well as the
original author. It is always possible to hear, however faintly,
the quoter's voice in words he or she has merely chosen.
Quotes are always, if minimally, coauthored. Tolstoy makes
them almost entirely his own.

To state the possibilities more generally: we can discern
a continuum from minimal to maximal personal imprint of
any quoter. Reference works seek to minimize this imprint.
They do so by employing multiple consultants, by instructing
each editor to build on predecessors, or by choosing arbitrary
principles of organization that render the search for the editor's voice difficult. By now, it would be utterly pointless to
divine John Bartlett's personality from the contents of the sixteenth edition of Bartlett's. Like Heinz, Bartlett is no longer a
person, just a brand. At the other end of the continuum is Tolstoy; and in between, however one chooses to place them, are
Erasmus, Forster, and Kronenberger and Auden.

One may also arrange anthologies of quotations along a

scale of increasing literariness. It extends from the impersonal reference work to a literary work made mostly from the words of others. At every point on this continuum there have been examples long before the present era. At one extreme we have the Oxford, Macmillan, and Yale dictionaries, and at the other Tolstoy's *Circle* and Burton's *Anatomy.* At various points in between we may discover Erasmus's *Adages,* Auden's *A Certain World,* and various other works to which we now turn.

We turn as well to the more general questions raised by such oddities. How separable can parts be from the whole that contains them?

XII
Whole and Part

What is "Literature"?

In the dying world I come from quotation is a national vice. No one would think of making an after-dinner speech without the help of poetry. It used to be classics, now it's lyric verse.

—*Evelyn Waugh (WoW, 298)*

He wrapped himself in quotations—as a beggar would enfold himself in the purple of emperors.

—*Rudyard Kipling (ODLQ, 237)*

When we speak of "literature," we usually think first of great epics, dramas, and novels, not proverbs, witticisms, and sayings. No survey of literature would be complete without considering works like the *Aeneid, Hamlet,* and *Anna Karenina,* but almost no one includes the ripostes of Samuel Johnson or the aphorisms of Pascal. Why should that be so?

From antiquity to the present, and from the Delphic oracle to the *Analects* of Confucius, numerous cultures have placed the shortest works, especially wise sayings, at the center of their canon. The biblical book of Proverbs begins by summoning us "to receive the instructions of wisdom. . . . To understand a proverb, and the interpretation; the words of the wise, and their dark sayings" (Proverbs 1:2–6). Great writers have expended considerable effort on short works, and some, like Mark Twain, Benjamin Franklin, and Oscar Wilde, are known as much for their quotations as for their longer masterpieces. Others, like La Rochefoucauld or Lichtenberg, are known for nothing else.

Quotations also play a key role in longer works. Sacred genres cite Scripture, lives repeat memorable words, and poems both quote and supply quotable lines. Pushkin and George Eliot not only loved to use quotations as chapter epigraphs, but also made up supposed quotations for that purpose. Great novelists wove maxims and aphorisms into the texture of their prose. I would venture that at least as many people know the aphoristic first line of *Pride and Prejudice* or *Anna Karenina* as have read the whole work. And yet, although quotations fascinate almost everyone, shape our language, inspire our thought, and supply key elements to longer literary works, we forget their very existence as literature.

Somehow, short works do not quite seem like the real thing. One reason, perhaps, is that for many well-read people, they no longer feel like "works" at all, just the residue of works or mere parts that have somehow seceded from the whole. They easily strike us as illegitimate short-cuts to education, as if people took too far Churchill's advice that "it's a good thing for an uneducated man to read books of quotations" (YBQ, 152). People who do not bother to read Shakespeare or Milton might still memorize lines from Bartlett's, which serves as a

sort of *Idiot's Guide to Literacy.* Euphonious phrases extracted
to stand in for masterpieces become the ultimate abridgment.
That view of quotations is presumably what A. E. Housman
had in mind when he cautioned his publisher: "You must not
treat my immortal works as quarries to be used at will by the
various hacks whom you may employ to compile anthologies"
(ODLQ, 237).

We have all witnessed great writers reduced to banality
when quoted by politicians, in the newspaper, or on Celestial
Seasonings boxes. A Jane Austen line suffused with irony becomes a sentimental platitude. We might assent to Hannah
Moore's account of such quoting: "He liked those literary
cooks, / Who skim the cream of others' books; / And ruin half
an author's graces / By plucking bon-mots from their places"
(ODLQ, 237). I draw this line, out of context, from an anthology to draw attention to a curious contradiction. Even in
pointing to the misuse of quotations, we use them. As we gossip about gossipers, and expatiate against prolixity, we seem
unable to resist the muse of quotations.

We all know many quotations and love repeating our
favorites, but we nevertheless turn to anthologies with a sort
of guilty pleasure. The way we speak of quotations does not
match our actual appreciation of them.

Quotation as Education

Many Renaissance humanists saw matters differently. For them,
quotations comprised an essential part of education. Erasmus
saw his amazingly popular anthology as fulfilling the most important purposes of literature, guiding the use of language and
conveying valuable lessons. Quotations distilled, and reading
them instilled, wisdom.

Used properly, an exemplary collection of quotations,

such as Erasmus sought to compile, would teach how good thinking and apt expression invigorate each other.[1] Later critics notwithstanding, it was not sheer pedantry or blind reverence for antiquity that shaped humanist learning. Rather, it was the conviction that clear ideas require clear writing, so mastering one meant mastering the other. As the greatest anthologizers have understood, true literacy involves more than the simple ability to process printed words. It also requires skill at grasping the profundities they convey and the way they do so. It is hard to imagine Erasmus spending so many decades on his work unless he had attached great importance to its power to shape the mind.[2]

Erasmus recommended his *Adages* as a compendium of insights not only from great authors but also from anonymous, ordinary people. He was neither the first nor the last to approach common sayings as expressions of primitive philosophy, derived from the worthiest reflections on shared, everyday experience. From trial and error come proverb and maxim.

At the same time, Erasmus explains, knowledge of sayings also contributes to mastery of Latin language and style: "When I considered the important contribution made to elegance and richness of style by brilliant aphorisms, apt metaphors, proverbs, and similar figures of speech, I made up my mind to collect the largest possible supply of such things from approved authors of every sort and arrange them each in its appropriate class, to make them more accessible to those who wish to practice composition with a view to securing a rich and ready diction" (AE, 11). Erasmus's collection exercised immense influence right through the eighteenth century, that is, about as long as a knowledge of the classics was considered essential to education. His anthology set a standard for Latin. Beyond Latin, it shaped educated use of vernacular languages. To know English required learning, if not Latin, then much of what study of Latin could teach. Translations of Erasmus therefore circulated throughout Europe, and his collection influenced style not only in Latin, but also in English, French, his native Dutch, and other European languages.

Almost immediately, the *Adages* was adapted and readapted, "rather in the way that Webster's dictionary has undergone constant rebirths long after Noah Webster died in the mid-nineteenth century" (EA, xxii). Epitomes shortened Erasmus's work by leaving out not only particular sayings but also the essays he often appended in explanation of them. On the other hand, some later editors expanded the work. A putative edition of 1574 really collects several collections of proverbs, while adding thousands of sayings assembled by others. By the end of the sixteenth century, Erasmus would not have recognized works that were still called Erasmus's Adages.

The process of adaptation occurred in numerous languages and for various audiences. In England, Richard Taverner translated and radically abridged the *Adages* for two editions (1539 and 1549). His cuttings were so extensive that one scholar referred to the book as having been "turkissed"— mangled (AE, xxxvii). When schoolboys studied Greek and Latin, they often encountered the *Adages,* and commonplace books frequently contained numerous selections from the collection. Latin-English dictionaries relied on it. It would appear that many English proverbs and sayings can be traced to Erasmus, whose work therefore shaped the English language in significant ways.

The existence of numerous anthologies of quotations across Europe should suggest that Erasmus, though the most famous collector, was far from the only one. Although he laid claim to the title of first humanist collector, he had eventually to admit that he was preceded by Polydore Vergil, who, two years before Erasmus's first edition, published his *Little Book of Proverbs*. In fact, neither originated the idea. Both relied on models from classical or medieval Greek collections by Johannes Stobaeus, Diogenianus, Zenobius, and Suidas and, closer to their own time, a collection of sententiae by Michael Apostolius.

Evidently, lines could be as valuable as, or more valuable than, the texts from which they were drawn.

The Aesthetic of Separation

One might almost say that Renaissance literature and thought were *about* quotation. Writers wondered whether true knowledge concerned, first and foremost, citing appropriate authorities or creating something better. Are we mere dwarves on the shoulders of giants, or do we see farther than our predecessors on whose shoulders we stand? The famous saying expressed both lessons.

Thinkers also wondered whether it was even possible to quote something from a different time and culture without significantly altering it. Culture changes; each period has its language and style, and so the very same words transposed across centuries could prove entirely different. The more things stay the same, the more they change. The Italian humanist Pietro Aretino observed that repeating old expressions can be as absurd as appearing in the costume of another era. The same clothes and words may be sensible in one era and senseless in another. The problem of quotation was intertwined with that of anachronism, the sense that periods could be radically different.[3]

Scholars have noted that the love of quotations in the humanist period corresponded not only to ideas about knowledge but also to a particular aesthetic. Humanists typically kept their own commonplace books and, as we say today, read for lines. The practice often accompanied an *aesthetic of parts.* Students of literature today are taught that to understand a work properly one must read it as a whole. For us, it is a truism that parts do not "mean directly," but as components of a structure. Every student learns that analyzing a section of a work as if it were itself a complete work risks radically misreading it. One might easily ascribe the opinions of a character or an "unreliable narrator" to the author. Or one might overlook the context shaping a passage's meaning. Irony, so inherently fragile, is particularly vulnerable to quotation. If so, then anthologies are inherently dangerous.

One can trace to Aristotle the view that parts properly have meaning only in relation to the whole. Today it unites many otherwise dissimilar kinds of critical theory, from formalism and structuralism to deconstruction, psychoanalysis, and the hyphenated hybrids they have generated. It hardly matters whether we attribute the whole to conscious intention, unconscious wishes, or social forces acting through the writer. Whatever the source of the whole, the part is properly mediated through it. We therefore often overlook that a quite different sense of reading is possible: sometimes the whole, though significant in itself, is nevertheless also—or perhaps even primarily—a container of parts that can stand on their own.

Rebecca Bushnell refers to an early sixteenth-century "disintegrative approach" to reading. A humanist who read this way "addressed the parts in great detail but was little concerned with seeing them as a whole. The point of reading a book was not to provide an 'anatomy' or understanding of its argument or structure; rather the end was a harvesting or mining of the book for its functional parts."[4] Reading was sorting, while quotations were the tangible results of a quest for wisdom. It was commonly said that one discovered great lines in works the way one gathered fruit in a forest. Erasmus regarded commonplace books as "treasuries" of specific jewels. Jewels, it must not be forgotten, are valuable on their own, not only as parts of a larger ornament.

One could literally decorate one's house with these verbal jewels. Erasmus suggested that one "should inscribe apophthegms, proverbs, and sententiae at the front and back of books, and engrave them on rings and cups, and paint them on doors and walls and even on window glass" (Bushnell, 133–134). Marsilio Ficino had quotations painted on the walls of his study, and Montaigne had fifty-seven maxims painted on the beam of his library. Hanging above him were the words of Sextus Empiricus about suspending judgment. These humanists literally lived among quotations; their home was their Bartlett's. More portable was the medal Montaigne had struck: on one side was his motto—*Que sais-je?* (What do I know?)—and on the other a visual representation of it, a pair of scales in suspense.[5]

"Harvesting" served as a common metaphor for such reading. One harvests the best parts and discards the rest, separating wheat from chaff. The metaphor suggests that *subtraction can improve,* that what we think of as the whole of a work may be little more than an earlier stage of the harvest requiring further labor. Erasmus and others used the same commonplace of the bee that we have already seen in Burton. The good reader, writes Erasmus, "flies about like a diligent bee through the whole garden of authors, where he would fall on every little flower, collecting a bit of nectar from each to carry to his hive" (cited in Bushnell, 135–136).

As Montaigne explained, one must harvest so as to assimilate, just as the bees do. "The bees plunder the flowers here and there, but afterward they make of them honey, which is all theirs; it is no longer thyme or marjoram. Even so with the pieces borrowed from others; he [the student who learns quotations] will transform and blend them to make a work that is all his own."[6] Unless one can, like a bee, take only what one needs, one cannot make anything one's own.

Far from being antithetical to borrowing, personality depends on it. Montaigne could not have disagreed more with those who regard quotation as a failure of originality and a surrender of individuality. The anthology *Words on Words* cites numerous thinkers who warn us not to quote others but to be ourselves: "Some for renown on scraps of learning doat, / And think they grow immortal as they *quote*" (Edward Young); "Don't quote Latin; say what you have to say and sit down" (Arthur Wellesley, Duke of Wellington); "He who has his head filled with other people's words will find no place where he may put his own" (Moorish proverb) (WoW, 208). Montaigne would have been much more sympathetic to twentieth-century Russian psychologists Lev Vygotsky and Mikhail Bakhtin, who saw the formation of selfhood as analogous to absorbing quotations so the expression changes to adapt to its new context. We form a self by assimilating the words of others until they become not externally demanding but "innerly persuasive." Still later, they may be gradually outgrown and then discarded as only *formerly* persuasive. This activity never ceases. "The relation of thought to [quoted] word," Vygotsky explained, "is not a thing but a process, a continual movement back and forth from thought to word and from word to thought."[7]

In the view of Montaigne and other Renaissance humanists, books resemble nature, which provides food to be collected: we do not consume an entire book any more than we eat everything in a cultivated field. It is not surprising, then, that gardening was a common metaphor for reading. In the early sixteenth century, the aesthetic of the garden was opposed to the aesthetic of the body. The body lives as a whole and cannot be dismembered, but the garden (in this conception) consists of a series of separate visual experiences. Skillfully planted, a garden draws the visitor's eye to the best parts rather than to any design of a whole. The good garden, like the good book, was "seen as brimming with remarkable, beautiful, or unusual stuff ready to be admired, plucked out, and used" (Bushnell, 138).[8]

Literary critics have lost this aesthetic of separability, which applies in varying degrees to many classics of the Western tradition. Which way of reading—as a total design or as an artful collection of separable parts—more accords with the spirit not only of Burton but also of Byron's *Don Juan* or the work of Rabelais? Even the supremely classical Pope explicitly states in the preface to his *Essay on Man* that he means his poem to be read with the purpose of extracting memorable lines and couplets. That is why the essay is in rhyme: "the principles, maxims, or precepts so written, both strike the reader more strongly at first, and are more easily retained by him afterwards."[9]

Pope has made the *Essay on Man* both a whole work and a collection of memorable passages that should themselves be read as whole works. To insist on only an integral reading is to mistake the author's intention and the nature of the poem. The very design of the *Essay on Man* demands that readers not just appreciate it as a whole artifact but also take it apart for its best lines. In this case, to dissect is to enliven.

Browsing

When an aesthetic of separability governs, it is sometimes hard to ascertain whether an extended text is a complete work at all. Valerius Maximus's first-century *Memorable Deeds and Sayings* proved immensely popular in the Middle Ages and Renaissance, and more copies of it survive than of any other prose work. But is it a single work? As its title suggests, it lends itself to excerpting, although it is also more or less readable as a whole. It was abridged in various ways and is perhaps best seen not as an integral whole but as a source for works. Is Plutarch's *Lives* a single work? It has one title, but the particular lives are usually read separately, or at times, in pairs ("The Lives of Demosthenes and Cicero Compared"). Diogenes Laertius's *Lives of the Philosophers* reads as a combination of separable biographies, while each biography reads in turn like a combination of separable anecdotes. These anecdotes, which have circulated freely on their own, typically set up an aphorism that has come to stand as a separate quotation.

In fact, quotations and anecdotes resemble each other in encouraging separability. An anecdote, after all, is a sort of quoted event. One may identify a distinct type of separable work—such as Diogenes Laertius's—that is typically and most easily read as a stringing together of anecdotes or lines.

Our theories notwithstanding, we in practice indulge an aesthetic of separability. Few feel compelled to insist that one must not read individual books of the Bible apart from the whole or individual psalms apart from the Books of Psalms.

No one squirms at a discussion of one of Shakespeare's sonnets. Without dismay we encounter Pascal's *Pensées* and the *Maxims* of La Rochefoucauld in editions that place their lines in different orders. We do not usually read these books through; we open them at random and read haphazardly.

In fact, one sign that an aesthetic of separability governs is this feeling that we are invited to read in any order, to thumb through, to *browse*. We are encouraged to introduce an element of randomness—of "exploratory zeal"—into our reading. Works of this sort necessarily lack closure: a book of quotations has a last page but no ending that completes a design. The encyclopedic impulse favors not only endless expansion but also separability.

Processuality

Some, but not all, separable works are what I like to think of as *processual*. Think of the two groups as overlapping ellipses in a Venn diagram. Separable works may or may not be processual. Processual works include some that are separable and others that might be called "continuable."

Whether separable or continuable, processual works are those that in principle can never be complete. By their very nature, they are always being made and must always be read as in process. Any stopping point or available text is dictated by some external contingency, like the author's death.

Works that are separable as well as processual—typically encyclopedic ones like Burton's—are designed to accrete *anywhere*. They grow from the end or from the middle, and specific parts expand. There are buds everywhere. They usually assume some sort of encyclopedic form that, like a dictionary, can add entries at any point. By contrast, continuable processual works are typically narrative: they tell a story that, like history, can always be continued, but only by explaining what happened next. They grow from the end, as new incidents are added. Tolstoy explicitly described *War and Peace,* which was serialized, as capable of indefinite expansion. It would always be possible to add another installment and a new set of incidents. The same is true of *Tristram Shandy,* and *Don Juan.* There is no possibility of an ending, only a temporary stopping point.

Continuable works are not made as collections of parts; they are made to be intrinsically partial. Let them be ever so long—as long as *War and Peace*—and the author can always add more.

Separable processual works are designed to grow anywhere. Even if short, like *The Devil's Dictionary,* they lend themselves to disassembly. Continuable processual works are also necessarily incomplete, but in a different way. They lend themselves not to being taken apart, but to being taken as *a* part.

Both types of processual works insist on being read as arbitrary pieces from some indefinitely large extension.

Passing on Wisdom

An aesthetic of separability reflects the very nature of quotations. Quotations pass on wisdom, convey values, and define situations. We learn our culture through them. So that they can be preserved, they are often collected, but in a form easily taken apart, so they can be used.

Today we have works like the Oxford and Bartlett's. Renaissance readers knew Erasmus and commonplace books. In the Middle Ages, collections called florilegia circulated. Classical anthologies of quotations (Stobaeus) and sets of lives presented memorable deeds and sayings. As we have seen, collections of quotations go back still further. The Book of Proverbs compiles compilations from diverse sources.

If one pauses to consider societies in which writing has not yet appeared or is limited to a few people, it becomes evident why quotations should be so important in passing on wisdom. It also becomes clear why sages should have been regarded as formulators not of complex arguments but of aphorisms or gnomic sayings. "Nothing to excess" not only imparts wisdom but also describes its own way of imparting it. Even in a highly literate culture, a great deal of what we need to know is learned through commonly repeated rules or maxims (put yourself in his place, look both ways, there's no free lunch, nobody ever washed a rental car, there but for the grace of God go I). We all know endless proverbs, reminders, sayings, and rules of thumb without quite knowing we know them. Written quotations add to the stock of spoken ones.

Proverbs recommend learning proverbs. The ancient Egyptian *Precepts of Ptah-hotep* tells us (as does Proverbs) that "a son who receives his father's instructions will grow old" (JHDP, 4). Why not describe that process of instructing along with the lessons it conveys? In fact, many cultures at many times have hit upon the idea of making a narrative about passing on wisdom. We learn how and what a parent or sage taught a child or youth. Cultures have devised numerous kinds of such narratives. Each gives an anthology dramatic form, and the story is valued for the many maxims it contains or situations it defines. By their very nature, these stories are adapted for dismemberment.

English anthologies in the form of a parent's instructions include (among others) the Anglo-Saxon *Fader Larcwidas, The Proverbs of Alfred* (thirteenth century), "How the Wise

Man Taught His Son," and "How the Good Wijf taughte Hir Doughtir" (both about 1430) (see JHDP, 4). Especially popular was the "Distichs of Cato," a manual of advice for the young composed in Latin in the fourth or fifth century and used as a schoolbook for a millennium. Caxton printed a translation of it in 1477, as well as four more editions during the next seven years. (See JHDP, 4–5.) It would be tedious to list many such works, but we may recall that Polonius's counsel to Laertes apparently parodies the form and so suggests how conventional it was.

Separability's Risk

Perhaps the most important English anthology in literary form is John Heywood's *Dialogue of Proverbs,* originally published 1546 under the title: *A dialogue conteinyng the number in effect of all the prouerbes in the englishe tongue, compacte in a matter concernyng two maner of marriages, made and set foorth by Iohn Heywood.* Heywood's *Dialogue* is our source for the English versions of over a thousand proverbs. Some appear to have been coined by Heywood himself. Despite the claim to exhaustiveness, of course, later editions included many more. Add a day, add a proverb.

Heywood's *Dialogue* draws not only on numerous collections of sayings in different languages, and not only on the then-popular theme of wise and unwise marriages, but also on the literary tradition of the "dialogue-debate" about abstract topics. The tradition includes William Cornysshe's *A Treatyse bytweene Enformacione & Musyke* (1504), William Nevill's *The castell of pleasure* (1518), and Heywood's own interludes, *A Play of Love* and *A Dialogue of Wit and Folly* (see JHDP, 53–54).

In the *Dialogue of Proverbs,* an older man recites stories

to a youth trying to decide whether to marry a beautiful poor woman or an ugly rich one. The poem has its own artistry, wisdom, and humor, but, as its 1963 editor Rudolph E. Habenicht observes, it has nevertheless essentially always been treated "as a mere collection of proverbs per se" (JHDP, 50). This fate illustrates one danger of works designed, like Pope's *Essay on Man,* to be separable: separation may go so far that the sense that there is a larger work, rather than a mere list, may be lost. Every aesthetic runs risks, and such loss consti- tutes the main risk of separability.

Far from guarding against this risk, Heywood's preface cautions us against the opposite danger. It insists, one would think unnecessarily, that the dialogue can be used as an an- thology of wisdom:

> Among other thyngs profitying in our tong
> Those whiche much may profit old & yong
> Suche as on their fruite will feede or take holde
> Are our comon playne pithy prouerbes olde.
> . . . .
>   . . . I write for this.
> Remembryng and consyderyng what the pith is
> That by remembrance of these prouerbes may grow
> In this tale, erst talked with a frende, I show
> As many of theim as we could fytly fynde,
> Fallyng to purpose, that might fall in mynde.
> To thentent the reader redyly may
> Fynde theim and mynde theim, when he will alway.
>   (JHDP, 97)

Some of Heywood's proverbs live in English as rephrased in Motteux's translation of *Don Quixote,* to which many English sayings are indebted. Hesketh Pearson laments that "it is a little mortifying to find so many of our pithiest sayings in the English translation of a Spanish author by a French writer."[10] Mortification is in the eye of the beholder.

Don Quoxote

Upon reflection, it makes sense that a version of Cervantes should have contributed so much to our verbal consciousness. Not only is Sancho Panza, like Erasmus's Folly, unable to stop reciting proverbs and droll sayings, but the *Quixote* as a whole is a book *about* quotation. It is not the only work to develop this theme, but it is probably the greatest. Its hero lives in a sea of other people's words and is always citing their phrases.

Cervantes's story opens with the author's recollection of how, for lack of quotations, he almost failed to publish the book until a friend helped him out of his difficulty. The author recalls complaining that, after so many years of writing, all he has is "a tale . . . devoid of all learning and instruction, without quotations" whereas other books "are so crammed with sentences from Aristotle and Plato and the whole mob of philosophers as to astound their readers. And when they quote Holy Scripture! You are sure to say they are so many Saint Thomases" (DQ, 42). Alas, "none of this will be found in my book, for I have nothing to quote. . . . Nor do I even know what authors I follow in it, so as to place their names at the beginning in alphabetical order, as they all do, commencing with Aristotle and ending with Xenophon or Zoilus, although one was a libeler and the other a painter" (DQ, 42–43). Readers, he continued, will detect that I am "too slack and indolent to go in search of authors to say for me what I myself can say without them" (DQ, 43).

Cervantes's friend was able to solve this problem quite easily. He advised: if you need sonnets, epigrams, and eulogies to begin your work, why, just write them yourself and then attribute them to someone famous—say, "Prester John of the Indies or the Emperor of Trebizond, who, it is rumored, were famous poets." If you need quotations in the margins, don't read widely, just look them up. If it is notes at the end you require, use the same ones everyone else uses, or just mention some names "and leave me the task of putting in the notes and quotations, and I swear I will fill your margins and fill up four sheets at the back of the book" (DQ, 46). It is particularly easy just "to search for a book that quotes them [authors] from A to Z" and copy. Reference works or books that have already pillaged them offer a marvelous shortcut to erudition. And none of this trickery will harm your book because you don't need quotations in the first place, since what you are aiming at is precisely to discredit, not repeat, the classics of chivalry.

In the suggestion that the sonnets and epigrams would carry more weight if attributed to a long-dead author, in the allusions to a culture of senseless citation, and in the mention of reference works as time-savers to wisdom, we may easily detect the seventeenth-century debates on the ancients and moderns, on authority and experience, on realism and a fog of learning. Overthrowing books of chivalry is evidently analogous to discrediting thinking by quotation. The *Quixote* repeatedly works by opposing quotation to its core values: direct experience, authenticity, common sense, and the complexity of life irreducible to a saying.

Nonverbal Quotation and Citational Lives

We have seen that quotation (or citation) need not be verbal. Don Quixote quotes not only the language, but also the action, of knight-errantry stories. His behavior, as well as his speech, is cited.

All that night he did not sleep, for he kept thinking
of his lady, Dulcinea. In this way, he imitated what
he had read in his books, where knights spent many
sleepless nights in forests and wastes, reveling in
memories of their fair ladies. (DQ, 101)

So imitating as closely as possible the exploits he
had read about in his books, he resolved now to
perform one that was admirably molded to present
circumstances. (DQ, 78)

"Oh, sir," cried the niece [to the curate], "you should
have them [pastorals] burned like the rest. For I
shall not be surprised if my uncle, when cured of
his disease of chivalry, does not start reading these
books, and suddenly take it into his head to turn
shepherd and roam through the woods and fields,
singing and piping, and what is worse, turning
poet, for it is said that disease is incurable and
catching." (DQ, 90)

Living by citing, quotation as a way of being: this is Cervantes's
theme, and, as the passage about pastorals and poets hints, he
was himself subject to the quixotic disease.

So many Western works have focused on quoted behavior and citational lives! The heroine of Pushkin's *Eugene Onegin* wanders through the hero's library, inspects the lines he
has marked for memory, and at last discovers what the reader
has long known, that the hero is a quotation incarnate:

What was he then? An imitation?
An empty phantom or a joke,
A Muscovite in Harold's cloak,

Compendium of affectation,
A lexicon of words in vogue? . . .
Is he not in fact a parody?[11]

Madame Bovary, Anna Karenina, Eugene Onegin, all live as if
they were the main character in a novel named after them, as,
of course, they are. Given natural egoism, perhaps each of us
lives in imagination as they do, eponymously.

Too Many Saws Is Like Too Much Salt, for What Flavors When Sprinkled Drowns When Ladled

> "A curse upon you, Sancho!" cried Don Quixote.
> "May sixty thousand devils take you and your prov-
> erbs! For the past hour you have been stringing
> them and choking me with them. Take my word for
> it, these proverbs will one day bring you to the gal-
> lows." (DQ, 831)

Don Quixote meets his most formidable match not in other
knights but in his own squire, whose repertoire of quotations
exceeds his own. He travels with a living anthology, who does
not seem able to open his mouth without voicing a glut of ir-
relevant proverbs and saws. Immersed in cited language and
action as he is, Don Quixote nevertheless becomes increas-
ingly irritated at speech that, with many sayings, says little. He
at last tells his squire that if, as they both expect, Sancho receives as his reward the governorship of an island, he must
learn to talk in his own words:

> "Furthermore, Sancho, you must not overload your
> conversation with such a glut of proverbs, for

though proverbs are concise and pithy sentences, you so often drag them in by the hair that they seem to be maxims of folly rather than of wisdom."

"God alone can remedy that," answered Sancho, "for I know more proverbs than would fill a book, and when I talk, they crowd so thick and fast into my mouth that they struggle to get out first. And the tongue starts firing off the first that comes, haphazard, no matter if it is to the point or no. However, in the future, I'll take good care to say only those that are beneficial to the dignity of my place, for 'Where there's plenty, the guests can't be empty'; and 'He that cuts doesn't deal'; and 'He's safe as a house who rings the bells'; and 'He's no fool who can spend and spare.'"

"There you are, Sancho!" said Don Quixote. "On you go, threading, tacking, stitching together proverb after proverb till nobody can make head or tail of you! With you it's a case of 'My mother whips me yet I spin the top!' Here am I warning you not to make an extravagant use of proverbs, and you then foist upon me a whole litany of old saws that have as much to do with our present business as over the hills of Ubeda." (DQ, 829)

Sancho does indeed know enough proverbs to fill a book, and, as actually happened, has supplied a significant number to many of them. These words of others seem to speak through him as if he was not quoting but they were using him to quote. With their own agency, they "crowd" into his mouth and "struggle" with each other for utterance, so that, even in promising to avoid them, Sancho uses them.

When Don Quixote points out the contradiction between Sancho's promise and the words with which he makes it, he, too, unwittingly uses a proverb of dubious relevance. He may criticize his squire's attachment to borrowed words, but he becomes infected with a similar habit, much as Sancho, though he can distinguish windmills from giants, somehow comes to believe in a great feat that will gain his island. Each lives in a world of citation and each suspects but somehow credits the other's quoting. From beginning to end, Cervantes's book narrates a tale of quote-errantry.

We easily take as original what we learned as quotations. For this reason, quotations can exercise enormous power over us when least expected. As inns may appear to be castles, the words of others may seem like our own.

The Continuum of Separability

Let us return to the problem of wholes supplying parts. We may identify another continuum, a continuum of separability.

At one extreme is the work as poetics from Aristotle to the present has usually taught us to regard it: a complete artifact in which the parts properly have meaning only by their participation in the entire structure. All elements maintain a precise place in a totality, "the structural union of the parts being such that, if any one of them is displaced or removed, the whole will be disjointed and disturbed. For a thing whose presence or absence makes no visible difference, is not an organic part of the whole."[12] Works like these are the ones most likely to be distorted by extraction or quotation. For even if a quotation does not mislead by losing an ironizing context, it nevertheless distorts simply by virtue of standing on its own. It necessarily acquires a different "implied author," who is, let us say, an aphorist or wit rather than a novelist.

Such distortion would not necessarily occur if one were to quote from works lying toward the middle of the continuum. Some compositions, like Pope's *Essay on Man,* are simultaneously *composites* and *wholes.* They depend on a double design, in which parts can mean either by participation in the structure of the whole or on their own. Still further on the continuum we encounter books like Valerius Maximus's *Memorable Deeds and Sayings.* The sense of a whole is vaguely present, but it would be hard to claim that nothing could be moved, added, or subtracted without damaging the work. One could easily imagine including a new memorable deed or rearranging some existing ones. At this point on the continuum, the whole is still more than the sum of its parts, but not much more. It does not depend on anything so all-encompassing as a structure.

The whole may exist but not be particularly interesting. In such cases, we are invited to read primarily for the parts, as in the aesthetics of similar types of gardening. These cases are easily mistaken for those still further along the continuum, in which the whole barely exists at all. The editor of Heywood's poem has to remind us that it *is* a poem and not just an anthology. Finally, at the end of the continuum, we reach books that, as mere containers, ask to be taken apart. These are, at best, mere shadows of wholes that are not really works at all.

The closer we come to this end of the continuum, the more quotations acquire their own energy. More and more, they struggle with each other, as they do in Sancho Panza's mouth, to break free, to forget their origins, and acquire independent status.

Aristotle speaks of an organic whole, but the biological metaphor may teach a different lesson. To be sure, an elephant or a person is a whole organism and when it dies, so do all its cells. But worms may be cut and survive as independent organisms. Hives and anthills function as a biological unit whose participants just happen to be physically separate. The world of nature, like that of art, displays a continuum of separability.

Conclusion

*We can say nothing but what hath been said, the
composition and method is ours only.*
—*Burton,* The Anatomy of Melancholy

*I do not speak the minds of others except to speak
my own mind better.*
—*Montaigne, "Of the Education of Children"*

We live by the words of others.

When he heard quotation censured as pedantry, Dr. Johnson replied: "No, it is a good thing; there is community of mind in it. Classical quotation is the *parole* of literary men all over the world" (WoW, 297). Mind and *parole:* quotation shapes thought and its instrument.

For Johnson, to know a civilization is to know its quotations. To write and speak one's language well, one needs to be familiar with important models of its use. In Johnson's view, language is in part made by important things said in it. Just as the actions of individuals or peoples do not just express but also create their character, so their utterances do not just illuminate but also change the medium. "Every quotation contributes something to the stability or enlargment of the language," Johnson observes in the Preface to the Dictionary.[1] That is yet another reason that Johnson regarded quotations as essential to his lexicographical project: more than just illustrating language, they constitute an intrinsic part of it. A dictionary without quotations would be as deficient as one lacking idioms.

So far as we know, quotation is unique to human beings. Animals repeat behavior by instinct or by copying, but they do not quote it. It is possible that some animals pass on learning by teaching—that is one definition of culture—but only people copy the behavior of others so as to point to it *as* the behavior of others. Animals imitate, but they do not mimic.

Quotation belongs to humanness. So far as we know, all people, and all peoples, quote. Among the oldest writings we have are collections of wise sayings, and every culture, whether it has developed writing or not, uses proverbs to pass on wisdom and define situations. "There appears to be no form of teaching that is older than the proverb," observes Erasmus (AE, 12). And what the wise teach first of all is to attend to the words of the wise. The Book of Proverbs tells us: "Wisdom crieth without: she uttereth her words in the streets," summoning us to listen to her counsel and reproof. "My son, if thou wilt receive my words, and hide my commandments with thee, so that thou incline thine ear unto wisdom, and apply thine heart to understanding . . . then shalt thou understand the fear of the lord" (2:1–5). Confucius, too, professes not to create but only to pass on words of wisdom: "The Master said: I transmit but do not create" (SCT, 50).

Transmission does not mean blind repetition: "The Master said, 'One who reanimates the old so as to understand the new may become a teacher'" (SCT, 47). Seneca agreed: "Knowing is making the thing your own" (Seneca, 187). Learning involves quoting, but quoting can itself be creative.

Knowledge of some quotations defines who we are. Others give us concepts and ways of looking at things we would not otherwise have. All help us overcome our separation from other people. We must quote each other or die.

Human beings love to socialize, are inclined to collect, and seek wisdom. Quotation anthologies satisfy all three impulses. They are verbal museums that each of us can assemble. When we know many profound or witty sayings, we can reflect on our own lives and share our knowledge with others.

Quotations live as long as they are used, and so long as they are used, they shape thought, language, and individual personalities. Collections inspire us with the muse of quotation, and encourage a special sort of reading as roaming. We get to make a new dialogue from words already spoken. We play, and grow wiser as we do.

No matter how inventive a culture may be, most of what it imagines and makes was invented somewhere else. Cultures grow by absorbing the truths of other cultures. Individuals, too, grow by adapting the words of other individuals. As Montaigne and Burton repeat, we assimilate the words of others and transform them into something of our own. That is what making a self entails. We are what we have learned and what we make of what we have learned. We are also what we have disavowed, the "dis-quotations" we once accepted but now have outgrown or rejected.

The process of quoting and disquoting never ends. No one is ever completely himself or herself, and time always promises more words to come. Humanity, too, is always incomplete. Pope was right: "Man never Is, but always To be blest" (Pope, 132).

Bakhtin was also right: "The ultimate word of the world and about the world has not yet been spoken, the world is open and free, everything is still in the future and will always be in the future."[2]

We have not yet begun to quote.

Abbreviations

AE = *The Adages of Erasmus,* ed. William Barker (Toronto: University of Toronto Press, 2001). The volume contains one introduction by the editor (ix–xlvii) and one by Erasmus (3–28), which first appeared in the 1508 edition.

AK = Leo Tolstoy, *Anna Karenina,* the Garnett translation revised by Leonard J. Kent and Nina Berberova (New York: Modern Library, 1950).

AVM = Louis Kronenberger, *Animal, Vegetable, Mineral: A Commonplace Book* (New York: Viking, 1972).

BBA = *Bartlett's Book of Anecdotes,* ed. Clifton Fadiman and André Bernard (Boston: Little, Brown, 2000). The volume is an updated version of *The Little, Brown Book of Anecdotes,* ed. Clifton Fadiman (1985).

BFQ15 = John Bartlett, *Familiar Quotations: A Collection of Passages, Phrases, and Proverbs Traced to Their Sources in Ancient and Modern Literature,* fifteenth edition, ed. Emily Morison Beck (Boston: Little, Brown, 1980).

BFQ16 = John Bartlett, *Familiar Quotations: A Collection of Passages, Phrases, and Proverbs Traced to Their Sources in Ancient and Modern Literature,* sixteenth edition, ed. Justin Kaplan (Boston: Little, Brown, 1992).

BoG = Gary Saul Morson, *The Boundaries of Genre: Dostoevsky's "Diary of a Writer" and the Traditions of Literary Utopia* (Austin: University of Texas Press, 1981).

CHQ = *Cassell's Humorous Quotations,* ed. Nigel Rees (London: Cassell, 2003).

DD = Ambrose Bierce, *The Devil's Dictionary* (Garden City, NY: Doubleday, n.d.)

DLW = *Dictionary of Last Words,* compiled by Edward S. Le Comte (New York: Philosophical Library, 1955).

DQ = Miguel de Cervantes Saavedra, *Don Quixote,* trans. Walter Starkie (New York: Macmillan, 1957).

EAD = *Epitaphs: A Dictionary of Grave Epigrams and Memorial Eloquence,* ed. Nigel Rees (London: Bloomsbury, 1993).

FLW = *Famous Last Words: The Ultimate Collection of Finales and Farewells,* ed. Laura Ward (London: PRC, 2004).

HiQ = *History in Quotations,* ed. M. J. Cohen and John Major (London: Cassell, 2004).

JHDP = *John Heywood's "A Dialogue of Proverbs,"* ed. Rudolph E. Habenicht (Berkeley: University of California Press, 1963).

MBCP = Gary Saul Morson and Caryl Emerson, *Mikhail Bakhtin: Creation of a Prosaics* (Stanford: Stanford University Press, 1990).

MBSSQ = *The Macmillan Book of Social Science Quotations: Who Said What, When, and Where,* ed. David L. Sills and Robert K. Merton (New York: Macmillan, 1991), originally published as volume 19 of the International Encyclopedia of the Social Sciences.

MDQ = *The Macmillan Dictionary of Quotations,* ed. John Dainith et al. (Edison, NJ: Chartwell, 2000).

NGFS = *"Nice Guys Finish Seventh": False Phrases, Spurious Sayings, and Familiar Misquotations,* ed. Ralph Keyes (New York: HarperCollins, 1993).

OBA = *The Oxford Book of Aphorisms,* ed. John Gross (Oxford: Oxford University Press, 1987).

OBLA = *The Oxford Book of Literary Anecdotes,* ed. James Sutherland (New York: Simon and Schuster, 1975).

OCEL = *The Oxford Companion to the English Language,* ed. Tom McArthur (New York: Oxford University Press, 1992).

ODPSQ = *Oxford Dictionary of Phrase, Saying, and Quotation,* third edition, ed. Susan Ratcliffe (Oxford: Oxford University Press, 2006). Elizabeth Knowles edited the first edition, and her interesting introduction (1997) to it appears in the third on pages xii–xv.

ODLQ = *Oxford Dictionary of Literary Quotations,* ed. Peter Kemp (Oxford: Oxford University Press, 2003).

ODQ = *The Oxford Dictionary of Quotations,* 6th edition, ed. Elizabeth Knowles (Oxford: Oxford University Press, 2004).

ODQ2 = *Oxford Dictionary of Quotations,* 2nd edition (London: Oxford University Press, 1966; originally 1953).

OTSOG = Robert K. Merton, *On the Shoulders of Giants: A Shandean Postscript. The Vicennial Edition* (San Diego: Harcourt Brace, 1985), originally published by the Free Press, 1965.

PCBQ = *Putnam's Complete Book of Quotations, Proverbs and Household*

Words: A Collection of Quotations from British and American Authors, with Many Thousands of Proverbs, Familiar Phrases and Sayings, from All Sources, including Hebrew, German, Italian, Spanish and Other Languages, ed. W. Gurney Benham (New York: G. P. Putnam, 1926). The first edition was published in 1907.

PSS = L. N. Tolstoi, *Polnoe sobranie sochinenii* [Complete Works] in ninety volumes, ed. V. G. Chertkov et al. (Moscow: Khudozhestvennaia literature, 1929–58).

QV = *The Quote Verifier: Who Said What, Where, and When* (New York: St. Martin's Griffin, 2006).

RQ = *Respectfully Quoted: A Dictionary of Quotations,* ed. Suzy Platt (New York: Barnes and Noble, 1993).

SCT = *Sources of Chinese Tradition,* 2nd edition, volume 1 (*From the Earliest Times to 1600*), compiled by Wm. Theodore de Bary and Irene Bloom (New York: Columbia University Press, 1999).

TNSI = Paul F. Bolger and John George, *They Never Said It: A Book of Fake Quotes, Misquotes, and Misleading Attributions* (New York: Oxford University Press, 1989).

VBA = *The Viking Book of Aphorisms: A Personal Selection,* "by" W. H. Auden and Louis Kronenberger (New York: Dorset, 1981).

WoW = *Words on Words: Quotations on Language and Languages,* ed. David Crystal and Hilary Crystal (Chicago: University of Chicago Press, 2000).

WTDS = *What They Didn't Say: A Book of Misquotations,* ed. Elizabeth Knowles (Oxford: Oxford University Press, 2006).

YBQ = *The Yale Book of Quotations,* ed. Fred R. Shapiro (New Haven: Yale University Press, 2006).

Notes

Epigraph: Yuri Olesha, *Envy,* trans. Marian Schwartz (New York: New York Review of Books, 2004), 9.

Introduction

1. *The Poet's Tongue: An Anthology,* ed. W. H. Auden and John Garrett (London: Bell, 1935), v. The introduction, in which this phrase appears twice, is actually signed by both editors.

2. See SCT, 42.

3. Lao Tzu, *Tao Te Ching,* trans. D. C. Lau (London: Penguin, 1983). See pages 22 (poem XVIII), 24 (poem XX), 42 (poem XXXVII), and 63 (poem LVI).

4. The first four of these quotations are from BFQ15, 62; the fifth from ODQ, 745; the sixth from PCBQ, 447.

5. William Blake, "The Marriage of Heaven and Hell," in *English Romantic Poetry,* vol. 1, ed. Harold Bloom (Garden City, NY: Doubleday, 1963), 59.

6. The first three maxims are from *The Maxims of La Rochefoucauld,* trans. Louis Kronenberger (New York: Random House, 1959), 33, 36, 49; the fourth is from ODQ, 469.

7. On La Rochefoucauld, and on quotationality in general, I am indebted to Joseph Epstein in the following essays: "Reading Montaigne" and "La Rochefoucauld: Maximum Maximist," *Life Sentences: Literary Essays* (New York: Norton, 1997), 17–36 and 205–223; "Quotatious," *A Line Out for a Walk: Familiar Essays* (New York: Norton, 1991), 88–107; "Chamfort, Artist of Truth," *Pertinent Players: Essays on the Literary Life* (New York: Norton, 1993), 160–178.

8. Or compare with the similar logic in John Wilmot, Earl of Rochester, in his misanthropic "Satire against Mankind": "For all men would be cowards if they durst" (ODQ, 651).

9. *The Jerusalem Bible,* ed. Alexander Jones (Garden City, NY: Doubleday, 1966), 804. For an important recent study of the special status of the King James Bible and its influence on American writing, see Robert Alter, *Pen of Iron: American Prose and the King James Bible* (Princeton: Princeton University Press, 2010).

10. The "historical Jesus" approach to such issues often strays into a blunt literalism. As some scholars leap to conclusions, others leap to questions. The recent bestseller by Bart D. Ehrman, *Misquoting Jesus: The Story Behind Who Changed the Bible, and Why* (San Francisco: HarperCollins, 2005), directs itself to readers interested in detecting the errors in biblical quotations and in "seeing how we might, through the application of some rather rigorous methods of analysis, reconstruct what those original words actually were" (15). "Rather rigorous" often means drawing a rather plausible inference from a rather plausible inference from a rather plausible inference.

11. For an example of intelligent people making plausible predictions that largely turned out wrong in their estimate of present trends or did not even guess at what inventions or issues would arise, see *The Fabulous Future: America in 1980* (New York: Time, 1955). John von Neumann predicts that "a few decades hence energy may be free—just like the unmetered air" (37).

12. W. H. Auden, "In Memory of W. B. Yeats," in *Modern Poetry,* ed. Maynard Mack, Leonard Dean, and William Frost, 2nd edition (Englewood Cliffs, NJ: Prentice Hall, 1965), 208.

Chapter 1:
What Is an Anthology?

1. *Key Quotations in Sociology,* ed. Kenneth Thompson (London: Routledge, 1996).

2. *A Dictionary of Economic Quotations,* 2nd ed., compiled Simon James (Towota, NJ: Rowman and Allanheld, 1984); *The Macmillan Book of Business and Economic Quotations,* ed. Michael Jackman (New York: Macmillan, 1984).

3. *Cassell Dictionary of Insulting Quotations,* ed. Jonathon Green (London: Cassell, 1999); *The Mammoth Book of Zingers, Quips and One-Liners,* ed. Geoff Tibballs (New York: Carroll and Graf, 2005); *The Nasty Quote Book,* compiled Colin M. Jarman (New York: Gramercy, 1999); *The*

Book of Poisonous Quotes, compiled Colin M. Jarman (Lincolnwood, IL: Contemporary, 1993); *Fighting Words: Writers Lambast Other Writers—From Aristotle to Anne Rice,* ed. James Charlton (Chapel Hill, NC: Algonquin, 1994); *Put Downs: A Collection of Acid Wit,* ed. Laura Ward (London: PRC, 2004); *Viva la Repartee: Clever Comebacks and Witty Retorts from History's Great Wits and Wordsmiths,* ed. Dr. Mardy Grothe (New York: HarperCollins, 2005).

4. *The Cynic's Lexicon,* ed. Jonathon Green (New York: St. Martin's, 1984); *The Portable Curmudgeon,* ed. Jon Winokur (New York: New American, 1987).

5. Clinton Bailey, *A Culture of Desert Survival: Bedouin Proverbs from Sinai and the Negev* (New Haven: Yale University Press, 2004); *The Literary Spy: The Ultimate Source for Quotations on Espionage and Intelligenece,* compiled Charles E. Lathrop (New Haven: Yale University Press, 2004).

6. *Great Treasury of Western Thought: A Compendium of Important Statements on Man and His Institutions by the Great Thinkers in Western History,* ed. Mortimer J. Adler and Charles Van Doren (New York: Bowker, 1977). See also the well-known Seldes anthology: *The Great Thoughts,* compiled George Seldes, revised David Laskin (New York: Ballantine, 1996), originally published by Seldes in 1995. Such collections of "great thoughts" typically include longer selections than are to be found in most quotation anthologies.

7. For example, see *The 776 Stupidest Things Ever Said,* ed. Ross and Kathryn Petras (New York: Broadway, 1993); *The 776 Even Stupider Things Ever Said,* ed. Ross and Kathryn Petras (New York: HarperCollins, 1994); *1001 Dumbest Things Ever Said,* ed. Steven D. Price (Guilford, CT: Lyons, 2004); *Don't Quote Me,* ed. Don Atyeo and Jonathon Green (London: Chancellor, 2002).

8. *Hoyt's New Cyclopedia of Practical Quotations,* compiled Kate Louise Roberts (New York: Grosset and Dunlap, 1940), vii–viii. This collection first appeared in 1922.

9. Anthony W. Shipps, *The Quote Sleuth: A Manual for the Tracer of Lost Quotations* (Urbana: University of Illinois Press, 1990).

10. *A Complete Dictionary of Poetical Quotations: Comprising the Most Excellent and Appropriate Passages in the Old English Poets; with Choice and Copious Selections from the Best Modern British and American Poets,* ed. Sarah Josepha Hale (Philadelphia: Lippincott, 1860), ii.

11. "The Compilers to the Reader (1941)," in ODQ2, vii.

12. See Rudolph E. Habenicht, "Introduction: The Proverb Tradition in the Early Sixteenth Century," in JHDP, 1–94. The two Caxton collections are mentioned on 20–21.

13. As cited in the editor's introduction to AE, xix; the Holbein marginal illustration of Erasmus writing the notebooks to which Folly refers is also reproduced here.

14. Also translated as *The Instructions of Ptah-hotep.* See J. D. Ray, "Egyptian Wisdom Literature," in *Wisdom in Ancient Israel: Essays in Honor of J. A. Emerton,* ed. John Day, Robert P. Gordon, and H. G. M. Williamson (Cambridge: Cambridge University Press, 1998), 19. In BFQ15 and BFQ16, which arrange contributors in chronological order, this one is the second. In his introduction to *The Anchor Bible: Proverbs,* ed. and trans. R. B. Y. Scott (Garden City, NY: Doubleday, 1981), Scott cites the claim in I Kings 4:30, "And Solomon's wisdom excelled the wisdom of all the children of the east country, and all the wisdom of Egypt," as one piece of evidence that Proverbs is indebted to Egyptian wisdom collections going back to *The Instructions of Ptah-hotep,* which apparently goes back to the fifth dynasty (c. 2400 BCE). Habenicht in JHDP gives the date as c. 3440 BCE and remarks that it has been called "the oldest book in the world" (JHDP, 4). See Scott's comments on "International Wisdom and Its Literature," xl–liii. *The Instructions of Ptah-hotep* takes the form of a king instructing his son, xlii–xliii.

15. Paula Findlen, *Possessing Nature: Museums, Collecting, and Scientific Culture in Early Modern Italy* (Berkeley: University of California Press, 1994), 1.

16. The phrase "draw dotted lines" in this sense is a favorite of the Russian thinker Mikhail Bakhtin.

Chapter 2:
Quotationality and Former Quotations

1. Here and elsewhere, my thinking has been shaped by the school of Mikhail Bakhtin. See V. N. Voloshinov, *Marxism and the Philosophy of Language,* trans. Ladislav Matejka and I. R. Titunik (New York: Seminar, 1973); M. M. Bakhtin, "Discourse in the Novel," in *The Dialogic Imagination: Four Essays by M. M. Bakhtin,* ed. Michael Holquist, trans. Caryl Emerson and Michael Holquist (Austin: University of Texas Press, 1981), 259–422. See also MBCP for a summary of these and other writings on related topics.

2. George Eliot, *Middlemarch* (New York: Modern Library, 1984), 395 (Book IV, chapter 40).

3. Anthony Grafton, *The Footnote: A Curious History* (Cambridge, MA: Harvard University Press, 1997), 140.

4. Samuel Johnson, "The Vanity of Human Wishes: The Tenth Satire

of Juvenal Imitated," in *Rasselas, Poems, and Selected Prose,* ed. Bertrand H. Bronson (New York: Holt, Rinehart, 1958), 53, line 222.

5. Fyodor Dostoevsky, *The Idiot,* trans. Constance Garnett (New York: Modern Library, 1962), 241.

6. Mikhail Bakhtin uses the word "remember" in this way to indicate how we associate words, phrases, ways of speaking, and many other phenomena with the contexts in which they typically appear. The personification "the word remembers its context" means that for listeners the context is more or less clearly evoked.

7. "When did my dentist begin using the word *pasta?* When did anyone? I have checked with friends who grew up in Italian families, and in their memory the word of choice was inevitably *spaghetti,* sometimes *macaroni.* I'm not sure I can nail down the exact date when *pasta* came into currency, but around that time, my guess is, one can discover the beginning of food snobbery in America." Joseph Epstein, *Snobbery: The American Version* (New York: Houghton Mifflin, 2002), 215.

8. David L. Sills and Robert K. Merton, eds., *The Macmillan Book of Social Science Quotations: Who Said What, When, and Where* (New York: Macmillan, 1991), xvii. This volume, one of the truly great quotation anthologies, was also published as volume 19 of the International Encyclopedia of the Social Sciences.

9. Or perhaps, still earlier, with Flip Wilson in *Rowan and Martin's Laugh-In* and *The Flip Wilson Show.*

10. New York: Random House, 1994.

11. As cited in James Geary, *The World in a Phrase: A Brief History of the Aphorism* (New York: Bloomsbury, 2005). Geary's book offers a readable, basic introduction to the traditional canon of "aphorists."

12. James Rogers, *The Dictionary of Clichés* (New York: Ballantine, 1985), vii.

13. Eric Partridge's introduction to *A Dictionary of Clichés* (New York: Dutton, 1963) offers some shrewd comments on quotations.

14. Or to take a celebrated example, the French negative "ne . . . pas" (*il ne marche pas*) began as one of a series of emphatic expressions: he does not walk a step, does not drink a drop (*il ne boit goutte*), and so forth. But when utterances are routinely formed this way, such expression simply becomes the way one says it. "Pas" spread from "walk" to other forms of locomotion and was reinterpreted as part of the negative, so it could spread to other verbs as it could not if one still sensed its meaning as "step." "Il ne boit pas" is possible only if "pas" has been, as the linguists say, completely grammaticalized. Now one can negate with "pas" alone. See John McWhorter, *The*

Power of Babel: A Natural History of Language (New York: HarperCollins, 2003), 25–27.

15. Ludwig Wittgenstein, *Philosophical Investigations,* trans. G. E. M. Anscombe (New York: Macmillan, 1968), 33e, 11e.

16. I am aware, of course, that the idea of language I have in mind is cultural rather than generative and pertains to usage and performance rather than to abstract competence. When one takes a cultural approach to language, language itself has fuzzy and changing boundaries.

Chapter 3:
What Is a Quotation?

1. OBA, ix. Gross continues: "I have included a fair number of slightly longer passages, some poetry, a few mock-aphorisms, a sprinkling of miscellaneous outbursts and oddities. Once or twice I have broken the rule which says that aphorisms ought to deal with universals rather than particulars—but only, I hope, when the epigram in question readily lends itself to more extensive application."

2. In his 1926 introduction, W. Gurney Benham explains that, after the first edition of Putnam's collection, subsequent ones had additions constrained by "the necessity of utilizing the original plates . . . in order to avoid the delay and heavy cost of an entire resetting of type" (PCBQ, v).

3. One listing of such reproductions, mostly British, can be found at Travel-quest: http://www.travel-quest.co.uk/historical-recreations.htm.

4. Fyodor Dostoevsky, *The Brothers Karamazov,* trans. Constance Garnett (New York: Modern Library, 1950), 4.

5. As cited in Paul Lawrence Farber, *Finding Order in Nature: The Naturalist Tradition from Linnaeus to E. O. Wilson* (Baltimore: Johns Hopkins University Press, 2000), 8–9.

6. Jack Anderson, "The Joffrey Ballet Restores Nijinsky's 'Rite of Spring,'" *New York Times,* October 25, 1987, http://www.nytimes.com/1987/10/25/arts/the-joffrey-ballet-restores-nijinsky-s-rite-of-spring.html.

7. One could add a third criterion: the quotation must itself be saying something, the way mimicry comments on the situation in which it occurs or on the person who would use such a gesture. Artworks that quote images from other artworks do so to make artistic statements of their own. If this criterion is adopted, then the quoted museum exhibit would be making a statement on what makes an exhibit a good one. A quoted place would need to be seen as saying something about that place, or our relationship to it.

8. I argued for this idea of literariness in Morson, *The Boundaries of Genre: Dostoevsky's "Diary of a Writer" and the Traditions of Literary Utopia* (Austin: University of Texas Press, 1981), 39–44. My argument is indebted to John M. Ellis, *The Theory of Literary Criticism: A Logical Analysis* (Berkeley: University of California Press, 1974), chapter 2. "Literary texts," writes Ellis, "are those that are used by the society in such a way that *the text is not taken as specifically relevant to the immediate context of its origin*" (44; italics in original).

9. Francis Bacon, "The Advancement of Learning," book 2 in *The Major Works,* ed. Brian Vickers (Oxford: Oxford University Press, 2002), 234.

10. *The Aphorisms of Hippocrates and the Sentences of Celsus, with Explanations and References To the most considerable Writers in Physic and Philosophy, both Ancient and Modern. To which are added, Aphorisms Upon several Distempers, not well distinguished by the Ancients,* 2nd edition, ed. Sir Conrad Sprengell (London: R. Wilkin, 1735; reprint as excerpts by Lederle Laboratories 1987), 1.

11. On medieval literature, see A. C. Spearing, *Textual Subjectivity: The Encoding of Subjectivity in Medieval Narratives and Lyrics* (Oxford: Oxford University Press, 2005). Spearing sagely stresses the anachronism involved in applying the modern sense of a cohesive literary whole. See also Berhnard Cerquiglini's *In Praise of the Variant: A Critical History of Philology,* trans. Betsy Wing (Baltimore: Johns Hopkins University Press, 1999). Cerquiglini argues that variance is not something that just happens to such works but is part of their very nature. They display "essential variance" (21) and "intrinsic plurality" (40). Because they are constantly rewritten, "the term *text* [in our usual sense today] is hardly applicable to these works" (34). Moreover, a special "pleasure," which may be foreign to the modern critical sensibility, "lay in variance" when "writing made minute shifts in what was already known, and the acts of reading and listening lent themselves to the vicissitudes of recognition and surprise" (37). On modern works that exist in a cloud of versions, see Jerome J. McGann, *A Critique of Modern Textual Criticism* (Chicago: University of Chicago Press, 1983). McGann cites the example of Byron's narrative poem *The Giaour,* which seems to be essentially a cloud irreducible to a point. We have it in "multiple manuscripts, multiple corrected and uncorrected proofs, a trial edition, a whole series of early editions at least three of which are known to have been proofed and revised by Byron" (McGann, 31–32). In this multitude of "prepublication and published forms" we may distinguish "the holograph draft (344 lines), the fair copy (375 lines), the trial proof (453 lines), the first edition (684 lines), second edition (816 lines), third edition, first issue (950 lines), and second issue (1,014 lines), fourth edition (1048 lines), fifth edition (1215 lines) and seventh edi-

tion (1344 lines)" (59). Byron's work seems to have spread and grown. As a result, it apparently demonstrates "a number of different wishes and intentions" (32) that cannot be easily separated or enumerated because they overlap with each other.

12. As cited in Ruth Finnegan, *Oral Poetry: Its Nature, Significance and Social Context* (Cambridge: Cambridge University Press, 1977), 141.

Chapter 4:
Making a Quotation

1. The editors of BBA caution: "We hope *Bartlett's Book of Anecdotes* has value as a work of reference as well as one of entertainment. It does not, however, claim to be a work of exact scholarship, and should not be used as an infallible encyclopedia. Anecdotes are by nature often well worn; while in circulation (and after decades or even centuries) attributions can be mixed up, dates can be changed, and the very point of the stories can be lost. But we have done our best to verify the historical accuracy of those anecdotes we have included in this volume" (BBA, ix). Accuracy to what?

2. The *New York Times* quoted Lenin as calling left-liberals "useful idiots" and this line, too, has lived a life of its own (YBQ, 452).

3. So Ralph Keyes cites Rousseau attributing the remark to "a great princess" and comments: "It was not actually cake that this unnamed princess recommended, but the fancy pastry called *brioche*" (NGFS, 43).

4. See the notes in HiQ, 517, and OBQ, 512. A similar remark—"Que ne mangent-ils de la croûte de pâté?"—was apparently attributed to Marie Thérèse (1638–83), wife of Louis XIV.

5. *I Said It My Way: The Guinness Dictionary of Humorous Misquotations,* ed. Colin Jarman (London: Guinness, 1994), 34.

6. The line is omitted entirely from ODQ but included as "attributed" in ODQ2; omitted from YDQ but included as attributed in MDQ. BFQ16 includes it as attributed and supplies the following note:

> This sentence is not Voltaire's, but was first used in quoting a letter from Voltaire to Helvétius in *The Friends of Voltaire* (1906) by S. G. Tallentyre (E. Beatrice Hall). She claims it was a paraphrase of Voltaire's words in the *Essay on Tolerance:* Think for yourselves and let others enjoy the privilege to do so too.
>
> Norbert Gutterman, in *A Book of French Quotations* [1963] suggests that the probable source for the quotation is from a line in a letter to M. le Riche [February 6, 1770]: "Monsieur

l'abbé, I detest what you write, but I would give my life to make it possible for you to continue to write." (BFQ16, 307n2)

7. "Liberty is precious—so precious that it must be rationed" is attributed to Lenin in Sidney and Beatrice Webb, *Soviet Communism* (1936) (OBQ, 480; YBQ, 452). The line is usually taken as reliable, perhaps because of the book's pro-Soviet sympathies.

8. See WTDS, 55, and NGFS, 44–45, as well as the note from BFQ16, 306n2.

9. *The Jerusalem Bible* (Garden City, NY: Doubleday, 1966), 19.

10. *The Five Books of Moses: Genesis, Exodus, Leviticus, Numbers, Deuteronomy,* trans. Everett Fox (New York: Schocken, 1995), 27.

11. I adapt this idea of memory from Mikhail Bakhtin's concept of "genre memory." See the discussion in Gary Saul Morson and Caryl Emerson, *Mikhail Bakhtin: Creation of a Prosaics* (Stanford: Stanford University Press, 1990), 295–297.

12. "Stickiness" suggests an ability to accumulate the sense and context of earlier usages, which "stick" to the words.

13. Robert Alter pointed out to me that there is no equivalent to the King James in French or, most likely, the language of any non-Protestant country.

14. The line belongs to Robert Benchley; in WoW, 297.

15. Raymond L. Gordon, *Basic Interviewing Skills* (Itasca, IL: Peacock, 1992), 176.

16. Alexander Pope, *Selected Poetry and Prose,* ed. William K. Wimsatt Jr. (New York: Holt, Rinehart, 1965), li–lii.

17. Roy Flannagan, *The Riverside Milton* (Boston: Houghton Mifflin, 1998), vii–viii.

Chapter 5:
What Is a Misquotation?

1. QV, blurb page before title page.

2. At the end of each entry in QV, Keyes provides his "verdict."

3. Keyes notes that in 1939, the year before the famous speech to the House of Commons, "Churchill (who had previously used the phrases 'blood and tears' and 'their sweat, their tears, their blood' in his writing) himself used the 'blood, sweat, and tears' version in an article on the Spanish Civil War. . . . Churchill himself (or his publisher) called a 1941 collection of his speeches *Blood, Sweat, and Tears*" (QV, 15–16).

4. *Boswell's Life of Samuel Johnson,* ed. and abridged Anne H. Ehrenpreis and Irvin Ehrenpreis (New York: Washington Square, 1965), 114.

5. TNSI, 12; for a different account, see NGFS, 46.

Chapter 6:
More Than Words Alone

1. Any extract (as opposed to a quotation) must have an author and textual location that is not part of the extract itself. By contrast, a quotation may (or may not) include authorship and textual location as an intrinsic part of itself.

Similar phenomena may be true of longer works. It is often not clear where to draw the boundaries of a work. "By Leo Tolstoy" is not part of the title of *War and Peace;* but the author is included in *The Gospel According to Saint Matthew.* Some works incorporate their author into their title over time, especially when the title has been used by many authors: thus we have a work now known as *Plutarch's Lives.* Autobiographies often come to incorporate their authors into their titles, as did *The Confessions of Saint Augustine* (he could not have called it that). It is often not clear whether to include a designation of genre in the title. Is the title of Tolstoy's novel *Anna Karenina* or is it *Anna Karenina: A Novel* (or, as we may also translate, *Anna Karenina: A Romance*)? Given the heroine's propensity to think in terms of romance or novels, one could make a case that the designation of genre is part of the title, although it is usually not treated as such. When a novel is narrated by a fictional character, it will usually be a matter of interpretation whether author or character has chosen the title.

2. *Quotations from Chairman Mao Tsetung* (Peking: Foreign Languages, 1972); *Everyman's Dictionary of Shakespeare Quotations,* compiled D. C. Browning (London: Dent, 1974).

3. And even before the existence of the Soviet Union, the phrase had been used by H. G. Wells. See QV, 100–101; NGFS, 54–55; YBQ, 154.

4. BFQ16 lists numerous uses before the 1946 speech at Fulton, Missouri.

5. See NGFS, 97.

6. *Sayings of the Fathers, or Pirke Aboth,* trans. with commentary by Sr. Joseph H. Herz (n.p.: Behrman, 1945). The introduction by Moses Schonfeld explains: "'Sayings of the Fathers' is the most widely known of all the sixty-three tractates of the Mishna. . . . It consists, for the greater part, of the favourite maxims—being the epitome of their wisdom and experience—of

some sixty-three Rabbis, extending over a period of nearly five hundred years, from 300 B.C.E. to 200 of the common era. It also contains anonymous sayings, and touches upon various historical and folk-lore themes" (7).

7. Keyes notes that "the Christophers themselves say their source was a Chinese proverb" (NGFS, 76). As I mentioned in chapter 5, "Chinese proverb" is one conventional way of indicating a "second-speaker only" quotation.

8. Usually given as "I frame no hypotheses" (BFQ15, 313; YBQ, 550), the line is sometimes "I do not feign hypotheses" (OBQ, 561), as the Oxford translates "Hypotheses non fingo."

9. Sometimes the borrowed title occurs only in a translation, as in the rendering of Proust's *À la recherche du temps perdu* as *Remembrance of Things Past* after Shakespeare's thirtieth sonnet: "When to the sessions of sweet silent thought / I summon up remembrance of things past. . . ."

10. Jonathan Lear, *Freud* (New York: Routledge, 2005), 90.

11. Sigmund Freud, *Gesammelte Werke,* vols. 2–3 (London: Imago, 1942), 613.

12. Sigmund Freud, *The Interpretation of Dreams,* trans. A. A. Brill (New York: Modern Library, 1950), 459. There is considerable controversy as to how to translate Freud.

13. I set aside the additional problem of textual variants. In the first edition of Freud's book (1900) the sentence does not appear at all: see the facsimile of the 1900 edition, Elibrion Classics (2005), 362. The quotation from Virgil does appear and still also serves as the book's epigraph. The famous sentence was evidently added to comment on the Latin line.

Chapter 7:
Mis-misquotations

1. Keyes refers to a once frequently repeated line as "a good test of quote collections." (The *Yale Book of Quotations* cites Keyes's analysis approvingly.) That line, ascribed to GM President Charles E. Wilson, is: "What's good for General Motors is good for the country." Keyes observes:

> That observation captured perfectly the smug arrogance of corporate titans. During General Motors's downsizing in the early 1990s, this fatuous remark was dusted to summarize GM's attitude in a sound bite. But that isn't what Wilson said. While testifying about his nomination as Secretary of Defense before the Senate Committee on Armed Services on January

15, 1953, Wilson was asked whether he could make a decision on behalf of the government which would adversely affect General Motors. "Yes, sir," "Wilson replied, "I could. I cannot conceive of one because for years I thought that what was good for our country was good for General Motors, and vice versa." This is similar to the more popular version, but not the same at all. We prefer the misquote, however, so that is the version which has stuck in the public mind. This version echoed a line from a corrupt banker in the 1939 movie *Stagecoach:* "And remember this: What's good for the bank is good for the country." (Keyes, NGFS, 8)

Keyes's indignation here is hard to understand. Does Keyes detect some difference in meaning that the "more popular version" creates? In any case, he relies on a transcript of an answer to a question, not a published essay or finished speech. How do we know that the transcriber has not already cleared up hums, ers, ems, coughs, corrections in mid-sentence or mid-word, and other infelicities, as transcribers typically do?

2. *Common Misquotations,* collected by Hesketh Pearson (n.p.: Folcroft 1973, and London: Hamish Hamilton, n.d.). Pearson's introduction (9–16) is a source of many quotations about quotation and misquotation.

3. Louis Menand, "Notable Quotables," *The New Yorker,* February 19, 2007, pp. 186–189.

4. MDQ, 368. The entry appears in the section entitled "Misquotation."

5. Of course, one might preserve a verbal slip as "Freudian," but even then one would be following not mere mechanical wording but a second, ascribed, intention. The quotographers ascribe no such significant error to Armstrong.

6. And for some, it might even serve as an expression of nationalism.

7. *I Said It My Way: The Guinness Dictionary of Humorous Misquotations,* compiled Colin Jarman (London: Guinness, 1994), 128.

8. *Parodies: An Anthology from Chaucer to Beerbohm—and After,* ed. Dwight Macdonald (New York: Random House, 1960), 450n.

Chapter 8:
How and Where Quotations Live

1. *Cassell Dictionary of Insulting Quotations,* ed. Jonathon Green (London: Cassell, 1999), 16.

2. For the farting comment, see ODQ, 423; for both, see YBQ, 398, 399.

3. YBQ, 44, relies on A. H. Saxon's biography *P. T. Barnum, The Leg-*

end and the Man (1989) for the con-man source, and on Robert Andrews collection, *Famous Lines,* for the quotation that "Barnum doubted" his authorship of the line.

4. *The World's Great Speeches,* ed. Lewis Copeland and Lawrence N. Kamm, 3rd edition (New York: Dover, 1973), 315. The title is given as "Address at Gettysburg."

5. Aristotle, "Poetics," in *Critical Theory Since Plato,* ed. Hazard Adams (New York: Harcourt Brace, 1971), 65.

6. ODQ, 25.

7. The Latin version, now largely replaced by Pope's, is *humanum est errare* (YBQ, 599) or *errare humanum est* (BFQ15, 133).

8. "When I go to Rome, I fast on Saturday, but here [Milan] I do not. Do you also follow the custom of whatever church you attend, if you do not want to give or receive scandal" (ODQ, 13).

9. CHQ, 622. Burdett was an American journalist. The quotation's very existence testifies to a kind of quotational futility.

10. "*Rabbit* is not a corruption of *rare-bit;* the term is on a par with 'mock-turtle', 'Bombay duck', etc." *Brewer's Dictionary of Phrase and Fable,* revised by Ivor H. Evans (New York: Harper and Row, 1970), 1147. Bombay duck is a fish dried and eaten with curries (133).

Chapter 9:
Famous Last Words

1. A. N. Wilson, *Tolstoy* (New York: Fawcett Columbine, 1988), 467. Wilson's source is N. N. Gusev, *Letopisi zhizni i tvorchestva L'va Nikolaevicha Tolstogo, 1981–1920* (Moscow, 1960), 411. Biographers differ on this story. Ernest J. Simmons has Chekhov telling a friend what Tolstoy said to him: "You know, he does not like my dramas. He swears I am not a playwright. There is only one thing that comforts me. . . . He said to me: 'You know, I cannot abide Shakespeare, but your plays are even worse. . . .'" Simmons continues: "At this point in his account Chekhov laughed so hard his pince-nez fell off his nose. 'But, really, Leo Nikolaevich is serious,' Chekhov continued. 'He was ill. I sat with him by his bedside. When I began to leave, he took my hand, looked me in the eye, and said: "Anton Pavlovich, you are a fine man." Then, smiling, he let my hand go and added, "But your plays are altogether vile."'" Simmons, *Leo Tolstoy,* volume 2 ("The Years of Maturity, 1880–1910") (New York: Vintage, 1960), 289–290.

2. Ward comments on her experience of "stumbling across a note, diary entry, telegram, or letter which, while not written from a deathbed—or

indeed anywhere near one—turns out, thanks to a cruel twist of fate, to be a 'famous last word.' The latter thereby becomes a form of farewell, an unintentional finality" (Ward, 10).

3. Aristotle, "Poetics," in *Critical Theory Since Plato,* ed. Hazard Adams (New York: Harcourt Brace, 1971), 33.

4. That is the key distinction between historical novels and the new genre of "virtual" (or "alternate") history, which imagines that, at a given turning point, something else took place. If historical novels narrate events that might or might not have happened (or at least, are not ruled out), alternate histories narrate events that did not happen but could have. See *Virtual History: Alternatives and Counterfactuals,* ed. Niall Ferguson (New York: Basic, 1997); *What Might Have Been: Leading Historians on Twelve "What Ifs" of History,* ed. Andrew Roberts (London: Phoenix, 2004); *The Best Alternate History Stories of the 20th Century,* ed. Harry Turtledove with Martin H. Greenberg (New York: Random House, 2001); and *Roads Not Taken: Tales of Alternate History,* ed. Gardner Dozois and Stanley Schmidt (New York: Ballantine, 1998). One may consider differences between accounts written by historians (the first two anthologies) and by fiction writers (the second two).

5. Sur le point d'être vu?

6. Walter Gratzer, *Eurekas and Euphorias: the Oxford Book of Scientific Anecdotes* (Oxford: Oxford University Press, 2004), 6.

7. See Lebedyev's remarkable meditation on these last words in Fyodor Dostoevsky, *The Idiot,* trans. Constance Garnett (New York: Modern Library, 1935), 186 (Part Two, chapter 2).

Chapter 10:
Epitaphs

1. Long epitaphs invite responses like the following: "Friend, in your epitaph I'm grieved / So very much is said: / One half will never be believed / The other never read." As cited in *Everybody's Book of Epitaphs: Being for the Most Part What the Living Think of the Dead,* compiled W. H. Howe (London: Saxon, 1995), 4.

2. Cited in *Life and Death: Being an Authentic Account of the Deaths of One Hundred Celebrated Men and Women, with Their Portraits,* collated Thomas H. Lewin (London: Constable, 1910), xviii; and in Richard Tuck, *Hobbes* (Oxford: Oxford University Press, 1990), 38–39.

3. Herodotus, *The History,* trans. Henry Cary (Buffalo: Prometheus, 1991), 489.

4. *The Oxford History of the Classical World,* ed. John Boardman, Jasper Griffin, and Oswyn Murray (Oxford: Oxford University Press, 1986), 44–45.

5. Mark Twain, *Pudd'nhead Wilson* (New York: Bantam, 1959), 48.

6. *English Romantic Poetry,* volume 1, ed. Harold Bloom (Garden City, NY: Doubleday, 1963), 166.

7. As printed in *English Prose and Poetry, 1660–1800: A Selection,* ed. Frank Brady and Martin Price (New York: Holt, 1966), 223–227.

Chapter 11:
The Anthology as Literature

1. Fyodor Dostoevsky, *A Writer's Diary,* two volumes, trans. Kenneth Lantz (Evanston, IL: Northwestern University Press, 1994). Volume 1 contains my discussion of the *Diary*'s ways of making a whole out of discrete parts (1:1–117).

2. I discuss precedents of the *Diary* in Morson, *The Boundaries of Genre: Dostoevsky's "Diary of a Writer" and the Traditions of Literary Utopia* (Austin: University of Texas Press, 1981), 3–38.

3. As cited in John Forster, *The Life of Charles Dickens,* ed. J. W. T. Ley (London: Cecil Palmer, 1928), 140.

4. Seneca, "Maxims," in *The Stoic Philosophy of Seneca: Essays and Letters,* trans. Moses Hadas (New York: Norton, 1958), 186.

5. Robert Burton, *The Anatomy of Melancholy: What It Is, with All the Kinds, Causes, Symptomes, Prognostickes, and Severall Cures of It,* ed. Holbrook Jackson (New York: Random House, 1977), 24–25. The name Democritus Junior is a quotation ("a substitute for Democritus") in the sense that the author intends to imitate and extend a project of the ancient philosopher Democritus, who, legend has it, dissected animals to discover the seat of melancholy. "Democritus Junior is therefore bold to imitate, and because he left it unperfect, and it is now lost, *quasi succenturiator Democriti* (as a substitute for Democritus), to revive again, prosecute, and finish in this treatise" (Burton, 20).

6. Peter Burke, "Montaigne," in *Renaissance Thinkers* (Oxford: Oxford University Press, 1993), 371.

7. Laurence Sterne, *The Life and Opinions of Tristram Shandy, Gentleman,* ed. James Aiken Work (New York: Odyssey, 1940), 339; and see Work's note, 339–340. Democritus Jr. has drawn the quotation from Erasmus's prefatory letter to More in *The Praise of Folly.*

8. See Work's note, in Sterne 343n2. See also the note in Laurence Sterne, *Tristram Shandy,* ed. Howard Anderson (New York: Norton, 1980), 239n5.

9. On the principle of expandability, see Robert Belknap, "The Literary List: A Survey of Its Uses and Deployments," *Literary Imagination: The Review of the Association of Literary Scholars and Critics,* 2.1 (2000), 52.

10. Anthologies with commentary are quite common. Erasmus's *Adages* has been succeeded by such more recent works as *Magill's Quotations in Context,* ed. Frank N. Magill (New York: Salem Press, 1965, 1969), and *History in Quotations.*

11. *The Complete Essays of Montaigne,* trans. Donald M. Frame (Stanford: Stanford University Press, 1965), 108.

12. *The 2,548 Best Things Anybody Ever Said,* compiled Robert Byrne (New York: Simon and Schuster, 2002).

13. *The Chatto Book of Cabbages and Kings: Lists in Literature,* ed. Francis Spufford (London: Chatto and Windus, 1989), 4.

14. *History in Quotations* seems to begin this process and invite the reader to continue it.

15. Nicholai V. Gogol, *Dead Souls,* trans. Bernard Guilbert Guerney (New York: Modern Library, 1965), 141–142.

16. *Common Misquotations,* collected by Hesketh Pearson (n.p.: Folcroft 1973, and London: Hamish Hamilton, n.d.), 9.

17. In Russian, *zapiski.* The word appears in the titles of many great works: Dostoevsky, *Notes from Underground;* Dostoevsky, *Notes from the Dead House* (usually given in English as *The House of the Dead);* Turgenev, *Notes of a Hunter* (in English, *A Sportsman's Sketches);* and Gogol, "Notes of a Madman" (usually translated as "Diary of a Madman").

18. *The Diary of Samuel Pepys,* ed. Richard Le Gallienne (New York: Modern Library, n.d.), 332.

19. E. M. Forster, *Commonplace Book,* ed. Philip Gardner (Stanford: Stanford University Press, 1987).

20. Citations in this paragraph from W. H. Auden, *A Certain World: A Commonplace Book* (New York: Viking, 1974), vii–viii.

21. Lev Tolstoi, "Neskol'ko slov po povodu knigi 'Voina I mir'" (Some Words about the Book *War and Peace*), PSS, 16:7. The article first appeared while the book was being serialized.

22. Volume 40 of his complete works contains some eighteen short collections of quotations—the longer *Circle of Reading* occupies volumes 41 and 42—including "Selected Thoughts of La Bruyère," "Selected Aphorisms and Maxims of La Rochefoucauld," "Selected Thoughts of Montesquieu," "Sayings of Mohammed, Not Included in the Koran," and two collections of

quotations from Lao Tzu. See S. M. Vreitberg's foreword to PSS 39 to 42, PSS 39:v–xxxviii.

　　23. Leo Tolstoy, *A Calendar of Wisdom: Daily Thoughts to Nourish the Soul,* trans. Peter Sekirin (New York: Scribner's, 1997), 11–12.

Chapter 12:
Whole and Part

　　1. I rely on the excellent editor's introduction to AE.

　　2. So, too, his *Colloquies,* which began as Latin exercises, grew into meditations; they shaped the mind in both interconnected ways.

　　3. On the importance of anachronism in Renaissance thought, see Thomas M. Greene, *The Light in Troy: Imitation and Discovery in Renaissance Poetry* (New Haven: Yale University Press, 1982). The Aretino example comes from Greene, "History and Anachronism," *Literature and History: Theoretical Problems and Russian Case Studies,* ed. Gary Saul Morson (Stanford: Stanford University Press, 1986), 270.

　　4. Rebecca W. Bushnell. *A Culture of Teaching: Early Modern Humanism in Theory and Practice* (Ithaca: Cornell University Press, 1996), 129. See Bushnell's chapter "Harvesting Books," 117–143.

　　5. Peter Burke, "Montaigne," in *Renaissance Thinkers* (Oxford: Oxford University Press, 1993), 313, 319.

　　6. *The Complete Essays of Montaigne,* trans. Donald M. Frame (Stanford: Stanford University Press, 1965), 111.

　　7. L. S. Vygotsky, *Thought and Language,* ed. and trans. Eugenia Haufmann and Gertrude Vakar (Cambridge, MA: MIT Press, 1962), 125. The book's title is perhaps better translated as "Thinking and Speaking."

　　8. The view opposed to separation and "plucking" was also common: "That sentences in Authors, like haires in an horse-taile, concurre in one roote of beauty and strength, but being pluckt out one by one, serve only for springes and snares" (John Donne, as cited in WoW, 297).

　　9. Alexander Pope, *Selected Poetry and Prose,* ed. William K. Wimsatt Jr. (New York: Holt, Rinehart, 1965), 128.

　　10. *Common Misquotations,* collected by Hesketh Pearson (n.p.: Folcroft 1973, and London: Hamish Hamilton, n.d.), 12.

　　11. Alexander Pushkin, *Eugene Onegin: A Novel in Verse,* trans. James E. Falen (Carbondale: Southern Illinois University Press, 1990), 177 (Canto 7, stanza 24). Instead of citing Falen's last line here, I have quoted it more literally.

12. Aristotle, "Poetics," in *Critical Theory Since Plato,* ed. Hazard Adams (New York: Harcourt Brace, 1971), 93.

Conclusion

Epigraphs: Robert Burton, *The Anatomy of Melancholy: What It Is, with All the Kinds, Causes, Symptomes, Prognostickes, and Severall Cures of It,* ed. Holbrook Jackson (New York: Random House, 1977), 24; *The Complete Essays of Montaigne,* trans. Donald M. Frame (Stanford: Stanford University Press, 1965), 108.

1. Samuel Johnson, *Rasselas, Poems, and Selected Prose*, ed. Bertrand H. Bronson (New York: Holt, Rinehart and Winston, 1958), 228.

2. Mikhail Bakhtin, *Problems of Dostoevsky's Poetics,* ed. and trans. Caryl Emerson (Minneapolis: University of Minnesota Press, 1984), 166.

Index

In this index an "f" after a page number indicates a separate reference on the next page; an "ff" indicates separate references on the next two pages. A continuous discussion is indicated by two page numbers separated by a hyphen. *Passim* indicates a cluster of references in close but not consecutive sequence.

This index uses the abbreviations on pages 285–287. In addition, the following abbreviations are used: E = Erasmus, flw = famous last words, g (or gs) = genre (or genres), l = literature, q (or qs) = quotation (or quotations).